# THE LUST FOR POWER:
## NATIONALISM, SLOVAKIA, AND THE COMMUNISTS
### 1918–1948

WITHDRAWN

YESHAYAHU A. JELINEK

EAST EUROPEAN MONOGRAPHS, BOULDER
DISTRIBUTED BY COLUMBIA UNIVERSITY PRESS, NEW YORK

1983

EAST EUROPEAN MONOGRAPHS, NO. CXXX

Yeshayahu Jelinek is Associate Professor of History
at the Ben Gurion University of the Negev

Printed in the United States of America

To Miri
To Noa'ah, Ori, and Hadass

# CONTENTS

# PREFACE

This work focuses on two topics very close to my mind: nationalism and the history of East Central Europe.

It sometimes appears as if the Lord decided on collective punishment for sinful mankind and gave it nationalism. Yet historians, so I believe, should deal not with the ideal, but with the here and now. Nationalism is a reality, and is discussed as such.

The Slovaks are a small nation in Central Europe. Their only period of independent statehood, and not too honorable at that, was during the Second World War, under the aegis of the Third Reich. This nation can easily serve as a prototype of the impact of strong nationalist feelings and of the tragedies of modern history.

Since the First World War, the Communists have been an integral component of Slovakia's political spectrum. Though never very strong in numbers, they were more successful than Communist parties in many other European countries. The Communist Party wished to rule and direct Slovakia's modern history, and thanks to the good services of the Nazis and their local collaborators, it achieved its aim. It is hard to envisage how this could have happened without the Second World War and its results, which thrust the relatively insignificant minority into the center of the arena. But the Slovak Communists, before they came to dominate the life and thought of Slovakia, were first influenced by the prevailing values of the country.

The powerful force of nationalism, which moved the Slovak masses, compelled the local Communists to take a stand of their own. This nationalism not only determined their fate but won many zealous converts among them. My study is devoted to the confrontation between Slovak nationalism and Slovak Communism and their influence on one another.

This work is not intended to be a formal history of Communism in Slovakia. I have avoided discussion of Trade Union activities, many facets of Party life, representation in the country's political bodies, and other interesting topics. Instead, I have tried to devote myself to the main topic defined in my title. However, life often breaks through set boundaries, and I often found it difficult to stay within the outlines I had set myself. In several cases, particularly in the discussion of the Second World War, I felt obliged to survey related topics in order to present as consistent a story as possible. I restricted myself to the period of 1918–1948, since it seems to me that after 1948, we are dealing with very different conditions. The Slovak society was no longer pluralistic—even the wartime rulers of Hlinka's Slovak People's Party were not able to enforce totalitarian forms in the way the Communists did—and the post 1948 "rules of the game" were new and unprecedented. Several Western political scientists and historians have discussed Slovak nationalism under the Communists, and hence the story is known.

Anyone dealing with the modern history of Eastern Europe, and particularly of the Communist parties, is well acquainted with the problems and frustrations I had to face during my research. Access to archival material in the so-called socialist countries is circumscribed. Even local historians have little to boast about in this respect. A Western historian, and in particular an Israeli, must content himself with whatever material he is able to track down and make his historical reconstruction on the basis of the restrictions imposed by objective conditions. To a large extent I relied on documents published in Czechoslovakia, which are often of dubious nature and, as Czechoslovak historians frequently warn us, may have been tampered with.

Several personalities inside Czechoslovakia and abroad talked to me and made available some of their papers. As I was sworn to silence by some, I shall abstain from mentioning all their names. But I am glad to express my appreciation for their assistance.

The following institutions and libraries were helpful in my research: the National Library, Jerusalem; Yad Vashem Archives and Library, Jerusalem; Central Zionist Archives, Jerusalem; the Labour Movement Archives and Library, Tel Aviv; University of Haifa Library; the International Institute for Social History, Amsterdam; the Political Achives of the German Foreign Office, Bonn; the Federal Archives, Koblenz; the Public Records Office, London; Columbia University Library, New York City; Indiana University Library, Bloomington; the Hoover Institution for Peace, War, and Revolution, Stanford; the United States National Archives, Washington; and the United States Library of Congress, Washington. I also made good use of personal papers of the late Dr. Vojtech Winterstein and of Mr. Emanuel Frieder. A Senior Fellowship at the Institute on East Central Europe, Columbia University, a grant of the Deutscher Akademischer Austauschdienst, and research funds of the Univeristy of Haifa allowed me to conduct parts of this research.

Dr. Ladislav Winterstein of Haifa, Israel, and Professor David W. Paul of University of Washington, Seattle, WA, read and commented on the manuscript. However the full responsibility for this work, its defects and shortcomings, lies only with me. The first chapter of this book was originally published in *Slavic Review,* XXXIV, 1 (March 1975), pp. 65–85, under the title "Nationalism in Slovakia and the Communists, 1918–1928." I wish to express my appreciation to that journal for permission to reprint the article.

# LIST OF ABBREVIATIONS

| | |
|---|---|
| CC | Central Committee |
| CC CPCS | Central Committee of the Communist Party of Czechoslovakia |
| CC CPS | Central Committee of the Communist Party of Slovakia |
| CI | Communist International |
| CIE | Communist International—the Executive |
| CPCS | Communist Party of Czechoslovakia |
| CPS | Communist Party of Slovakia |
| DP | Democratic Party |
| HSPP | Hlinka's Slovak People's Party |
| NFCS | National Front of Czechs and Slovaks |
| PNA | Provisional National Assembly |
| SNC | Slovak National Council |
| UNCP | Ukrainian National Council of Priashevschchina |

## Chapter 1

# IN THE FIRST REPUBLIC: ŠMERAL'S LEADERSHIP

In Czechoslovakia "the attitude toward the national question always constituted the touchstone for political understanding of the defence of revolutionary positions." Thus, Paul Reimann,[1] the Czech-German-Jewish historian of Communism in Czechoslovakia, wrote in 1931.

In fall 1918, the Habsburg Empire disappeared. The multinational structure of that ancient monarchy was among the causes of its weakness and downfall. Several succession states filled the empty space. The nature of the region was such, however, that any political entity was bound to include different nationalities and ethnic groups. Consequently, the new states inherited many of the problems of the disintegrated Empire. Czechoslovakia could offer an illustration of the above. Although two major nations, Czechs and Slovaks, created the new Republic, they shared the fatherland with a host of other people. Any political party, movement, group, or ideology, intending to influence the fate of Czechoslovakia, was bound to face the challenge of nationalism. The Communists constituted no exception.

In Slovakia, the Communist movement took an indigenous form. The nationalistic and irredintistic pressures forced the left-wing Socialists to pay attention to the prevailing problem.

This study intends to probe the Communist reaction to the desires, aspirations, and dreams of the various nationalities in Slovakia. It presupposes that the Communist party had no ready-made answers. The responses chosen were mostly those which were to serve the party's ideology and pragmatic aims. And since the ideology could not provide clear cut solutions as how to reach the aims (i.e., attainment of power), external influences, internal disputes, and objective conditions, local and general, gave birth to several schools of thought. The study will follow these schools, their attempts to apply their own recipes, and the outcome of their deeds. We shall claim that the ultimate objective of Communism in Slovakia was to become the country's master, and that it regarded nationalism as a mere tool to achieve that end.

Slovakia in 1918 was inhabited by several peoples: Slovaks, Magyars, Germans, Ruthenians (Russians, Ukrainians), Jews and gypsies.[2] To these should be added an ever-increasing number of Czechs taking jobs in Slovakia and replacing the emigrating Magyars. While the Slovaks formed the main part of the territory's inhabitants, the Czechoslovak constitution did not recognize them as an independent national entity. The constitution's preamble talked only about a "Czechoslovak nation" speaking a "Czechoslovak language."[3] Although the doctrine of racial, ethnic, historic, and linguistic unity of the Czechs and the Slovaks had a long history, it was received in Slovakia with mixed feelings and often with open resistance.[4] The Communists had to form their own viewpoint on the "Czechoslovak question." They also faced the problems of Magyar and German adjustment to the Republic, the ethnic identity and territorial affiliation of the Ruthenians, and anti-Semitism. In this maze of quarrels, demands, and clashes, the Communists in Slovakia frequently lost their way or were misled by outside influences.

## Slovak Social Democracy in Austria-Hungary

Before the First World War the socialists in Slovakia belonged to the Social Democratic Part of Hungary. This party was not sufficiently aware of the deep emotions underlying the national consciousness of the minorities in the Kingdom. Taking an orthodox stand, the Magyar leaders believed that there existed no national problem, only the problem of exploiters and exploited. Only under pressure did the Party in 1906 resign itself to the creation of national committees in the territories populated by minorities.[5] Even before this concession by the Budapest leaders, the Slovak Social Democrats gathered in the city of Bratislava in June 1905, for what later came to be known as the First Convention of the Slovak Social Democrats. Other gatherings followed in later years. The First Convention expressed several Slovak national demands and also demonstrated Slovak-Czech fellowship.[6] The local *Slovenské robotnické noviny* (Slovak worker press) constantly voiced the specific aspirations of Slovakia. Thus Slovak Social Democrats joined the more veteran bourgeois parties in the struggle for some sort of free and unhindered national existence for their people.

The major Social Democratic move, aimed at the separation of Slovakia from Hungary and creation of a common state with the Czechs, took place on May 1st, 1918, in the city of Liptovský Svätý Mikuláš. The participants, in a public meeting initiated by the Social Democrats, adopted a resolution calling for the right of self-

determination for the "Hungarian branch of the Czechoslovak tribe."[7]
Later, at a gathering of Slovak political leaders on October 30th, 1918,
described as a meeting of the "Slovak National Council," the Social
Democrats expressed support to establishment of a new state with the
Czechs.[8] From then on, Social Democracy in Slovakia faithfully advocated the "Czechoslovak idea." However the party did not escape the
fate of its sister-parties elsewhere: separation into right and left wings,
and eventual development of a Communist movement.

## Magyar Communists and Slovakia

The first indication of the new socialist school of thought in Slovakia
came from Hungary, during the Soviet Republic there. Because of
conflicting statements and sources, it is hard to ascertain to what extent,
if at all, the Communists planned the creation of an independent Soviet
state in Slovakia.[9] It seems that the emphasis of the Budapest Revolutionary Governing Council on international worker solidarity, the invasion of Slovakia and the subsequent proclamation of the Slovak Soviet
Republic on May 16th was aimed at preserving the pre-war territorial
unity of Hungary. Declarations and statements published during the
short-lived republic represent three variant approaches. Primarily, the
Slovak Soviet Republic was to constitute a common body with the
Hungarian Soviet Republic, the model being the relations between
Russia and the Ukraine. Moreover, the Communists would thus save
Slovakia from occupation by the Czech bourgeoisie.[10] Second, this
Republic was to serve as a nucleus for the socialization of all of
Czechoslovakia. The Czech representation among the leaders of the
Slovak Soviet Republic lent plausibility to this approach.[11] Last, at
least a part of the Slovak Communist activists hoped for genuine
self-determination, and separation both from the Czechs and the Magyars. (The concept of a Central European Soviet Federative Republic
loomed in the background of each of the approaches.) The last
approach is of particular relevance to our study, as it suggested that
national independence was close to the hearts of some Slovak Communists. Indeed, contemporary writers in Slovakia and abroad were quick
to point this out.[12]

Slovaks were not the only left-wing Socialists in Slovakia. In fact, it is
our impression that they were outnumbered by the Magyars. Magyars
constituted only about one-sixth of the population of post-war Slovakia, but a considerable part of them were city-dwellers and industrial
workers.[13] They sympathized with Hungary, and many of them pledged

their allegiance to the Soviet Republics, whether Magyar or Slovak. The Magyar workers, who were active in the struggle against Slovakian affiliation to the Czechoslovak Republic, or at least against annexations of certain regions as stipulated by the Treaty of Trianon, felt defeated and frustrated.[14] True, they later learned to appreciate the democratic regime of Czechoslovakia, the White Terror of Admiral Miklos Horthy held out few charms and Magyar Communist activists began to cross the borders and join their comrades in Slovakia.[15] It was thus that the number of Magyar revolutionaries increased, and made an impact on the Slovakian left. The Magyar revolutionary leadership had little sympathy for the bourgeois Czechoslovak Republic. Supported by the solid vote of their co-nationals, the Magyars were the pioneers of "internationalism" among the workers and impoverished peasants. Social ills, national discrimination, and the frustration of being forced to live under Slovaks inspired their protest vote.[16] The Magyar labor leaders, experienced, intelligent, educated, and bitter, brought to the extreme left a certain coolness and doctrinaire attitude toward the national grievances of the dominant people in Slovakia. Years later Communist historians accused the idols of yesterday of national nihilism, ultra-left deviations, sectarianism, and lack of ability to understand the Slovak masses.[17] But at that time the Czechoslovak Communist movement was strongly sympathetic towards the pain of the Magyar minority. The outstanding Czech Communist, Dr. Bohumír Šmeral, favored border revisions with Hungary at least as early as June 14, 1921.[18] The Fifth Congress of the Communist International (1924) adopted a similar stand.[19]

## Slovakia in the New Republic

The Magyars were not the main concern of the left socialists in Slovakia. Czech-Slovak relations, and above all, the increasing national consciousness of the Slovaks and their demands, were more important. The new republic liberated the Slovaks from the political and cultural oppression they had suffered under the defunct monarchy. The leaders of the nation, and a good many of its people, appreciated the new conditions. Nevertheless, the threat from Hungary and her partisans in Slovakia was still acute. The majority of the population regarded the Hungarian Red Army as merely another Magyar attempt to subjugate the Slovaks.[20] The sentiments on the Czech side were no less intense.[21] The Czechs, including the working class, were overwhelmed by the creation of their own state, which was regarded by many as a continuation of the medieval Bohemian kingdom. This patriotic fervor served as the background for the discussion in the leftist camp about the position of Slovakia in the Republic. Workers in Bohemia and Moravia shared with other sectors of the population the concept of an indivisible Czechoslovak nation. Socialist thinkers also remembered the Austro-Marxian concepts of nations as cultural entities.[22] Others, including a great number of Germans and Magyars, argued, in the spirit of Rosa Luxemburg, that the first and main task of a revolutionary party was the overthrow of capitalism.[23] The Leninist approach to the national question was little known or used in those early days.[24] Those who referred to the right of self-determination had the Wilsonian formula in mind. In addition to ideas emanating in their own camp, the left-wing Socialists had to cope with the plans of other political powers.

From the very beginning, the establishment preferred to confine the reins of power to the capital, Prague.[25] On the other hand, some Slovak Catholic nationalists, headed by Father Andrej Hlinka, developed a design for territorial autonomy as early as 1919 and continued to promote it.[26] For a part of the population, religion constituted an inseparable element in their national consciousness. Eventually, many of the Catholics who were the prevailing majority of Slovakia's population, stood in opposition to the centralistic line of the Prague authorities, while Protestants tended to accept it. In the past, the Catholic Church had acted as a willing agent of Magyarization, and subsequently it contributed to the Slovak particularism. But, above all, the often liberal-minded and freethinking Czechs alarmed the Slovak clergy and pious believers. Some of the local priests and laymen had an honorable record of participation in the Slovak struggle for self-determination and against Magyar supremacy. They were disappointed when the Czechs preferred the Protestants in manning positions of power and influence. Some sort of political separation for Slovakia— perhaps autonomy—was thought to be the panacea for all ills. Hlinka started to object to centralism even before the details of the so-called Pittsburgh agreement of May 30th, 1918, signed by Czech and Slovak emigré groups, reached the country. This agreement, which stipulated separate administration, parliament, and courts for Slovakia, came to the attention of the public in 1919 and encouraged the autonomists.[27]

At the same time Slovakia turned restless. The population became dissatisfied with the manner in which the military authorities were governing the region. Social and economic problems plagued large sections of the population. The influx of Czechs was a special cause for discontent.[28] The left-wing Czech socialists had to pay close attention to the status of Slovakia and the Slovaks. This was an uncomfortable problem for them, as in addition to the Czech-Slovak-Magyar problem, they had their own sizable German minority. Czech Socialists of all types well understood that the ideology of the "Czechoslovak nation" was aimed, *inter alia,* at inflating the number of Slavs vis-à-vis Germans in the Republic. Most of the Czech leftist leaders indeed accepted this ideology and acted accordingly at least until 1924 and, with some modifications, even later.[29] Only then was the ideology awarded the doubtful distinction of "Czech chauvinism."

During the first decade, the Republic was in the process of reorganization. In comparison to the scenery of the Empire, the body politic took now a new look and a new form. The trend was toward the left. While the conservatives (the "National-Democrats") were losing, the leading force in the state became the Agrarians (the "Republicans"), the Social-Democrats, and the National-Socialists (Edward Beneš' own party). The Catholics were divided into two Populist parties: a Czech and a Slovak. Considerable strength—but with little influence—gathered the political organizations on the nationalities and the minorities, the German, the Magyar, and even the Ruthene and the Jewish. Several lesser groups completed the picture.

During the period between the wars, three parties were at the helm and manned many of the changing coalitions: the Agrarians—who provided most of the Premiers; the Social Democrats; and the National Socialists. Leaders of the ruling parties, in company with the President Thomas G. Masaryk and his heir Beneš, constituted the so-called "Bourg group," the real heart of Czechoslovak democracy and the men who pulled the strings behind the scene. The Communists were a party of opposition *par exellence.* Together with several representatives of the nationalities and minorities, they consituted what in the political dictionary was termed "the state-demolishing" *(štátoborné)* parties.

The Slovaks were confused as well. When polarization began to occur in social democracy, the experienced and educated Slovak leaders leaned to the right. Slovakia's leftists regarded with awe their sophisticated and broadly-educated Czech counterparts, whom they met in Prague's Parliament.[30] The Germans and incoming Czech socialists gave the Slovak left socialists a sense of direction. Small wonder then that the internationalist spirit in Slovakia was deeply entrenched from the outset. In addition, Slovak left socialists were less susceptible to the ideology of a "Czechoslovak nation," though they did not dismiss it entirely. Its impact was not as profound as among the Czechs and the Slovaks soon discarded it.[31]

## The First Leftist Attempts to Solve the "Slovak Question"

Theoreticians and ideologists were lacking in Slovakia. The leftists there failed to give proper attention to the national problem at the outset. Šmeral was among the first left-wing socialists to take a close look at the Slovak question. Though not entirely free of the "Czechoslovak nation" ideology, Šmeral was well aware of the looming dangers. His long experience in the Austrian worker movement stood him in good stead. He warned the Czech proletariat against emotional nationalism, and recognized the individuality of the Slovaks. Hoping for an early settlement of the Slovak question, Šmeral wished to find a suitable solution, thus strengthening the bourgeois republic and facilitating its evolution into a socialist republic. Šmeral objected to small political units, which he regarded as non-viable in the modern world. He preferred a socialist federation, but until the ideal solution would materialize, he supported Czechoslovakia. He considered a cantonal system the best form for the multi-national republic. For Slovakia Šmeral proposed autonomous status. But the party held to a centralist line at least until 1924.[32]

Šmeral developed his views in 1920–1921, before the Communist Part of Czechoslovakia (CPCS) was founded. CPCS, a latecomer to the Communist International (Comintern, CI), nevertheless turned out to be one of its most valuable components.[33] With regard to shaping the party, the Czech section was the last to act. The German leftists, together with leftists of other nationalities in Slovakia, urged early formation of the party and affiliation to the International. In Slovakia, Magyars and Germans pioneered the unification of the various leftist cells into one group. At the "unification meeting" of the Left in Slovakia and Transcarpathian Ukraine ("Subcarpathian Russia"), which took place on January 16th, 1921, at Lubochňa spa, the national question was a secondary topic. After a plenary session, the meeting split into sections by nationality.[34] Only the proceedings of the plenary session and of the Slovak section are now available. In these documents, definition of the right to self-determination recalls the Wilsonian formula.[35] The speakers used the expressions "Slovak proletariat" and "Czechoslovak proletariat" interchangeably, and occasionally recalled the patriotism of the working class.[36] Karel Kreibich, who addressed the meeting in the name of the German-Bohemian left, already spoke of Slovakia as a "colony," a designation which was to recur frequently.[37] The low priority accorded to the national question was reflected in the fact that it was discussed only in connection with the tiny Jewish faction.[38]

Shortly after the meeting the organ of the Slovak left, *Pravda Chudoby*, published the Action Program of the "Czechoslovak Social-Democratic Workers' Party in Slovakia," a misleading title, to say the least. The ninth and last point called for creation of national sections in the whole territory of Slovakia and Subcarpathian Russia, in order to advance indoctrination of the members. Although the sections were subordinated to the Territorial Executive Committee, they were entirely free in the cultural sphere. All nationalities were to be represented in the proposed Territorial Executive Committee. Each nationality was also to have its own Executive Committee.[39] This was hardly a Bolshevik solution. Recalling the tenets of Austro-Marxism, the Action Program clearly demonstrated the full national consciousness of its authors. The Lubochňa meeting accepted the twenty-one conditions of the CI, leaving the name of the party (Condition No. 17) open.[40]

Slovakian Communists met with Czechs and Transcarpathians in Prague on May 14-16, 1921, and formally founded the Communist Party of Czechoslovakia. At this convention the Slovak delegates expressed their loyalty to the united Czechoslovak Republic and professed their faith in one inseparable Czechoslovak nation.[41] From October 30-November 4, 1921, German, Polish and Jewish Communists united with the CPCS and the Slovakian issue was not raised at all, while Šmeral exhorted against nationalistic exhibitionism.[42] The confusion on the national question remained after the convention ended; nor was clarity of thought rewarded by the Comintern, which spoke routinely about the *Czechoslovak*, Hungarian, German, Carpathorussian, and Polish proletariat in Czechoslovakia (the emphasis is mine).[43]

## The Early Nationalism of Slovak Communists

In any case, as early as 1921, the Slovak Communists disputed the issue of centralism versus autonomy. The debates notwithstanding, centralism prevailed not only in the state but also in the Party. The November convention abolished independent Slovak party institutions and trade unions. Instead, the convention established the function of Party Instructor for Slovakia. The trade unions were designated branches of centers located in Prague. The official explanation for the reorganization was the necessity for centralization in a party of the Bolshevik type plus the shortage of qualified functionaries, but Czech— and Magyar—suspicions of Slovak particularism played an important role in this arrangement.[44] Indeed, the nationalism of Slovak and of Czech workers was soon to clash inside the Communist Party.[45] The Communists followed the trend in the Republic, where nationalism was on the increase, with Slovakia no exception. In the first election of 1920, the Social Democratic Party polled 510,300 out of 1,341,100 votes in Slovakia. The nationalistic Hlinka's Slovak People's Party (HSPP; also nicknamed L'udáks) collected only 235,300 votes.[46] Three years later, in the municipal elections of 1923 (1,177,400 voters) HSPP polled 430,000, CPCS 241,000, and SDP 56,100 votes.[47] In comparison, in 1925 the Ludaks received 489,000 votes, the Communists 198,000 votes and the Social Democrats 60,600 votes out of 1,425,200 cast.[48] The trend toward an increase in nationalistic voting and a corresponding decrease of the socialist bloc is clear.

In Slovakia, where social problems and administrative oppression were plaguing the lower classes, the Communists inclined toward nationalism. In their propaganda they attacked what they termed "the robbing of Slovakia" by Czech capital. Party speakers described the territory as a colony of the Czech lands, while they characterized the entire state as a colony of French imperialism.[49] Only a socialist republic—or better still, a federation of soviet republics—and the dictatorship of the proletariat could improve the situation of the various nationalities in Czechoslovakia.[50] In this analysis of the nation's position, the Czechoslovak Bolsheviks emulated the CI hostility to the various peace treaties. The Communists criticized the government for not fulfilling promises such as autonomy for Slovakia and Transcarpathian Ukraine.[51] Yet, such argumentation proved problematic when it was confronted with a powerful, if no less demagogic, adversary: the Hlinka Party. The struggle of this Party for territorial autonomy placed the Slovak Communists in an awkward position: support of autonomy would make them seem to agree with the leading local bourgeois nationalists, who were violently anti-Communist! Still, quite a few Slovak Communists sensed the strong spell of the concept of autonomy. Unfortunately for them, the official party program recognized the unified nation and state, and objected to autonomistic designs. Hence, the speeches and publications of the various spokesmen revealed their confusion and embarrassment.[52]

The first regular congress of CPCS on Feburary 2–5, 1923, reiterated the old line, with Slovak delegates expressing unequivocal support. The congress denounced government policies for weakening the ties unifying the Czechoslovak nation, and thus exposing the state to external dangers. Also denounced were the L'udák slogans of autonomy, intended to prevent the influence of Western culture on Slovakia and hinder the national unification of the two kindred peoples. The Congress proposed broad self-government in all existing municipal, administrative and educational institutions, and objected to national and linguistic discrimination.[53] The decisions were a far cry from the concept of the right of self-determination, including creation of independent states, which was voiced so explicity by the Comintern at that time.[54] Historians argue that Šmeral and the Party were not fully aware of the Leninist principle of self-determination to the point of secession. Šmeral discovered Lenin's pre-war writings on nationalism only in 1924 and then started to publish them in the Party's press.[55] But the "Czechoslovak nation" ideology apparently remained a congenial idea for many Czech Communists.

The Slovaks were not happy, however. They objected, for example, to the liquidation of territorial party and trade-union institutions in Slovakia. The year 1923, in particular, witnessed attempts to set up a Slovak (National) Communist Party. Some trade unions declined to submit to Prague's leadership. Entire branches rebelled and followed the dissidents. Although none of these attempts succeeded, they bear witness to the restless national spirit of the rank and file.[56] Another sign of the true feelings was the almost open cooperation with the L'udáks. In 1922 deputies of Hlinka and Communist Parties were already joining in the attack on the government's deeds and misdeeds in Slovakia.[57] During the next year *Pravda Chudoby,* the Communist Slovak language paper, repeatedly described the HSPP as a representative of the genuine feelings of the people, while not forgetting to mention what it termed "L'udák intentions to mislead the plain folk."[58] During 1923 and also later, there were hints that negotiations were being held between the two parties.[59] The ambivalent stand of the two parties vis-à-vis one another became evident several times in the coming years. A contemporary historian suggested that the existence and appeal of Communist propaganda forced the HSPP to pay attention to social questions. *Mutatis mutandis,* the Communists became more aware of the awakening of local nationalism.[60]

After the Congress, as before, the CPCS continued to attack "the robbing" of Slovakia and its "colonial status." An interesting sideline was the campaign against local capitalists of non-Slovak origin, such as Magyars, Germans and Jews. Perhaps this was yet another indication of the mood of the Slovak party members. The outbursts against Jews often displayed a general anti-Semitic tone. From time to time, writers denounced "Jews" as such rather than "Jewish capitalists."[61] It should be recalled that the Party did not recognize the existence of a "Jewish nation."[62] It is also illuminating to consider the extremely harsh anti-Jewish pronouncements by Party personalities of Jewish origin.[63] Jewish Communists, whether Magyar, German, or Slovak, excelled in orthodox radicalism.

The German Communists were a special case. Less influential than the Magyars, less conspicious than the Jews, they relied on their co-nationals, who were strongly represented in industry and mining, and enjoyed the support of fellow Germans in Bohemia and Moravia. The Germans in Slovakia had undergone extensive Magyarization and traditionally cooperated with the Hungarians. Nor did Bohemian Germans exert a moderating influence. Radicalism was not unusual among the Germans. In other words, the various components of the Slovakian national spectrum stood to the left of their Czech comrades. Even if we disregard the social, economic, and political causes of extremism, the nationalist fervor made many Slovaks and Transcarpathian Ukrainians faithful supporters of the extremists in CPCS.

The decisions of the first party congress conciliated neither the "internationalists" nor the "nationalists" in the country. Magyars and Germans on the one hand, and Slovaks on the other, continued to press for clarifications and changes in the guidelines. They took issue with the Czechs, who were satisfied by and large with the accepted national platform. Notable exceptions were several Czechs politically active in Slovakia, such as Klement Gottwald, Eduard Urx, Karol Bacílek and others. Some of them were destined to hold important positions in Czechoslovak Stalinism. Did the Slovak experience influence these men? When the established leaders of the Party, well acquainted with the feelings of the Czech workers, proved immovable, Communists from Slovakia addressed their grievances to the Communist International.

### The Fifth Congress of CI and Slovakia

At that time the Comintern was in the midst of the Stalin-Trotsky conflict. Under the guise of "Bolshevization," the Executive of the CI was purging the affiliated parties of elements considered unreliable by the victors, and was increasing its control over the national sections.[64] The national and colonial problems proved to be an extremely sensitive and vital issue, particularly in the "successor states." The Comintern was hostile to the series of peace treaties, which it regarded as a new imperialist division of the world and of Europe. The new states, natural hotbeds of nationalist feelings, were regarded as hindrances to the victorious march of socialism. The Fifth Congress of CI (June–July, 1924) gave time and attention to the national problems of Central and Southeastern Europe, and censured the centralistic and chauvinistic policies of the region's governments. The Comintern commanded the Communist parties to adopt a "Leninist line in national problems."[65] With special reference to Yugoslavia and Czechoslovakia, but no less to Rumania, Poland and Greece, CI emphasized the "right of self-determination to the point of secession" of nations. In its resolutions addressed directly to the CPCS, the Congress enumerated the various nationalities living in Czechoslovakia, including Czechs and Slovaks, *separately*. The Party was requested to support "Slovakia's struggle for independence." The Comintern qualified the proclamation by adding that all nationalities of the Republic must cooperate in the common effort to overthrow the rule of capital and establish the dictatorship of the proletariat.[66] The Comintern failed to differentiate between nationalities and nations in Czechoslovakia, as the situation of Czechs and Slovaks was different from Germans, Magyars, or Poles. Nevertheless, the CPCS was forced to modify its views on the "Czechoslovak nation" and, at least verbally, to admit Slovakia's "right to self-determination to the point of secession." Later Communist writers complained however that the Party did not carry the new line into practice.[67] Significantly, the International's intervention constituted part and parcel of the effort to "bolshevize" CPCS. In practice, bolshevization meant an attack on the veteran and experienced leadership of Šmeral, Kreibich, and Antonín Zápotocký, and conversely an endorsement of the left opposition. In the ensuing discussion, the Slovak question ranked high.

The bourgeois press claimed that, by demanding Slovakia's independence, the CI was inciting the destruction of Czechoslovakia.[68] The Communists now gave much thought to analyzing Slovakia's place in the state. Kreibich, the Party's specialist on questions of nationality, had long bruited the slogan of territorial autonomy. He hoped that by this method democratic forces in the Slovak nation would gain power, while at the same time the position of the Hlinka Party would be undermined.[69] The prominent fellow-traveler, Professor Zdeněk Nejedlý, denied the existence of separate Slovak nation altogether.[70] The leading Slovak Communist, Julius Verčík, accused Šmeral and "Šmeralism" of willful discrimination against the former's fatherland.[71] Gottwald proposed complete separation of Slovakia from the Republic,[72] whereupon the Comintern's emissary Dmitrij Z. Manuilskij cautioned that the right to secede did not mean the obligation to do so.[73]

The Second Congress of CPCS (October 31–November 4, 1924) adopted the International's decisions.[74]

The Moravian Communist, Edmund Burian, who reported on the national question in the Congress, listed nine tasks for the Party. Of particular interest were the third and fourth points.[75] Burian denounced what he called "national bolshevism" and called for more involvement in real national problems.[76] The speaker warned against too extensive an interest in national rights, which might lead to support for one's "own" bourgeoisie. In demanding attention to "real problems," he actually seemed to be striving to avoid "national nihilism," meaning detachment from national emotions. Here we come up against the Scylla and Charybdis of Communism in Slovakia. Being completely radical in their general approach, Communists of Slovak nationality inclined to "national bolshevism," while comrades of Magyar, German, and Jewish origin were predisposed toward "national nihilism." The Second Congress turned down Kreibich's (and Šmeral's) model of "territorial autonomy" as being borrowed from the L'udáks.[77] Verčík saw in autonomy a "division of spoils among thieves."[78] He meant that the national bourgeoisie, by ridding itself of rivals, would gain a monopoly of exploitation in the autonomous region. This was a fundamental notion in the CPCS.[79] (A recent historian, Ján Mlynárik, regretted the acceptance of the dogma of the "right to self-determination to the point of secession" which he called "the frozen right to self-determination."[80] The resolution also envisaged the creation of a federal republic, which would eventually turn into a Soviet Union of Republics in Czechoslovakia.[81]

The resolution of the Congress did not reflect the pressures of the CI alone. The national set-up of the CPCS, and especially in Slovakia, forced a compromise. Postponement of the solution to some distant future may have increased the immediate tensions in the Party, but in the long run prevented a major explosion. All elements, whether Czech patriots, Slovak nationalists or radicals of the splinter nationalities, could derive some satisfaction from the resolution. Unfortunately for the Party, its unsteady policies on the agrarian question and on the national problem compelled the Communists in Slovakia to renounce voluntarily participation in the search for valid solutions to the territory's ills. The dogmatic solutions satisfied few, and the dissatisfied sought remedies in Slovak, Magyar, and German nationalistic parties. Evidently the CPCS failed to appreciate the subtleties and dangers of Slovak nationalism and its special flavor. The Communists saw in the exploitation of national tensions merely a convenient way of outweighing capitalism and introducing a socialist revolution. For them, the national problem was secondary to the social issue. When they analyzed nationalism with the assistance of the Marxist vocabulary of base and super structure, the Communists were insensitive to the irrational and emotional drives of the newly awakened Slovaks. There is little doubt that the radicalism of the Slovak Communists stemmed from a variety of objective causes, such as increasing exploitation, rising unemployment, extreme poverty in some parts of the country, and the mistakes and failures of Prague. To these should be added the impact of foreign developments and of rising radicalism abroad. Yet the subjective elements should be remembered as well: the thirst for self-expression and self-rule, national pride, and the hatred of all capitalist systems. The decisions of the Second Congress contributed to the theoretical but not to the practical solution of the Slovak question.

The year 1924 saw the appearance of a new kind of Communist in Slovakia: the young intellectuals educated and raised in the Republic. Among them Vladimír (Vlado) Clementis and Ladislav (Laco) Novomeský should be mentioned. They were part of that young Slovak generation which was then taking the helm in other parties as well, and excelling in original approaches to the problems of their nation. (They included, *inter alia,* the L'udak Karol Sidor and the Agrarian Dr. Imrich Karvaš.) The young communists published a journal of their own, named *Dav* (the masses; the multitude), which strove to develop original solutions for Slovakia. National pride and a warm love for Slovakdom and Slovakia characterized this journal. It wished to import humanistic and socialistic values in order to enrich the indigenous culture. The ambition to create a Slovak socialist culture—several of the youngsters displayed considerable talent as writers, poets and scholars—indicated their future path: a desire to combine nationalism with Marxism-Leninism.[83]

## The "Communist Separatism"

The achievements of the Second Congress satisfied neither the Comintern nor local leftists. A struggle between various factions continued within the Party. Slovak Communists spearheaded the struggle against what was nicknamed "Šmeralism", i.e., the balanced and self-confident line of Šmeral, Kreibich, and their associates. The Executive Committee of the CI intervened when Verčík became a victim of the struggle. His reinstatement lent him enormous prestige, and for years he was the darling of the Slovak radicals.[84] Verčík and his allies attacked Šmeral furiously at a conference held on May 10, 1925.[85] Observers felt that the tensions among the nationalities poisoned the atmosphere within the Party.[86] In spite of the "Leninist stand," Hlinka's slogan of autonomy continued to cause trouble. Such speakers as Verčík and Emanuel Šafranko proclaimed the Party's willingness, under certain conditions, to support the slogan. More seriously, Šmeral and Kreibich once again prepared an autonomistic design for Slovakia.[87] They recalled the wartime promises of Masaryk and others to grant Slovakia and Transcarpathian Ukraine autonomy and national diets. The Party reiterated to the charge that Slovakia was a mere colony.[88]

Characteristically, the Third Congress of the Party (September 26-28, 1925) glossed over the right to secession and the national question.[89] The general election of November 1925, in which the Hlinka and Magyar parties won great victories, again demonstrated the key importance of nationalism in Slovakia. The results of the elections caused a political crisis in the Republic. The strength of the various oppositionist groups, such as the German, Magyar, Hlinka, and Communist parties, forced the traditional political leadership to retreat; a new rightist coalition came into existence. The Hlinka Party participated in this coalition.[90]

The change in the political constellation and climate forced th Communists into new activity. They hoped to exploit the volte-face of Hlinka's followers. The Central Committee issued a communique accusing the HSPP of betrayal to Slovak autonomy, and demanded independence for the country. The Slovak people should decide for themselves their future political existence.[91] The party members were told, as they had been told before and would be again, that while the non-Slovaks should struggle for the right to Slovakia's self-determination, the local Communists and proletarians should insist on staying voluntarily in the Republic.[92] Characteristically, the Czech press charged the Party with conspiring with Hungary to annex Slovakia.[93] This notorious accusation, often hurled also at the Hlinka Party, did more harm than good. In spite of the existence of pro-Magyar or Magyar personalities in both parties, there was little doubt that they preferred Masaryk to Horthy. The charges did not alter the Party's line, and the Slovak functionaries greatly appreciated the new tactics.[94]

The Communist speakers continued to attack the Ľudáks, citing their hypocrisy and alledged national treachery. Conspicuous in this respect were the moderate parliamentary debates on the "Law of the State Language,"[95] previously of overriding importance for the Ľudáks; and the agreement to pay salaries to priests (congrua), one of the conditions for Hlinka's joining the coalition.[96] The CPCS continued to call for a plebiscite in Slovakia and for independence for that country. Most important in the anti-governmental and anti-L'udák campaign was the proclamation "Remove the oppressing apparatus of the Czech bourgeoisie from Slovakia!" published by a Party conference in the city of Žilina on July 25th, 1926.[97] The proclamation described the country's condition in an aggressive and exaggerated manner, and repeated the demand for a plebiscite and for independence. Independent Slovakia should become a part of the Union of Soviet Republics. This provocative proclamation, with its harsh call to the Czechs to leave immediately, caused much dispute.[98] It was Gottwald who initiated this document and composed it with the approval of Verčík and the Central Committee. This however did not deter him from pinning responsibility for its publication on Verčík, when authorship became an embarassment.[99] Doctrinaire thinking, such as the proposal to establish Worker, Farmer, and Small Craftsmen Security Units, or subordination of national liberation to social freedom, ruined this clever attempt to beat the Hlinka Party with its own weapons.

Despite Gottwald's authorship, the above proclamation reflected the confusion and radicalism of the Slovak Communists. Should Slovakia stay in the Republic? What did "right of self-determintion to the point of secession" mean? Should Slovakia demand autonomy or independence? Who were the true allies—Czech Communists or Slovak nationalists? Would the solution be reached before a socialist revolution or after it? There were no definitive and unequivocal answers, and there were no theoreticians of stature to give the answers.

The Communists sensed that the Hlinka Party represented a real power and spoke for a great part of Slovakia's population. But all the Communists were able to do was blame their nationalistic adversaries for misleading the toiling masses. The CPCS analyzed and described the HSPP as representative of the Slovak bourgeoisie competing bitterly with Czech capital.[100]

The new government presented the Parliament with a law reorganizing the state administration. The law was to extend to self-rule in Slovakia, thus satisfying the Hlinka Party. In reality, however, the new organization was far from HSPP demands, as the Communist deputies recognized.[101] In presenting the Party's views, Šmeral and Kreibich criticized the government policies in Slovakia. They returned to the old proposals of self-determination, territorial autonomy, and a local diet. In speeches free of the demagogy of the proclamation of Žilina, the two protested against further curtailment of the municipal government's freedom of action.[102] Nevertheless, two years of intensive activity ended in nothing.

## The "Slovak Question" and Gottwald's Victory in the CPCS

In 1927, Party interest in Slovakia decreased. The Fourth Congress of the CPCS (May 25–28, 1927) had little of relevance to say.[103] The main reason for the silence probably lay in the intensified factional struggle and the Comintern interference in it. But the state's administrative reorganization brought to light a misunderstanding between the Slovak and Transcarpathian Communists over several Ruthenian villages on the border of the two regions.[104] Again nationalism within the Party got the better of the proclaimed internationalism.

The low priority accorded to the national question was also evident in the next year (1928) and subsequently. This was a fateful period in the history of the Party. Political failures, continuous in-fighting, and the dictates of the Comintern caused a major upheaval, which ended in replacement of the entire leadership. The new leaders, an extremist coterie around Gottwald, nicknamed "the boys of Karlin" (Karlinští Kluci),[105] were a group of young fanatics, whose greatest qualification was their willingness to accept Moscow's orders unconditionally.[106] The change of guard brought about the retirement of many members in Slovakia as well. Nonetheless, Slovakia remained radical. Quite a few young Magyars, Jews, Dav contributors and others rallied around Gottwald.[107] The Sixth Congress of the CI (August 1928) discussed the changes, as the Fifth Congress of the CPCS had already done (February 18–23, 1929).[108] The national question was on the agenda of both, and the latter congress in fact adopted the decisions of the former.[109] Gottwald reported to both congresses, addressing himself, inter alia, to the national question as well.[110] In the debates, all thought of autonomy for Slovakia, including the proclamation of Žilina, was rejected and branded as a bourgeois slogan. The participants denied the idea of colonial status for the Republic and Slovakia, defining Czechoslovakia instead as an imperialist country.[111] The Fifth Congress reaffirmed the right of self-determination to the point of separation.[112] Years later, Ján Mlynárik maintained that the new leadership had not bothered with ingenious and original thinking. By again copying formalistic prescriptions, it guaranteed further divisions within the Party in the future.[113]

One can hardly say that in the described period, the CPCS displayed consistency in dealing with nationalism in Slovakia. Being abundantly supplied with formulas, it vacillated between them. The Party moved ahead in convoluted fashion and, apparently, reached a major turning point at the Fifth Congress. This meeting was also to decide on the direction in which Slovakia's Communism would move from then on.

## Chapter 2

# THE FIRST REPUBLIC: GOTTWALD'S LEADERSHIP

The Fifth Congress constituted a watershed in the Party's history. The generation of the anti-Habsburg struggle had to yield its place to the younger generation, mostly graduates of Czechoslovak schools. This happened just as the fateful period in the Republic's history entered the gate: the period of economic and political upheaval—the one to end with the Munich dictate. Czechoslovakia faced now an increasing pressure from the nationalities and minorities. The political atmosphere changed. Winds were blowing in the rightist direction: not only division of seats in the state's Parliament and Senate but also power-relations within the parties testified to this. The developing force of authoritarian states, big powers and lesser neighbors, could not go unnoticed. The Communists were to learn hard realities as the time went by; their attempts to escape the political ghetto came to nil.

## After the Fifth Congress of the CPCS

Changes instituted at the Fifth Congress were of signal importance in the life of the Party. The Congress hoped that its policies toward the nationalities would have a lasting impact, but these expectations were not fulfilled.[1] On the contrary, the Party showed laxity and passivity on the Slovak question and particularly toward concrete, immediate problems.[2]

A major crisis followed the Congress. Hundreds of members left the Party or were purged by the new leadership. Cells and entire organizations disintegrated and disappeared. In Slovakia, zealous leftists brought the generation problem into the political arena, expelling experienced senior comrades. The Party's following and its influence on the public decreased enormously.[3] The crisis and the reform of Czechoslovak Communism occurred at the time when the Great Depression enveloped and crippled the world's and Republic's economy. The Comintern exhorted the forces of the proletariat to begin the decisive battle against capitalism; it declared war on Fascism, whether of "national" or "social" brand.[4] The brunt of the attack was aimed at the Social Democrats. In short, there were many adverse circumstances which prevented the CPCS from paying closer attention to the national question. But the objective conditions just described should not be separated from the Party's thinking on the subject. Indeed, ideological considerations and practical actions were intertwined in the Party's work.

The Communist Party in Slovakia could hardly rely on theoretical analysis and high-standard planning, for it was always short of intellectuals trained in Marxism-Leninism. Unlike its Czech counterpart, Slovak Communism could draw little inspiration from the heritage of the Austro-Hungarian days. The few experienced Communist leaders in Slovakia were mostly of Magyar nationality, and not fully in tune with the dreams and wishes of the Slovak masses.[5] The CPCS was slow to prepare sufficient Slovak "cadres".[6] To make matters worse, the CPCS bosses in Slovakia were hostile to intellectuals. Distrusting "petty-bourgeois" elements, they discouraged young members of the intelligentsia from joining the Party.[7] Like the developing working class, a considerable portion of the young Slovak intelligentsia was of peasant origin. As mentioned, in pre-1918, predominantly agrarian Slovakia, Germans, Magyars, and Jews constituted large parts of the urban and industrial population. Sizable aggregates of the Party following were of the peasant origin or from the agrarian proletariat. Still, the Party bosses resented "petty-bourgeois" intellectuals—these peasant sons dressed in waistcoats. The price the Party paid for its attitude toward intellectuals was a shortage of theoreticians and above all of propagandists attuned to the masses. In Slovakia, as elsewhere, the intellectuals were the carriers of new ideas.

The Party was not sufficiently aware of the intensity of Slovak nationalism and was out of step with its development. One of the Party's sources of strength lay in the regions populated by national minorities. The vote of protest of the Magyars, and to a certain degree also of the (Communist) Germans, was obvious and explicable. Similarly understandable was the coolness toward Slovak nationalism injected into the Party tactics by functionaries from the minorities.[8] It should again be emphasized that the CRCS saw in nationalism, above all, a lever to weaken and counterbalance capitalism. Since in the Communist view social liberation meant, *ipso facto,* national liberation as well, the struggle for national liberation was subordinated to the struggle for social emancipation. Consequently, Communist theorists provided few detailed analyses of problems relating to Slovak national grievances on cultural matters, language and education. If the establishment of the dictatorship of the proletariat would automatically cure all these ills, why bother with them now? Unsatisfied national aspirations (Magyar no less than Slovak) intensified the dissatisfaction of the masses, which could prove useful to the Communist cause. During the period under discussion, however, the Party's policy of ignoring Slovak national aspirations enjoyed the hearty support of young radicals, of the Party's non-Slovak leaders, and of activists whose social origins had inculcated in them feelings of insecurity (in particular the sons of rich Jewish families).[9]

The importance of the Comintern's promotion of a policy of social, rather than national, awareness can hardly be overstated. If the bourgeois state was in fact a fascist dictatorship, if there was little difference between the various bourgeois parties, or between them and the socialist parties, then any positive action by the Communists on behalf of the national minorities would only strengthen the class enemy.

It would be hard to describe Czechoslovakia as a "Fascist state," however. The rightist coalition broke down, in a considerable degree because of the problems accrued by the Hlinka Party during its participation in the government, and the 1929 elections returned to power the traditional components of the Czechoslovak body politic. The new government, although forced into defense by attacks from the left and from the right, and in particular from the more aggressive elements within the national minorities, preserved the basic democratic set-up of the state. The Agrarian-led cabinet responded to the political and economic pressures by appropriate legislative and administrative measures. It took steps to combat the tensions in the economic life and to tighten the surveillance in the socio-political sphere. The Communist leadership concluded that these measures initiate "Fasczization of the State." During the early thirties, the Communist propaganda described the Republic's regime as "Fascist dictatorship," and aimed at increasing alienation of the workers toward the "bourgois state." Thus the CPCS followed closely the line prescribed by the CI, and abstained from applying independent, original strategy and tactics.

In one sphere, namely the Party's organization, a change did take place. The new leadership under Gottwald decided to lower the number of Party regions, while expanding their prerogatives. The entire territory of Slovakia was recognized as a single region, headed by local functionaries. It is not clear whether there was any intention to satisfy the demands of the Slovak comrades, who had clamored for their own region ever since 1921. Perhaps we are dealing here only with the logical consequence of a natural process and with a need for increased efficiency.[10] Nevertheless, the step was in harmony with the Party's program for Slovakia: the right to self-determination to the point of separation.

The basic doctrine of the CPCS did not regard the survival of the Republic as a necessity. Communist declarations were quick to point out first that, in the given circumstances, self-determination could come about only after the achievement of the Party's ultimate aim, the establishment of the dictatorship of the proletariat; and secondly that the proletariat of various nationalities should try to maintain proletarian unity in one state. The possibility that national minorities might secede from Czechoslovakia and join their mother nations instead of Czechoslovakia was not, however, excluded.[11] In spite of these statements, the Party made it clear to its members that the existing Czechoslovak Republic was only a temporary arrangement. Thus the CPCS singled out the minorities for special attention, approving their desire to destroy the status quo in the Czechoslovak state. On the other hand, the Party now revealed little appreciation for the hopes and dreams of the Czech people, who wanted to see the state preserved. Czechs, by and large, regarded Czechoslovakia's sizable German minority and the Slovak nationalists with suspicion. Since Gottwald's leadership regarded the minorities as more promising from the revolutionary point of view, the CPCS concentrated its efforts in the areas of Czechoslovakia populated by non-Czech peoples.[12]

Yet, as already indicated, the Slovaks were not officially classified as a minority. Czechoslovakia's founding fathers had created the state for the Slovaks no less than for the Czechs. While most Slovaks appreciated the Republic and the freedom it had brought them, many of them criticized its real or imaginary shortcomings, especially the alleged discrimination against them. The Prague government obstinately clung to the centralist system of governing the country. It did not do enough to develop Slovakia's backward economy or to protect its industries from the competition of the better developed Czech industries. As a result, Slovakia underwent a painful process of deindustrialization in the 1920s. Slovak nationalists saw in the enforcement of policies based on the doctrine of a single Czechoslovak nation a conscious design to Czechify them. In their efforts to suppress industrial and agricultural strikes and to overcome resistance to foreclosures for nonpayment of taxes and debts, the Czechoslovak authorities did not hesitate to use force, even armed force,[13] against workers and peasants in Slovakia. (The authorities used similar means in the Czech lands and Transcarpathian Ukraine.) Because of Prague's fear of the threat of Hungarian irridenta, the Magyar minority in Slovakia was subjected to political, cultural, and social discrimination.[14]

Basing its arguments on the wrongs done to Slovakia, the CPCS included the Slovaks among the oppressed minorities. (The HSPP likewise regarded the Slovaks as one of Czechoslovakia's oppressed minority groups.) The Party hoped that Slovakia, where political and social discontent were more intense than in the Czech lands, might become the fuse igniting the proletarian revolution in Czechoslovakia.[15] During the winter of 1929–1930, Party propaganda held up before the Slovak working class the vision of a "Soviet Slovakia," that is, a country administered by workers' councils (soviets) and free to determine its future by itself.[16] In fact, the Party envisaged Czechoslovakia as a soviet socialist federation.[17] However, this was to be decided only after the preliminary task of creating Soviet states had been accomplished. The Communists were not alone in proposing a division of the centralist Republic into its component parts. The Hlinka Party and other groups advocated the same solution. In countering the L'udáks, the Communists insisted that autonomy would grant the Slovak bourgeoisie a monopoly in exploiting the working man, but would not change his living conditions.[18] As we have seen, during the twenties the concept of autonomy had its partisans among Communists as well.[19] Under Gottwald's leadership, however, the CPCS sought to highlight the differences between itself and the HSPP. A slogan promoted by a bourgeois party could not be used by the Communist Party. Still, observers felt that both parties were competing on a similar platform, and even learning from each other.[20]

As pointed out above, the decisions of the Fifth Congress had only a modest impact on the nationality policy of the CPCS in Slovakia. Nevertheless the new leadership and the CI hoped for quick revolutionary achievements. For them, the national question was an important tool in their efforts to establish the dictatorship of the proletariat in Czechoslovakia. The slogan "Soviet Slovakia" was not an end, but merely a means, an interpretation of the doctrine of self-determination to the point of secession, designed by the CI to promote socialism in Central Europe. This slogan, however, fell on fertile ground, and was revived several times, whenever Slovak Communists considered separation from Czechoslovakia (most recently in 1968–1969).

## The Sixth Congress of the CPCS

The Sixth Congress of the CPCS took place on March 7–11, 1931. It discussed the question of nationalism at considerable length, criticizing the Party for its inertia. The thesis on the national question equated Czechoslovakia with the Austro-Hungarian monarchy. It borrowed

Mazzini's famous epithet for the Habsburg empire, "prison of nations," to describe Czechoslovakia.[21] Slovakia was said to be worse off under the Republic than it had been under the Magyars.[22] The Congress called upon Czechoslovakia's nationalities to fight for self-determination to the point of secession. It emphasized once again that this did not exclude the possibility of the ultimate creation of a common state on a basis of autonomy and complete equality of all nationalities.[23] In accordance with the CI policy, the Party leaders admonished the members not to practice "nihilism on the national question," i.e., to consider the struggle for social liberation not "purely" a class struggle, but also a struggle for national liberation.

The Party also warned the proletariat not to engage in a "pure" national liberation struggle, without simultaneous class war, and not to believe that partial reforms in the bourgeois state could significantly improve the life of the minorities. The Party's advocacy of some of the minorities' demands combined with its attention to agrarian problems, signified an important step toward understanding the needs of the non-Czech people.[24] Finally, the Congress branded the government's policies "Czech imperialism" instead of "Czechoslovak imperialism," thus absolving the Slovaks from responsibility, and recognizing their status as similar to that of the other national minorities. Václav Kopecký, who reported on nationality questions, rejected and denounced the slogan "Soviet Slovakia."[25] Although the views expressed by the CPCS on the national question at this time were witness to a sensitive and sensible attitude, one still wonders why plans were not outlined for individual nations, particularly for the Slovaks. The generalities voiced were far from satisfactory.

**The Great Depression**

Faithful to the orders of the CI, the Czechoslovak Communists undertook to prepare for the revolution which Comintern theoreticians anticipated as a result of the Great Depression and the advance of fascism.[26] The aim was to intensify class war, in the form of "class against class" in disregard of nationalities. Czechoslovak Communists once more reduced the national question to a tool of class warfare. In Slovakia, the Party suffered an assortment of "deviations" after the Fifth Congress, and was not able to exploit fully the adverse economic conditions for its own ends. Slovakia's branch of the Party was notoriously short of card-carrying members and functionaries.[27] The organizational and propaganda activities of the Party in Slovakia left much to be desired, although election returns did not clearly reveal this fact.[28] During the depression years, Communist undertakings suffered several bitter setbacks, in spite of repeated assessments by Party theorists that conditions in Slovakia were ripe for revolution. The slogans of "Soviet Slovakia" experienced a revival. Party leaflets described Slovakia as the "weak link in the decaying imperialist regime in Czechoslovakia."[29] The period between the Sixth and the Seventh Congresses of the CPCS was one of extreme aggressiveness and strident language. Provocative and militant elements had their day. Communist activity led to increased tension within and around the Party. In accordance with the CI's analysis, the CPCS affirmed that the "Fascist Czechoslovak regime" was determined to outlaw and destroy the Party.[30]

The regime was, indeed, quite efficient in fighting the Communists. It prohibited meetings and closed sections of the Party press, and a spy network reported on Communist activities. The Party chose to move some of its work underground to avoid open clash with the authorities. Living in a timorous atmosphere, the Party members vented their frustration and fear in harangues in the illegal press and publications. This semi-legal, quasi-conspiratorial existence tended to create a barrier between the Party and the people. Because of overconcentration on matters of revolutionary politics, the CPCS left the nationally-conscious Slovak masses unmoved. The Party thus missed one of the great opportunities in Slovakia under the First Republic. During the years of the Depression, the population lent a willing ear to radical voices. Moreover, the Communists' principal rival in radicalism, the Hlinka Party, was in deep trouble. The HSPP joined the government in 1927, thereby exposing itself to the charge that it had sold out to the Prague government. In 1929, the well-publicized trial and conviction of Hlinka's trusted advisor, Professor Vojtech (Béla) Tuka, for military espionage and high treason, caused the Party's tremendous decline in prestige. Although Hlinka promptly pulled the Party out of the government, he weakened its traditional leadership by expelling those of his associates who had ventured to criticize him for his support of Tuka.[31]

The election returns of 1929 (nationwide) and 1931 (municipal) demonstrated the L'udák downward trend. One should state to the credit of the Czechoslovak regime that it succeeded in paralyzing radicals of the right and left during the difficult times of the Depression, through both firm police intervention and proper moderation in economic policies. In addition, the CPCS and the HSPP neutralized each other. They weakened their own influence on the public, one by underestimating the intensity of the nationality problem, the other by giving insufficient attention to social discontent.[32]

The year 1932 witnessed promising contacts between the Communist and L'udák (academic) youth. In June of that year, a meeting of young Slovak intellectuals was held at the spa of Trenčianské Teplice, for the purpose of discussing Slovakia's future. The array of speeches of diverse political schools was characterized by the tendency to condemn the existing system and the position of Slovakia in the Republic. Although the participants did not agree on what the Slovak future course should be, they severely criticized the prevailing state of affairs. The *Dav* group represented the Communist side. By now, the Davists had freed themselves both from the sterile internationalism of the Stalin-led Comintern and from L'udák-inspired Slovak nationalism, which was parochial and obsurantist. In their appearance they represented, in the wider sense, the secular, nationally-minded Slovak intelligentsia. As such, they were also appreciated by members of other political streams.[33] Against the "bourgeois" nationalism of the Slovak political parties the Davist Novomeský proposed raising the banner of a nationalism with a "proletarian-revolutionary" content. Party Chairman Gottwald, however, harshly attacked Novomeský's ideas.[34] Actually, at the time when the Comintern was discouraging Communists from cooperating with non-Communists, the Davists rightly recognized the importance of the Trencianske Teplice meeting, and participated in it with the Party's consent. They did not even exclude further cooperation with other participants in the meeting.[35]

The Davists shared in Slovak national undertakings; they were among key-note speakers at the first convention of Slovak writers in May 1936 at the spa of Trenčianské Teplice, and firmly defended the independent entity *(svojbytnost')* of the Slovak nation.[36] The Slovak Communist intellectuals easily developed contacts with Slovak non-Communists and with their Communist and non-Communist counterparts. They lived, however, in intellectual and emotional isolation from the local Communist functionaries.[37] During the bleak doctrinaire years of the Depression, the young Communist intellectuals took a more realistic, down-to-earth attitude to Slovak national problems than did the rest of the Party.

In 1934, during the parliamentary debate on President Thomas G. Masaryk's re-election, the CPCS opened a concentrated attack on the Republic. It savagely denounced Masaryk and put up Gottwald as a presidential candidate.[38] The Communist actions caused a major commotion, and the State Prosecutor issued a warrant of arrest against Gottwald and three of his colleagues, which they evaded by fleeing to Moscow. Gottwald's disappearance from Czechoslovakia for eighteen months closed a rather unhappy chapter in the history of the Party, a chapter marked by much outward aggressiveness but few tangible results.

## In the Shadow of Nazism

In the midst of the Depression, a drama was played out in Germany: Adolf Hitler became Chancellor. The Czechoslovak Communists did not differ from comrades elsewhere in their reaction to this event. They refused to be overly impressed by the new dictator, and anticipated his quick downfall in the wake of a proletarian revolution. In the meantime, the CPCS preferred to fight the "Social Fascists," i.e., the Social Democrats. Those who replaced the exiled leaders, however, chose to change Party strategy. Ján Šverma, *pro tempore* head of the Party (from August 1934 to February 1936), was more cognizant of the dangers budding in Germany, and veteran leader, Dr. Bohumír Šmeral, rushed to his aid. Šverma, Šmeral, Rudolf Slánsky and the rest of their colleagues took the Nazi threat seriously. Independent of the Comintern, the CPCS started to elaborate a sort of popular front concept *(socialistické souručenství).*[39] This spelled the end of the Party's indifference to the "bourgeois state;" indeed, the Party even looked for ways of cooperating with this state. Communist deputies voted, for the first time, in favor of parts of the state budget. After Masaryk's resignation in 1935, they no longer put up a presidential candidate of their own, but voted for Dr. Eduard Beneš.[40] (The Ľudáks had done likewise.) The Communists gave favorable consideration, in accordance with the CI, to the armament program of the Republic.

These innovations in the Party were the result of a reassessment of the position of the Republic *and* of the Czech nation, vis-à-vis the Nazi danger. Although not free of CI directives, Šverma and friends evolved decisions of their own. The Czech Communist leaders became sympathetic to Czech statehood. They considered it to be a way of defending the Czech nation, a safeguard for the future. If Nazi expansionism questioned the Czech's right of existence as a nation, the Communists should rally to the aid of their people.

Consequently, the Party shifted its activity from the minorities, including the Slovaks, to the dominant Czech ethnic group. The concept of the right of self-determination to the point of secession lost popularity. Only enemies of the state would welcome the weakening of Czechoslovakia through the secession of individual parts. The slogan of "Soviet Slovakia" fell into oblivion, and harsh attacks on the Republic became a thing of the past.[41] Communists in Slovakia discovered that much could be improved through local reform. Reform and not the complete overthrow of the bourgeois state became the motto of the day. The autonomy advocated by the Ludaks came under stronger fire than ever. Now autonomy was criticized not merely as a "bourgeois demand;" the Communist claimed, with a great deal of justice, that in the circumstances of the day autonomy would weaken the common homeland.[42] Again, temporizing won out. It was not the needs and dreams of the Slovak people that determined the CPCS stand toward Slovakia, but the broader overall policy of the Party. And again, the Party lost a critical chance to establish itself among the Slovak people. The Hlinka Party was left alone (if the miniscule Slovak National Party is discounted) to argue the case of Slovakia's autonomy in Czechoslovakia. The Communists, thanks to their new policy, succeeded in gaining popularity among the Czechs, but lost it among the other nationalities.[43] At a meeting of the CI Executive Commission's Presidium, participants attacked Šverma and Slánsky, and the latter were removed from leadership of CPCS. Gottwald was reinstated and with him many of the stringent policies of the past.

With a new president in office, the government extended an amnesty to those accused of political crimes, and the Moscow exiles returned home. Gottwald did not lose much time asserting the Comintern line in Party policy. He condemned the conciliatory policy of the temporary leadership, and those duly submitted to self-criticism.

Self-determination to the point of secession regained favor for a short while. Šverma's policy lost support, even while the Comintern prepared the popular-front strategy. Yet Gottwald had to find a proper answer for the new conditions in Central Europe. The right of separation was soon discarded again. Instead, the Party recalled the Leninist principle of proletarian obligation to combat separatism in a multinational state after the victorious revolution. The Stalinist maxim of a country national in form and socialist in essence was also invoked to deny national minorities the right of separation. Later, the Party launched a full-scale attack on all separatist (and autonomist) tendencies. When they were chided for betraying their own programs and slogans, the Communist speakers answered by professing their faith in socialism as their ultimate aim. They explained that in the given situation the battle against the bourgeois dictatorship—fascism—required dialectic adjustments in strategy and tactics.[44]

In plain terms, the new Communist line held that if the bourgeoisie of the national minorities clamored for separation (or autonomy), it was the duty of Communists to offer determined opposition. Communists learned how to differentiate between bourgeois parties, contrary to their previous indiscriminate condemnation of all of them. Pragmatism and not ideology seemed to guide the Party's day-to-day actions. In Slovakia, Communist policy was expressed in condemnations of the HSPP's autonomist designs, and in objections to the surrender of any Slovak territory to Hungary or to Poland. The CPCS intensified its activity among the Magyar and German minorities, hoping thus to paralyze the growing strength of irridentist parties.[45] The fascist danger finally aroused the Czechoslovak Communists from their doctrinaire dreams. In close correlation with the CI line, they proclaimed the necessity to defend the Republic from its mortal enemies abroad and within. The Communists began to display an ostentatious patriotism, adopting and adapting national symbols, figures, and traditions in their public appearances. The new image met with favorable response among the Czechs. The Slovak autonomists, Magyars, Germans and other minorities started to wonder whether the CPCS had jumped on the government bandwagon.[46]

The new Party line was formally proclaimed at the Seventh Congress of the CPCS on April 11–14, 1936. The Congress argued for improvement of the economic, social, cultural and administrative situation of non-Czech groups, so as to answer their needs and bind them more closely to the Republic. It claimed equality of all nations in the state, and asked the Czechs to fight on behalf of the just demands of the national minorities in Czechoslovakia.[47]

It should be stressed, however, that even in 1936 a Communist Congress had nothing specific to say about Slovakia, as distinct from the other non-Czech nationalities in the country. Students of CPCS history agree that the Party was late in realizing the separate needs of Slovakia.[48] Although speakers often returned to the matter, only in May 1937 did a regional conference prepare an elaborate plan of action for Slovakia.

## On the Eve

The Party was slow to come to grips with Slovakia's problems, in large degree because of ignorance and an uninspired program. The lack of theoreticians may explain, at least in part, the Party's shortcomings in this respect. Years later a Communist historian stated that the condition for the Communist Party's retaining the initiative in Slovakia was the ability to lead a national movement and to translate this leadership into a written program.[49] To give another illustration of the critical approach, the poet Novomeský approved of the struggle of the

HSPP, yet objected to the obsurantist-parochial elements and final objectives of that movement.[50]

A decisive step forward was the unequivocal demand for equality in relations between the Czechs and the Slovaks. Although the Party had, in the past, demanded equality for all nationalities in the Republic, it was only in 1937 that it publicly recognized that some national groups were more equal than others. The Communists learned to regard Slovaks as a nation equal with the Czechs, unlike minorities, which were mere fragments of larger ethnic groups living abroad. The treatment of Slovaks as a minority was shelved. The maxim "Equal with Equal" *(rovný s rovným)*, which expressed the Slovaks' right to be treated on an equal footing with the Czechs and their desire to be recognized as a separate *(svojbytný)* entity similar to the Slavonic population of Bohemia and Moravia, was to receive increasing importance in Party parlance, valid up to the present day.[51]

Another important point of progress was represented by the so-called Plan of Economic, Social and Cultural Construction for Slovakia, drawn up on May 16–17, 1937, in the city of Banská Bystrica. The Plan coincided with similar Party undertakings elaborated during the same period on behalf of the Transcarpathian Ukraine, the Germans, and the Magyars (and with many other vague plans bruited in the Republic during the critical years before Munich). Nonetheless, it was the first time that the Party had taken the trouble to consider Slovakia's problems in a comprehensive manner, and to prepare a plan relatively free of dogmatism and demagogy. The document was in seven parts, of which the first—the call for industrialization of Slovakia—was probably the most important. Other economic-social demands were made for the improvement of agriculture and the raising of the living standards of the middle class. Two chapters dealt with cultural matters, with education, and with linguistic rights. Finally, under separate headings, democratization and liberalization of the administration were discussed.[52] The cardinal shortcoming of this document was the lack of attention to the status of Slovakia in the Republic. The authors of the Plan were evidently afraid that by referring to it, they might arouse suspicion that they were in agreement with the Slovak, Magyar, and German bourgeois parties. Yet while the Plan responded to numerous immediate demands, it left open the central issue, namely the right of self-determination. Although more than a few of its details had an anti-capitalist tinge and others could not be realized in the contemporary Czechoslovak Republic, still the plan was an outline for reform rather than revolution.[53] The Plan was in line with a variety of pronouncements aimed at countering HSPP demands, particularly that of autonomy.[54] However, the Party failed to give the Plan adequate publicity.

The position of Communist agitators was not easy. On one hand, they had to criticize Czechoslovakia's capitalist system and demand changes, for which they were accused of unpatriotic behavior and of giving support to L'udák autonomists and Magyar irridentists in Slovakia. On the other hand, national minorities accused the CPCS of betraying the right to self-determination and turning into "Czechoslovaks." The Party found it difficult to explain its about-face. In spite of the important innovations, Communism was in retreat in the last year of the Republic.

## The Year of Munich

To say that the Hlinka Party actually convinced the Slovak people of the justice of its cause would be a gross overstatement. During the years of the Depression, when objective conditions favored radicalism, Slovakia's population displayed relative moderation. But in a period of rising nationalism all over Europe, when Hitler and the Sudeten German leader Konrad Henlein were battering Prague, and a growing number of citizens of Slovakia became restless, the HSPP harvested the hatred it had sown. The non-Czech nationalities were ignorant of the mortal danger developing in Berlin. And the nationalist parties, including the Hlinka Party, adopted the "Leninist" view that a defeat for Prague was a gain for them. The Communists had long been accustomed to speak of the HSPP in the same terms as they referred to other bourgeois parties: while parading anti-Czechism at home, the L'udáks willingly allied themselves with the right-wing Czech politicians against the working people to perpetuate capitalist exploitation.[55] Once the L'udáks moved closer to the Sudeten German and Magyar parties, the Communists realized that they could expect little from the HSPP.[56] In its appeals to members of the HSPP, the CPCS pleaded with them to return to their original and traditional pro-Republican policy. The Communists recognized that the L'udáks had succeeded in making themselves the spokesmen of Slovak restlessness, but warned the HSPP against playing with the nation's future.[57] The Communists now began to take a greater interest in the Slovak qustion. They no longer classified the Slovaks among the country's national minorities. They also took a more understanding view of the old "Czechoslovak" doctrine which, by combining the Czechs and Slovaks into a single nation, increased the numerical strength of the "people of the state" *(Staatvolk)* vis-à-vis the Germans and other national minorities. A regional meeting in the city of Košice (July 30–31, 1938) recognized that the "Czechs and Slovaks are two nations closely related, which are naturally bound together and should evolve toward an even closer relationship."[58] The statement was based on the thesis that the idea of a single Czechoslovak nation was a relatively progressive one for this period of increased oppression.[59] In plain language, this meant that when external dangers threatened the existence of the Czech nation, the Slovaks should lend it every possible support. They ought to do so in their own interests, because of the dangers which Hungarian and Polish revisionism posed to the territorial and ethnic integrity of their own land. The Czechs, on the other hand, should back the just demands of Slovakia.[60] It should be taken into consideration that Slovak nationalists regarded Hungary, and not Germany, as their Fatherland's historical enemy. Whether Czechoslovak authorities or Communists, both were required to convince Slovakia that the tragedy befalling the Czechs would unfavorably affect Slovaks too. The Party argued the need to satisfy all the nationalities, and grant them a status of genuine equality, thus giving them an interest in the defense of the Republic.

The L'udák Deputy, Karol Sidor, served as a particular target of Communist attacks. Sidor headed the radical, pro-Polish wing of the HSPP, which demanded Slovakia's close cooperation with Poland. In its campaign for autonomy, the radical wing of the HSPP virtually echoed Nazi anti-Czechoslovak propaganda, which claimed that the Republic was not a state. The Communists also opposed anti-Semitic agitation of the Hlinka Party.[61] But the CPCS was not sure of itself in battling the HSPP. That can be seen in its vacillating approach toward the so-called Pittsburgh agreement. The L'udáks argued that Prague had failed to honor the agreement, and on the occasion of the 20th anniversary of its signing they appealed to public opinion. The Communists either denounced the agreement altogether, saying that it was not tolerant of minorities and disregarded social and economic issues; or, alternately, they pointed to its democratic spirit. The Pittsburg agreement, declared the Communists, was in opposition to the pro-Nazi and authoritarian demands of the HSPP. They appealed to the pristine democratic, patriotic, and anti-Magyar heritage of the veteran leader of the HSPP, Father Andrej Hlinka. Although numerous L'udák complaints were justified, said the CPCS, this was neither the proper hour nor the way to fight for the realization of the Pittsburg program. Instead, the nation, the country, and the state should unite against the foreign danger.[62] The situation in Slovakia, the advance of the L'udáks, and mounting pressure from abroad had evidently induced the Communist movement to search for new approaches and new solutions.

In proposing administrative reorganization of Slovakia, the CPCS demanded far-going decentralization and representative institutions, and toyed with the concept of regionalism of the Agrarian Party (the Czechoslovak leading non-Communist political body). This concept provided for territorial regions, and for government according to local needs. One interesting notion sprang from these projects and the others mentioned earlier: the Communists asked to leave actual power in the hands of the central government in Prague. Not a single one of the Communists' projects envisaged turning a nationality-inhabited area over to the control of the local population. The Communist Party was willing to make many concessions to Slovakia, but the reins of power were still to be concentrated at the center of power in Prague. In 1938 the CI was considering the division of the CPCS into national-regional components, but it scrapped the plan.[63]

Perhaps the most surprising change in CPCS tactics—possibly indicating a real change of heart—was the admission that Czechoslovakia was a liberal state. The Communists repeatedly vowed their readiness to defend the Republic by any possible means. They recognized the extensive liberties granted to minorities in Czechoslovakia.[64] The leading Davist, Clementis, wondered whether Slovakia was at all prepared for independent existence. His answer was essentially negative.[65] But these considerations came too late to change anything.

The minority problems of Czechoslovakia, and Berlin's intervention in the Republic's internal affairs, led to international tension. It culminated on September 29th with the summit conference in Munich. The results of the "Munich Agreement" sapped the moral strength of the Czechoslovak people. The state lay prostrate at the mercy of its foreign and internal enemies. These confused and dark days presented the Hlinka Party with unexpected opportunities.

On October 6, the HSPP, still under the effect of the Munich verdict, met with the representatives of the Slovak centralist parties at Žilina and forced them to accept its program of Slovak autonomy. Then it exacted approval of the program by the government in Prague. The Communists hurried to join the victors. "Let us give the Slovaks everything necessary!" cried *Rudé Právo*, the Prague-based central organ of the CPCS, on the previous day. And on October 6, a Slovak regional meeting of CPCS, which was also held in Žilina, hastened to endorse Slovak autonomy.[66] Several weeks later, at a meeting of the Executive Committee of the CI in Moscow on December 26, 1938, Klement Gottwald and the Slovak Party boss, Viliam Široký, confessed to their failure in dealing with nationalism in Slovakia. Said Široký:

"We Communists represented in Slovakia the national interests of the Czech nation, while Slovak national interests were better represented by the Hlinka Party. . . .

Only at the last moment, as the Czechoslovak crisis was reaching a climax, did we put forward a demand for the democratic solution of the Slovak problem, i.e., the granting of full autonomy."[67]

And Gottwald added:

"There is no doubt that the Achilles heel of Czechoslovakia was its national integrity. Only Czechs and Slovaks—and these last only partially—see in Czechoslovakia their own state."[68]

The total failure of the national policies of the CPCS in Slovakia during the First Republic was confirmed by two of its leading figures. The Second Republic and the Slovak State which followed it created entirely new conditions for the development of the Party and for its national policies.

## Chapter 3

# THE SLOVAK STATE

Slovakian autonomy was not long lived. Incited by extremist elements, Bratislava's provincial government frequently clashed with the Republic's central institutions located in Prague. The Czech politicians were rapidly losing patience—in direct proportion to the Slovak radicals' increasing appetite for additional prerogatives.[1] The Nazi authorities encouraged the dissident Slovaks: an unruly Bratislava would provide a good pretext for the destruction of Czecho-Slovakia. Concomitently, the Nazis advised Prague to take decisive steps against the "rebellious Slovaks." All these elements converged during the Ides of March 1939. At this point Berlin goaded, browbeat, and cajoled the Slovak politicians into proclaiming an independent state. Mixed feelings accompanied this act. Leaders of the ruling Hlinka's Slovak People's Party were aware of the dangers posed by scheming Magyars, Poles, and Germans. Sudden independence had an intoxicating impact and also offered definite advantages. Loyalty to Czecho-Slovakia was neutralized by the German *force majeure*. Countless Slovaks responded with a kind of euphoria, and even the less emotional were elated. Others were genuinely regretful or even shocked. But the majority of the population probably faced the future with curiosity and expectation mixed with feelings of uncertainty.

It is essential to take into account the circumstances of Slovakia's independence, as Bratislava's actions engendered profound bitterness in the Czech people. The charge of "Slovakia's betrayal" was widely voiced, and was also a political slogan. Though they aroused envy, occasionally camouflaged by half-hearted congratulations, Slovakia's actions since October 1938 and its status after the Ides of March 1939 were a permanent reality which had to be taken into account by the Communists in any future action or decision.

## During the Autonomy

Slovak Communists met legally for the last time on October 6, 1938 in Žilina in convening the Territorial Executive and ranking officials.

They acted similarly to other Slovak political parties. It may be assumed that they hoped to be invited to participate with other political groups in discussions on Slovakia's future.[2] Concurrently, they prepared blueprints for future activity. The Communists approved Slovakia's autonomy and volunteered assistance. Yet instead of accepting them, the new regime outlawed the Communist, Social Democratic and Jewish parties on October 9, 1939. A new chapter then opened in the annals of Slovak Communism.

In Žilina the Communists formed a new territorial leadership (krajinské vedenie) of the party in Slovakia. It included Julius Ďuriš, Karol Bacílek, and Koloman Moskowicz (Moško). They discussed the eventual necessity to go underground, but prepared little for such a contingency. The CIE (Communist International Executive) ordered the movement's leading Czech and Slovak personalities out of the country. Among the first to go to Moscow were Viliam Široký, Istvan (Štefan) Major, Karol Schmidtke (Šmidke), and others. Jozef Valló (Valo) and Vladimír Clementis escaped to the West. Gottwald, Václav Kopecký, and Josef Slánsky organized the Central Committee of CPCS (CC CPCS) in Moscow. It is remarkable that not a single Slovak became a member of Moscow's CC, then or later. Široký, Šverma, and the German Bruno Kohler left on May 1939 for France, where they manned the Paris bureau of CC CPCS.

After March 1939, Bacílek and Moskowicz preferred to go to Moscow as well. In Prague, an illegal Secretariat of CPCS had to coordinate the activity in the entire territory of what had previously been Czecho-Slovakia. Members of the Slovak CC visited Prague frequently, and for some time all of them hid in the city of Brno.[3] CIE decided to change the status of the Slovak and Transcarpath-Ukrainian Communist sections. The Communist Party of Slovakia (CPS) now came into existence, although the name of the entire party (CPCS) remained unchanged. Prague continued to bear overall responsibility and reported to the CC CPCS in Moscow.[4]

### After the Proclamation of Slovakia's Independence

After the proclamation of Slovakia's independence, and the escape of Bacílek and Moskowicz, Ďuriš reorganized Slovakia's CC, which now included Ján Osoha and L'udovít Benada. As Ďuriš spent a considerable part of 1939 in Prague, Osoha emerged as the central personality of Slovakian Communism.[5]

Among the three, Osoha was the most interesting. A peasant boy from Moravia, he left his country in 1925 for the Soviet Union. There he received party schooling, and in 1935 returned home. The party assigned him to political work in Eastern Slovakia, a location fitting well Osoha's predisposition for doctrinaire thinking and narrow-mindness. Ďuriš, a journalist, belonged during the First Republic to the second echelon of the party's activists. The last one, Benada, also spent six years in the Soviet Union, until 1937. He was just another "aparatchik."

It was not immediately clear to Slovakia's Communists that their party was heading toward virtual independence. Even when outlawed in autonomous Slovakia—an act which took them by surprise—they continued to depend on Prague, unlike the remaining political parties in the country. They did not expect the proclamation of independence and were again taken by surprise. CPS leaders were slow in severing the ties with Prague. The rank and file forced the leaders to rethink the Party's conditions. Communists of Slovak nationality were obviously confused and affected by the prevailing atmosphere of suspense and anticipation in the new state. Was not the Slovak State a fulfillment of national dreams, a realization of the slogan of self-determination and independence to the point of secession?! The problems of the CPS differed from those of its Czech counterpart, Bohemia and Moravia being ruled by the Germans directly. Even the leaders started to wonder why it was necessary to take orders from Prague, from people who were unfamiliar with conditions in Slovakia, and to undertake trips fraught with dangers. Quarrels occurred between the Czech and the Slovak comrades. The Slovaks disagreed with the evaluation and directives of Prague's Central Committee, and were particularly incensed by the CPCS boss Emanuel Klíma. By the end of 1939 the CPS was acting independently of Prague, and turning for instructions directly to Moscow. Organizational complications reflected the uncertainties and search for answers to national questions, which characterized the CPS in 1939. Naturally, under such conditons, the party's freedom of action was limited, and 1939 was not the most momentous year in the annals of Communism in Slovakia.

## The Problem of Program and Slogans

The Communist meeting of October 6, 1938, in Žilina expressed the hope that Slovak demands would be satisfied and the country would have a democratic regime. The meeting called for preservation of the Czechoslovak state and offered every assistance to this end.[6] Moreover, Czech and Slovak Communists were and remained in contact with local politicians known for their "Czechoslovak" convictions. The old "national front" tactics took on new meaning.[7] Party spokesmen censored the L'udáks for cooperation with the Nazis, although admitting that the official policies of the First Republic had boosted the fortunes of its enemies. Slovak nationalism, so they claimed, opposed the political structure of Czechoslovakia and turned to Berlin for assistance.[8] Yet the times were dynamic and the need for changes in the party-line occurred frequently. The Party lacked a firm line. Characteristically, the proclamation of Slovakia's independence drew no comments from the CPS, and no evaluation of the new stance.[9] The Manifesto of the CPCS was aimed largely at the Czechs.[10] This Manifesto denounced the destruction of the Czechoslovak Republic and demanded its renewal. The Party representatives talked in a similar fashion abroad. They used the slogan "For a new Czechoslovakia," while emphasizing the need for a new approach to Czech-Slovak coexistence. Ranking Czechoslovak Communists were ready to cooperate with the "bourgeois" exiles in the West.[11] The CPS also remained committed to the old slogans, at least for the time being.[12]

The Communist efforts to digest the new reality in the country were not uniformly successful. With the passage of time, the status of independence won more and more hearts. Slovakia now enjoyed advantages; problems, particularly those related to the War and the crude Nazi interventions in the state's life, were still in the future. The Hlinka Party engaged in intensive propaganda aimed at gaining popular support for independence, and blotting memories of the late Republic. This campaign was not unsuccessful. It is not surprising that the Communist call for renewal of the belated state won little sympathy. The Slovak comrades had a thankless task and were caught between the orders of the Comintern and their own experience. Members were fleeing the Party ranks, which in any case were never filled to capacity. It is understandable that the CPS sought new slogans. The Ribbentrop-Molotov Treaty, so shocking to many Communists elsewhere, had a mild impact on Slovakia. Soon the Soviet Union recognized Slovak independence. Only a few months before, after the Ides of March, Moscow had protested Berlin's action and the separation of Slovakia from the Czech lands. Now it posted a well-staffed legation in Bratislava. With the Russian invasion of Poland, the Soviet borders moved close to Slovakia. The local Communists had much admiration for Soviet incorporation of Western Ukraine and White Russia. The Ukrainians in Eastern Slovakia displayed considerable interest as well. Rumors in Slovakia told about annexation of the country to the Soviet Union in the near future. The vision of Soviet liberation, of socialist expansion, dazzled the eyes. Osoha, familiar with Eastern Slovakia, was aware of the new geographic realities, and of geopolitics—to use the term so popular with the Nazis.

After the conclusion of the Soviet-Nazi treaty, the Comintern saw the green light and discovered the "imperialist nature" of the War. Under Czechoslovak conditions, the Comintern directives obscured the slogan of renewal of the Republic. Moscow policymakers modified this slogan with demands for socialization and for social and economic reconstruction of the future state. The Communists denounced the Czechoslovak exiles as hostile to the Soviet Union and for assisting imperialist powers. The exiles were blamed for intending to revive the bourgeois state, which was branded by the Communists as "hell for the working people."[13] Cooperation with the exiles, with Beneš, or with their followers in the Czech and Slovak underground was equaled to helping class enemies, and this was the basis for a change of slogans and tactics in Slovakia.

In the fall of 1939, new instructions reached Prague from Moscow on the basis of which Ďuriš prepared in October the "Guide for the Party's Internal Activity and Organization, and Ideological Campaign." Moscow instructions induced Ďuriš to spread the slogan "For a free Slovakia in a liberated Republic." Prague leaders approved the slogan, but Osoha, Benada, and others in Slovakia objected. Slovak activists argued that the slogan was a contradiction of the nationalist mood prevalent in the country.[14] The leading Communists prepared a more elaborate slogan, which called for a "Liberated Slovakia in liberated Czechoslovakia and in free Europe, for strong ties with the Soviet Union, for unity of the working class and the toiling people under the flag of Comintern."[15]

While the leaders argued, an old-new slogan reappeared: the call for a Soviet Slovakia. During the early thirties, this slogan had been used to mobilize the masses against the bourgeois republic. Later, the "National Front" tactic and increasing struggle against fascism pushed the "Soviet Slovakia" slogan into the background. Party extremists, many of them in Eastern Slovakia, regretted this. Now "Soviet Slovakia" staged a comeback.

The slogan may have been introduced from abroad,[16] or reborn in the minds of local activists,[17] and could even have been revived by Osoha himself.[18] There is no doubt, however, that both slogans, the "Czechoslovak" and the "Soviet," were used at the same time.[19]

The new slogans, that elaborated by Ďuriš and the popular "Soviet Slovakia," annoyed the Czech Communist leaders. In the Protectorate, the Communists continued to talk about revival of Czechoslovakia in a diversity of forms ("new Czechoslovakia," "socialist Czechoslovakia," "liberated Czechoslovakia"). The slogans used in Slovakia, and above all the "Soviet Slovakia" variant, emphasized the quest for social liberation of a nationally fulfilled people. The main Czech problem was national liberation from German supremacy. Acceptance of a Slovakia separated for the Czech countries—be it even in a Soviet form—would legitimize the Nazi *fait accompli*. Public opinion in the Czech countries regarded the Slovaks as traitors who deserved punishment rather than reward. We are dealing here with a strange *volte-face* in comparison to 1918: at that time the Czechs had been the satisfied element, and the Slovaks the struggling nation. Now the roles were transposed, and Czech Communists could not dare approve the slogans raised in Slovakia. What is more, they saw that their task was to suppress these slogans. Both sides forwarded the dispute to Moscow for a decision.

## Moscow and Slovakia

It seems appropriate to comment on the Communist leadership and decision-making. We have seen the Czechoslovak Communist leadership at several levels and locations. There was the Central Committee in Moscow, which was subordinated to the Comintern. The CC had an executive bureau in Paris, a Secretariat in Prague, and a Central Committee in Bratislava. London-based Czechoslovak Communists received their orders from Paris and Moscow. The lines of communication were imperfect, to say the least. Prague used wireless in its exchanges with Moscow, probably through the local Soviet mission. Some written messages reached their destination in spite of numerous obstacles. There was secret courier service and underground channels were provided for personal visits. At least until Spring 1941, Moscow emissaries reached Slovakia and returned to their base. The Paris bureau reached Prague via Belgrade and Bratislava. Slovak Communists, and particularly Ďuriš, were frequent visitors in Prague. Nevertheless, it is not out of place to ask how people living in the security of their offices far from home—some of whom had actually fled the dangers of underground living—could know of and decide on problems occurring at home. Even the Czechs could hardly appreciate the current state of mind in Slovakia. How could a Široký in Paris or a Gottwald in Moscow, with their limited contacts with the fatherland, comprehend and direct the Party in Slovakia? It was probably also for this reason that Czechoslovak Communists spoke in several voices, and tactics employed were scarcely identical. To this confused picture should be added Soviet official representatives, who tempered their *modus oper-*

*andi* to the troubled route of Moscow's foreign policy. With regard to the national Czechoslovak (-Slovak) question the confusion was great. Such conditions—and worse—became commonplace in the years to come.

A cable concerning the Slovakian problem reached Moscow on January 26, 1940.[20] The sender wrote:

"Let us know whether we should speak in our slogans about a new Czechoslovakia. The slogan of national and social liberation of Czechs and Slovaks does not exhaust the entire problem. There is the question of Czech-Slovak relations, and thus the future organization of the State. The present slogan in Slovakia 'For a free Slovakia in liberated Czechoslovakia' is therefore debatable. We are asking whether the slogan of free right for self-determination . . . can be regarded as the slogan of the CPCS."

The reply arrived only on March 15, 1940, after repeated reminders from Prague.[21] Why did it take so long?

"The Czech-Slovak relations have now taken on a new form. Slovak separatism now plays a different role. Therefore the old slogans affecting Slovakia should be rescinded. The Slovak State is the given basis for the struggle for complete Slovak freedom. The future relations between the Czech and Slovak states is a question of the self-determination of both nations, and depends on the result of the war. The term Czecho-Slovakia should be understood in its ethnographic meaning. . . . We emphasize again the need for an independent policy for Slovakia."

Gottwald's answer testifies to a new change in the line toward Slovakia, and must have had quite a shocking impact on the Czech comrades. (They were later expected to swallow even more bitter pills.) Thereafter, the Party in Bohemia and Moravia continued to speak about Czechoslovakia; the new directives were aimed at Slovakia alone. According to Moscow, the demand to recreate Czechoslovakia involved imperialist and anti-Soviet designs. Both nations had the unconditional right of self-determination, including the right for independent state existence. Moscow advised the Slovaks to struggle for genuine independence and for democratization of the state. The CPS was expected to influence the Slovak state through the working class. Gottwald demonstrated his "grasp" of the situation in Central Europe by advising his comrades to learn from the socialist struggle in old Austria![22]

The new policy virtually buried the Czechoslovak republic. Although the door was open for talks between the two nationalities in the future, Czecho-Slovakia (the name of the Second Republic was regularly hyphenated) was only an ethnographic term. The Slovak historian

Stvrtecká remarked that the Secretary of the CI Dimitrov did not believe in a revival of Czechoslovakia, and Gottwald's cable was based on the Bulgarian's views. Significantly, neither Sovietization nor dictatorship of the proletariat was demanded for Slovakia.[23]

## To Make White Slovakia Red

It appears that Gottwald not only accepted the *fait accompli* of the Ides of March, but in retrospect also granted them formal recognition. The views of Osoha and his friends were legalized. Subsequently, the Slovak comrades shifted their train of thought from political to social matters: could a nationally-fulfilled Slovakia be made socialist? The slogan "Soviet Slovakia" appeared more frequently in the Party's pronouncements. In spite of the Party's numerical and organizational weakness[24] (and perhaps because of it), Osoha plunged enthusiastically into the task of making Slovakia red. One may wonder about Osoha's optimism, or perhaps about his limited capacity to think realistically: in a country with a minute working class, immersed in nationalistic euphoria, with a large and backward peasantry, he had chosen the most advanced form of statehood offered by the Communist consumers' catalog. The first stage in his design was a call for "a genuinely free and independent Slovakia." This concept, based on Moscow directives, accepted at least in theory the existing state and asked only for improvements.[25] The next stage proposed a "Soviet Slovakia," the heart of the CPS's main program.

Ján Osoha was the leading personality behind the national program, but he was not alone. Some of his close collaborators identified themselves with his views, and he found considerable agreement among the rank and file. During the last quarter of 1940, the Party numbered some 2000 members, but had few officers.[26] The Nazi intelligence was disturbed even by the activity of such a small group.[27] Leaflets and inscriptions painted on walls and recorded in German archives present a rather doctrinaire Communist approach, which could hardly have had an extensive influence on the masses. For this reason the potentially unpopular slogan requires further explanation. A few explanations were offered earlier.[28] The addenda hereafter were pertinent to the year under discussion and to the later period.

Slovak Communists lived a lonely life. In the First Republic, they had been effectively persecuted, but now their suffering became extreme. Radicalism characterized Slovakia in general, the radicalism of an underdeveloped country with sharp class contrasts. The population was by and large conservative and intensely religious, while the Communist minority turned to the opposite extreme. Given the conditions, Slovak Communists had to believe in miracles in order to advance.

The Party could not and did not trust its own power. Yet with the pretension and arrogance, so typical of an extremist movement, the Communists were convinced that they, and only they, possessed the key to the nation's happiness. After annexation of the Polish and Finnish territories, the Soviet Union swallowed the Baltic States in June 1940. The vision of being incorporated into the Soviet Union became a reality. Like the Slovak government officials the Communists also greatly exaggerated the international significance of Slovakia. They believed that if Slovakia turned into a socialist country, the whole of Central Europe would follow.[29] We have already pointed out that the number of Slovakian Communist thinkers were few and the War reduced their number further.[30] In this country provincialism and narrow-mindedness became widespread during the War, both in the government and in the opposition. Naturally, the Osoha-like personalities were less able to adopt a broad all-inclusive view. For them, the Messiah riding on Soviet tanks was a reality rather than a vision.

Osoha was aware of Slovakia's shortcomings. He did not believe that the country would be able to keep step with the Czech lands, but feared that it might instead hinder their progress. With outside intervention Slovakia would advance rapidly, perhaps becoming the pioneer of Communism, for Slovakia was now the weak link in the capitalist chain.

Because of the variety of slogans used in the country ("Soviet Slovakia," "Slovak Soviet Socialist Republic," "Socialist Slovakia," and "Red Slovakia"), one can assume that the Party did not clarify its own aims. Did it wish to be annexed by the Soviet Union, or to stay completely independent but socialist; to adhere to a new Central European Federation, or something else. The Slovak Communists tended to identify Soviet power politics with the revolution. Formerly they had toyed with such models; now they adopted them easily. The narrow outlook and limited vision, so common to the great majority of the men under discussion, were branded by the later-days analysts as "sectarian thinking." Contemporary Slovak Communists argue that the slogans had no anti-Czech implications. Such activity on the basis of the existing state was only natural. It was Soviet, rather than national, incentives which led Osoha to choose his program.[31] Osoha's Czech descent served this kind of argumentation well.[32] A "Soviet Slovakia" of any kind could and had to neutralize the pro-Czechoslovak propaganda and feelings of the non-Communist underground and of the London exiles.

The London exiles remained addicted to the old doctrine of a "Czechoslovak nation," and were unwilling to accept the new conditions. This bigotry of the exiles frightened many sincere Slovak anti-Fascists and believers in the idea of a common Czech-Slovak state. Many who remained loyal to the old Republic did not shelve their old credos in spite of hard times. The ostensible calmness of London on national questions offended the faithful. London exiles' policies served the Slovak State's official propaganda well and provided it with ammunition.[33] The historians claim that a pro-Czechoslovak Communist propaganda campaign would carry the danger of alienating potential followers. On the other hand, the "Soviet Slovakia" slogan reflected the emotions of its originators and at the same time constituted a valuable substitute for an unpopular slogan.[34] Thus both flags could be held aloft: the standard of Slovak independence and the flag of social justice. The "Soviet Slovakia" slogan was employed in dialectical fashion. While directed toward Slovak workers, it advocated Slovak statehood and emphasized ties to the Soviet Union, the largest Slav state. Slovak Communists played in subtle—and sometimes not so subtle—fashion on the Pan-Slavic emotions deeply rooted in the country. They did this long before Pan-Slavism was rediscovered in Moscow.[35] Yet when the slogan was addressed to ethnic German or Magyar workers, it emphasized "internationalist" and "proletarian" aspects. Thus, the feelings of non-Slavic elements were taken into account. Perhaps Bratislava, with its varied population, influenced the Party bosses living there to adopt a more "internationalist" stand. In the past Magyar, German, and Jewish members had pushed Slovak communism toward a more pronounced extremism. It could be that such was the case now as well.

The year 1940 saw the establishment of virtual independence of the CPS vis-à-vis the Prague center. This development took place with the approval or initiative of Moscow, and still left the Party under control and direction of the CC CPCS in the Soviet Union.[36] Karol Bacílek returned in December 1940 to Slovakia in order to establish the liaison with Moscow.[37] September 1940 also witnessed the first war-time Communist attempt to create in Slovakia an anti-Fascist front with some bourgeois groups. Failure of this undertaking may be attributed in a considerable part to the doctrinaire mind of the Communists.[38] The CPS was still straying in the dark.

The second year of the War was a difficult time for the anti-Fascist powers. The conquering Wehrmacht subdued almost half of the continent. The Comintern divided Europe into villains and angels, naturally assigning the latter role to itself and its allies. Communism presented the Axis powers and their victims on an equal footing: as imperialists fighting for primacy. Slovakia of 1940 had seen the expansion of German domination and the power-hunger of Berlin's disciples in the country. In July, Berlin dictated changes in the local government, and a new leadership took the place of the old. Persecutions of the regime's adversaries also increased.

Under such conditions, Osoha and his colleagues saw in Sovietization the only natural way for Slovakia. The Slovak Central Committee regarded the Eastern Power as the only source of encouragement and of future liberation. "Soviet Slovakia" and similar slogans held uncontested sway in the Party's pronouncements. The next year, the year of the German invasion of the Soviet Union and of Soviet recognition of Czechoslovakia, again heavily taxed the intellectual abilities of the Slovak Communists.

## The Invasion and Afterwards

In some respects, for the Slovak Communists the new calendar year did not signify a change in established routine, at least up to June 22, 1941. The first months of the year brought more of the same, although on a higher level of sophistication.

In honor of May Day of 1941, CPS prepared some of its most important documents on current national and social politics: "The May Day 1941 Program of CPS,"[39] written by Osoha, and Ďuriš's leaflet "The Road to Freedom of the Slovak Nation."[40] Emphasis of the Program is on the dictatorship of the proletariat in Slovakia, which Osoha elaborated in detail. Ďuriš demonstrated Slovakia's similarity to the Baltic states, Bessarabia, Moldavia, Bucovina, Belorussia, and West Ukraine. He concluded that the local war for national liberation should lead to creation of a republic in the Soviet Union. Both documents can be regarded as a test-tube treatise of the social and national thought of the CPS's First Central Committee. The documents made no mention of Czechoslovakia, and directed the readers toward a struggle for "Soviet Slovakia."

A clash between Osoha and Ďuriš preceded formulation of these documents. Ďuriš, who had just returned from a longer stay in the capital of Bohemia, was still faithful to the concept of the primacy of Prague's Central Secretariat. He was also more flexible in bruiting social and national slogans. Osoha, jealous of Ďuriš and in favor of the independence of CPS, demanded clear-cut ("Leninist-Stalinist") slogans. Bacílek participated in the debate and sided with Osoha. Anna Štvrtecká, Osoha's biographer, claims to see in these documents the first independent and original Slovak thought in the field of Marxist theory. While taking note of the "Sectarian" and unrealistic aspects, she finds the documents understandable against the background of the current international and national situation.[41]

Shortly after the discussions in the CC CPS, Bacílek and another emissary Karol Černocký returned to Moscow, and on April 10, 1941, presented their report to the CC CPCS there. The report was not well accepted; in fact, the Central Comittee criticized the authors for its tactics of "Soviet Slovakia." The ensuing discussion took place under the impact of the Nazi invasion of Yugoslavia.[42] The Central Committee published a summary of the discussion on May 17, 1941, under the title "The Resolution on Tasks of CPCS". The Resolution dropped the slogans of "Soviet Czech Lands" and "Soviet Slovakia," and called for an increased struggle against Nazism. In Slovakia, said the Resolution, the slogan of a Soviet state came too early and was fraught with the danger of the Party's isolation. Instead, Moscow called on the CPS to propagate an independent foreign policy for the Slovak State, which could be done by weakening ties with the Reich and strengthening links with the Soviet Union. The premise that the Slovak people were enjoying national, political, and state independence should guide the CPS in its work.[43] Moscow Communists approved the CPS's formal independence of Prague. They failed to include in their resolution a call for the revival of Czechoslovakia as such.

The Moscow Resolution did not condemn the slogan of "Soviet Slovakia," and only considered it inopportune—for political reasons. By omitting Czechoslovakia and approving the CPS's independence, Gottwald and his comrades suggested that in principle they did not object to the line taken by Bratislava. The Osoha circle was willing to listen to the voices of Slovak nationalism, and with Moscow's blessing, to exploit it for their own ends. Twenty years earlier, Šmeral had not failed to condemn the nationalism of Czech workers. Instead of taking an opportunistic stand, he tried to educate his fellow nationals.[44]

In June 1941, Moscow dispatched Viliam Široký and Vincent Škrabala to Bratislava. The Slovak Secret Police captured Široký soon after his arrival—some three weeks after the German invasion of the Soviet Union. The wave of arrests, which accompanied the invasion, resulted in the capture of several leading Communists, including members of CC Ďuriš and Benada. Osoha escaped and with Škrabala and Oto Krajňák (Klein), created the Second CC of the CPS, in August 1941.

Personal troubles of the Second CC involved a whole gallery of Communist functionaries. Široký was the most prestigious among them. He became the Slovak Communist Number One in the late thirties, and returned to this rank in 1945. Ambitious and ruthless, he had the bad luck to be of Magyarized parentage and to be married to a Jewish spouse. The blacksmith Škrabala owed his position to the almost accidental escape to the Soviet Union, and to the lack of more qualified personalities. Of Jewish proletarian descent, Krajňák was a not too well known party activist.

Osoha continued to promote the slogan of "Soviet Slovakia." Široký had not time to convey the new orders, and CPS lacked direct connections with Moscow. The invasion took the First CC by surprise, and only in July did it publish a proclamation condemning the Nazi action. The proclamation described the war as an imperialist crime, and more specificially, as a confrontation between socialism and capitalism.[45] Osoha was not able to comprehend the epic change, and its significance for the national question.

The Soviet statesmen were, naturally, wiser. On July 18, 1941, the Soviet Union recognized the Czechoslovak government in exile. Czechoslovak Communists in Moscow followed suit, and supported revival of the Republic.[46] It is not without interest, however, that the CC continued to address the Czechs and the Slovaks in separate broadcasts and different concepts.[47] Now and later, Moscow—and London-based—Communists would discuss the Republic's future in uncertain terms.

Slovak Communists monitored the conclusion of the Soviet-Czechoslovak Treaty of cooperation on Radio Moscow. Osoha, sensing the unpleasant situation, stated that the Treaty did not change the basic premise of the right of every nation to self-determination even to the point of secession and the need for a proletarian revolution, which alone could solve Slovakia's national and social problems. The most important task was to fight the enemy, and relations with the Czech nation should be relegated to the future.[48]

Observers greeted with interest the Convention of the All-Slavic Congress in Moscow. At this Congress, the Slovaks appeared as a separate nation. British diplomats saw in the pan-Slavic propaganda an encourgement of the separatist tendencies in Czechoslovakia.[49] CPS continued to promote a nationalistic, anti-Nazi line.[50] Osoha's strategy was, in retrospect, self-defeating, as contemporary historians tend to point out. It became obvious to him and his colleagues that a policy of national unity could and would promote the anti-Nazi struggle. The CC tried to induce non-Communist forces to cooperate, yet without giving up the "Soviet Slovakia" slogan. The results were not encouraging, as one would expect.[51] Moreover, the Communist line indirectly assisted the regime's propaganda in fostering the war against the Soviet Union.

Thus 1941 saw a stable nationalistic policy of the Slovak Communists, but Moscow's tactics were marked by sharp fluctuations. The situation was similar in the following year. Osoha jealously resisted changes—hardships notwithstanding. The Moscovites tended toward a more flexible policy.

The year which ended with El-Alamein and Stalingrad was the best in the annals of the Slovak State. The President, Dr. Josef Tiso, reached the pinnacle of his power. This was also the year in which major persecutions of the Communist underground took place. The Second CC were jailed in April 1942. Osoha, who again eluded the Secret Police, brought in two more comrades, Jozef Lietavec and Štefan Dubček,[52] and established the Third CC of the CPS. The Third CC followed in the footsteps of the Second, with one difference: in July 1942 the Secret Police caught Osoha as well. The Fourth CC, formed by Štefan Bašťovanský and Miloš Hrušovský, could hardly fill the void left by the well-informed Osoha. And since many members accompanied the leaders to jail, the Communist network was breached in many places.

The jailed Communists represented the available stock of leadership. Lietavec was active in Central Slovakia, but hardly a driving personality. His companion Dubček, the father of Alexander Dubček of 1968 fame, was a minor Communist Trade-Unionist. Not much different was Bašťovanský, an official of the Slovak Railways. He was capable of independent scholarship, however, and of ideological creativity, something the others could hardly do. Intellectually highest ranking was Hrušovský, a philosopher and a member of the party's intelligentsia. After their apprehension, CPS remained for the time being headless.

Only in one respect was there almost no interruption—in the propaganda of "Soviet Slovakia." It would be false to say that the slogan was universally accepted. In June 1942 Široký succeeded in smuggling a letter from prison. Addressing himself to contemporary problems and the line taken by the CPS, he argued that the Party ought to demand a "Free Slovakia," which meant complete freedom for the state and for the people. Everybody willing to work toward this end was welcome to cooperate. The major aim was to defeat Nazism, and the war for social liberation would only constitute the next step. Naturally, a war in which the Western Powers played a positive role could not be presented as an encounter between socialism and imperialism. In Slovakia one should try to find a way to Tiso's camp, which was objectively anti-Nazi, and opposed to the loyal pro-Nazis (headed by the Premier Professor Vojtech Tuka and the Minister of the Interior Alexander Mach). Only through a broad coalition of the opponents could fascism be defeated.[53]

Osoha, supported by numerous comrades, rejected Široký's views. He attacked Široký's concept of stages: the war for national and social liberation was one struggle. Only the defeat of fascism could bring about the establishment of socialism. To this end one should cooperate with bourgeois groups as well. Yet cooperation was only temporary and the contest for primacy between capitalism and socialism would continue durig the whole period. There was no room for rapprochement with any of the governing groups.[54]

In dispute, Osoha did not use polite language. He suspected Široký of being his rival for leadership, just as he had regarded Ďuriš in the past. It would be wrong, therefore, to search for the source of difference in the realm of Marxist analysis and ideology alone. When applied in practice, however, Osoha's views had negative effects. A renewed attempt to cooperate with non-Communist anti-Fascists came to nothing. The "bourgeois" were not very fond of Communism, but nevertheless, a common ground could be found. The Communist monopolistic aspirations constituted the major obstacle to cooperation.[55] But Osoha prophesied the future. In wartime the CPS constituted only one among several forces of opposition, but after the war its position became stronger.

We cannot establish with certainty the Party's size and influence at that time, for documentary evidence is contradictory. Documents released by Czechoslovak historians suggest that the Party was relatively strong compared to other forces. In the German archives and the war-time Slovakian press the Party was frequently mentioned; this meant that it was under constant surveillance. One should keep in mind, however, the propagandistic aims of the above publications, the boast of Nazi intelligence officers about watching Communists, and their considerable success in persecuting the leftist opponents. The fact that the Party was so frequently mentioned, as stated above, also proves that the German and Slovak authorities feared and hated them more than other local opposition groups. Communist prisoners, with a few exceptions which did not include Široký and Ďuriš, told their captors everything. Sometimes they acted under duress of torture, sometimes not.[56] It seems logical, therefore, to assume that the attention paid to the Communist underground could have been greater than it deserved. In their monthly reports to the Slovak Ministry of Interior, County Chiefs were requested to record the CPS's activity. A great part of these reports were preserved in *Sicherheitdienst* (SD-SS Secret Service) files, covering all the years of the Slovak State's existence. The reader of these reports does not gain the impression of extensive Communist activity, at least until the year 1944.

Documents in the files of the British Foreign Office, the US Department of State and US Office of Strategic Services, as well as in files of the Polish Foreign Office in Exile, do not point to extensive Communist influence in Slovakia. The source of information is important, however. One may assume that the agencies of the Western Allies were supplied with this information at least partly by the Czechoslovak authorities in exile who were interested in concealing Communist activity. The Czechoslovak agencies themselves received much of their information from loyalists in Slovakia, whose views on the Communists were not always flattering (although, according to some published documents, they occasionally praised left-wingers). The Polish reporters acquired a considerable amount of their information from Karol Sidor, the "Polonophile" Slovak Minister to the Holy See, and from his people who were also unsympathetic to the Communists. The intelligence in Western archives is not completely reliable. Slovak exiles, whether partisans of the Slovak State or its opponents, who arrived in the West after the war, consider themselves victims of Communism. They deliberately disparage the impact of Communism in Slovakia. Their evidence, even when given in good faith, must be taken with utmost caution.

In summary, Communist influence on the Slovak public until 1944 can be regarded as noticeable, but not considerable. Communist activity was concentrated in the field of propaganda and in social struggles, but was less pronounced in the field of "inter-party" and "oppositionist" politics, and very little in effective resistance (such as intelligence, sabotage, and armed struggle).[57]

The non-Communist centers were active in politics and in resistance. They branched out into numerous groups, representing a variety of political views, circles of friends and relatives, groups with similar interests and occupations. The non-Communist underground lacked coordination and leadership. Conspiratorial tactics and discipline were often disorganized, and political activities tended to concentrate on talk and negotiations with no tangible results. Several groups gathered and transmitted intelligence to the government in exile in London and assisted Czechs escaping the Protectorate and other persecuted persons in Slovakia. The activities of the non-Communist underground resistance were hardly noticed by the public in general.[58]

If we compare the Communist and non-Communist underground movements, it is the cohesiveness, central command, and a sense of purpose, which gave the former its advantage. Their *modus operandi* and the closer attention awarded them by pro-Nazi agencies made the Communists the more visible movement. As effective results go, one can hardly overestimate Communist activity. It was precisely this highly propaganda-oriented effort to influence public opinion which helped the secret services to neutralize the Communists. How much impact this had on the public we can only guess. The activities of the (Slavic) Soviet Union and of the Red Army amplified the Communist pronouncements in Slovakia, lent them prestige and extended their impact. The non-Communists were more effective in voluntary active engagement in the anti-Fascist struggle. In contrast to the Communists, they had limited specific aims. The wish to dominate the country was the determining factor in Communist efforts.

Osoha's ambition to control a unified underground was related more to his Party's plans and less to anti-Nazi realities. It is typical of contemporary Czechoslovak historiography that it depicts anti-Fascist activities as a monopoly of the Communist Party, while a historian outside the Soviet Bloc can hardly confirm the claim of his Eastern colleagues.

The men who opened talks with the Communists could not accept Osoha's pretensions. The Slovak Secret Police unconsciously served the anti-Nazi underground by removing Osoha, one of the major obstacles to the unification of anti-Fascist forces. Until his imprisonment however, the disappointed Osoha strengthened the "Sovietization" path of the CPS. He explained to his questioning comrades that the talks which had taken place during summer and spring of 1941-1942 proved the impossibility of cooperation with the bourgeoisie.[59] Evidently the whole question of an anti-Fascist front centered in Slovakia on the national problem. Only an understanding of this issue could further cooperation.

## Moscow Views After the Invasion

The Moscow Communists took a stand different from that of Slovakia. After the imprisonment of Široký and Škrabala, the direct link of communication with home was broken. All that remained was the radio. Moscow had no communication with Slovakia and was short of up-to-date news. Some insight on events could be gathered from Slovak soldiers who deserted to the Soviets. The deserters enlisted regularly in the Czechoslovak military units of the Soviet Union. The flight from the colors of the Slovak Army, an ally of the Wehrmacht, served as evidence of Slovakia's loyalty to the Czechoslovak Republic, and of the gradual fragmentation of the Axis.[60] But the Moscow Communists were well aware of the increase in intensity of national feelings in

Slovakia, and of the danger inherent in the call for revival of Czechoslovakia as a state. Soviet policy committed them to the tactical support of the government in exile in London, and consequently to the renewal of the Republic. The line taken was an opportunistic one. When talking to London, to the Czechs at home, and to other allies, the CPCS favored revival of Czechoslovakia. When broadcasting to Slovakia, the Party's "secret" radio called "for a Free Slovakia," and omitted Czech-Slovak statehood.[61]

Indeed, CPCS propaganda broadcasts to Slovakia appear more nationalistic than feelings at home. There, the idea of a single Czechoslovak nation lost support, but not so the idea of a common state with the Czechs. Even before Germany's defeats in the Fall of 1942, several leading Slovak politicians were willing to accept a renewal of the Republic, in a modified form.[62] After Fall 1942 these tendencies naturally increased. The common people demonstrated their sympathies toward the Czechs in countless ways. A typical example was assistance to refugees from the Protectorate during 1939.[63] SD documents include numerous testimonies of the ordinary Slovak who was also willing to return to Czechoslovakia. Moscow seemed to go out of its way to make concessions to Slovak nationalism.[64] Baštovanský's article "The National Development of the Slovaks in the Light of Marxism," is worth mentioning in this context as a serious attempt to understand the nation's past in order to study the present. The author of this document discovered further sanction for the current Party line: a social revolution is the key to national development.[65] Baštovanský's work suggests an awareness that the Party line needed something more basic than a mere analysis of the present.

The Fourth CC remained faithful by and large to Osoha's program. The pro-Czechoslovak policies of the Kremlin could not go unnoticed, however. Leaflets celebrating "Free Czechoslovakia" again circulated among the population.[66] Moscow's Communists also adjusted themselves to Soviet policies. The conviction that Slovaks should be brought into the fold of Czechoslovak thinking grew there. On January 5, 1943, the Cominform Executive passed a decision in favor of Czechoslovakia, on condition of and with equality between the two nations. Czech and Slovaks should be interdependent, said the Executive, and it appealed to the latter to overthrow the existing state.[67] The policy was therefore officially altered again.

### The Breakthrough

The year 1943 was a turning point in the modern history of Slovakia. Communists and non-Communists agreed upon a formula supporting local nationalism, which made possible future cooperation between them. Thus they paved the way toward a wartime partnership.

In May of that year the Secret Police discovered and jailed the Fourth CC, and with it numerous veteran Communists. The Old Guard was deprived of all its leading personalities, and the field was open to newcomers. In the summer of 1943 Karol Šmidke and Karol Bacílek parachuted into Poland, and crossed the border into Slovakia. The Moscow CC sent Šmidke to force a new line on the Slovak Party.[68] Bacílek's task was to operate a broadcasting apparatus for communication with Moscow. Šmidke found the Communists to be without leadership. He brought in two younger Party members, Dr. Gustav Husák and Ladislav Novomeský, and in the fall of 1943 he established the so-called Fifth CC.[69] We assume that the shortage of leaders opened the way for Husák and Novomeský to the top.

Šmidke, a party veteran, an experienced leader, was a carpenter by profession. Of Czech Silesian—German stock, he spent a lifetime as a party emissary in Slovakia. He left for the Soviet Union in 1939, where he received ideological training. Sources describe him as a quiet, level-headed, and devoted Communist. Husák was different. Originally from a Catholic background, he lost his father in early age and held grudges against the Church which allegedly little helped his widowed mother. His first student year—he studied law—he spent in the Catholic dormitory Svoradov, for which a clergy recommendation was needed. Husák gained the fame of one of the leaders of the Communist academic youth. During the war he was detained for three short periods, briefly active in the Communist underground in 1939-1940, and forcefully sent by the government to see for himself the "communist paradise" in the German-occupied territories of the Soviet Union. Since May 1942 Husák held a well paid job in the Slovak economy, and moved around freely. People who knew Husák described him as determined, calculating, and power-hungry. His close comrade Novomeský was nine years Husák's senior. A noted poet—a surrealist—and an experienced journalist, in spite his Communist conviction Novomeský was well known in the Slovak intellectual circles. Among his friends there were the Slovak Minister of Interior Alexander (Šaňo) Mach and the happy Franciscan brother and surrealist poet Rudolf Dilong. Since 1939 Novemeský edited a business journal and was not active in the party.

Šmidke and his younger colleagues analyzed the Party's past activity, and confronted it with Moscow's directives. Moscow required the Party to prepare Slovakia for an armed struggle. They ordered a complete halt to its widespread propaganda which had had hardly any results, and called instead for work toward a very concrete aim. They also decided to abandon those slogans which had become obstacles in the path of cooperation with non-Communist elements. Finally, they turned to sophisticated conspiratorial tactics.

The aim was a popular front: cooperation with opponents, a compromise—at least temporary—with regard to ultimate goals; and enforcement of coordination and discipline as required for the management of a larger group. Husák and Novomeský, familiar with Slovakia's political scene, launched a plan for building up a broader anti-Fascist coalition. Šmidke, living the clandestine life of an outlaw, devoted himself to constructing a new party network. The new bosses agreed that any action which might betray the Party to the police should be abandoned. The Fifth CC adopted the Comintern's orders, and gave up "Soviet Slovakia" and similar slogans. Instead, it furthered the plan for the renewal of Czechoslovakia. True, this was to be an improved state, both socially and economically, nationally just, but for all that, Czechoslovakia. On such a platform, Husák and Novomeský could seek friends outside the Party for their coalition.

Independently of developments elsewhere, the Communists in prison led an intellectual life of their own. As faith in a German victory diminished, the number of people willing to stretch out a helping hand to those Communists in prison had increased. Sympathetic friends and fellow travelers could be found in the Slovak judiciary as well.[70] Guarded by the pro-Communist procurators and wards, a quite extraordinary assembly took place in June 1943 in the office of Bratislava prison: a symposium on CPS ideology and tactics. Among the participants were Široký, several members of the First, Second, and Third CC, and other CP leaders. Among the interesting features of this debate was the split in the ranks of the Communist functionaries. One group headed by Široký was composed mostly of Moscovite emigrants, who had secretly returned home and been caught. The others who sided with Osoha, represented mainly the native underground.

The indigenous Communists took a "class struggle" stand. The war was an imperialist one, and should end in a socialist revolution and dictatorship of the proletariat. In other words, Osoha again defended the slogan of "Soviet Slovakia." He did not mention the national aims of the struggle and did not recognize the need for cooperation with the class enemy for national ends.[71] Široký argued that the supreme enemy of the proletariat was at the same time the supreme enemy of the Slovak nation, and that a struggle for national ends was also a struggle for class goals. Allies from other strata of the population were objectively playing a progressive role by opposing fascism. Cooperation with the bourgeoisie was just and right even if the price was a temporary betrayal of some final aims. Dictatorship of the proletariat remained the Party's goal, but now defeat of Fascism was of the greatest importance.[72] Another Moscow emissary, Karol Černocký, concluded the debate:

"We shall grant the nation liberty, sovereignty in its desires, and freedom to decide its own fate. We shall give it the right to self-determination, while the Slovak Communists will work toward a decision in favour of the Soviet Government."[73]

Evidently, the "Moscow" Communists, familiar with the Spring 1941 decisions of the Comintern (which set victory over Fascism as the primary goal), were closer to the February 1942 decision than those living in Slovakia. Siroký had predicted the future Communist tactics which would be used to conquer Czechoslovakia. Osoha, by his narrow approach, would deprive the communists of possible allies, and perhaps of victory as well. Not in vain had Široký dubbed his opponent an "unreconcilable sectarian."[74] Although the debate had no immediate results, it presaged future Communist policies.

## Activities Abroad

During the first half of 1943, Moscow had no direct communication with Slovakia. The non-Communist underground groups, on the other hand, had channels to London and were aware of the beginning of friendly relations between the exile government and the Kremlin. It seemed strange therefore when the local Communists pursued a different policy to that of the Kremlin. Slovak resistance repeatedly asked London to intervene with Slovak Communists and to persuade them to embrace a Czechoslovak program.[75] Stalin's efforts to convince Dr. Beneš that he had no intention of annexing parts of Czechoslovak territory or intervening in the internal affairs of the future state, added urgency to the demands of the non-Communists.[76] Klement Gottwald repeatedly broadcast to the population at home about the renewed Republic.[77] Communists living in England and in the United States generally assumed an outspoken pro-Czechoslovak attitude.[78] It seems logical that Šmidke's mission was to enforce the new strategy; considerations of the war-time coalition certainly played a role in sending him to Slovakia. The change in the official line left many doubts: the Communists had to clarify to themselves and others in detail what they had to offer to Czechoslovakia, to the Czechs and to the Slovaks.

It was the government in exile which forced the Communists to become immediately involved in the problem by broadcasting, on

June 30, 1943, a proclamation re-emphasizing its belief in a single
Czechoslovak nation and a unified Czechoslovak state.[79] The wisdom
of this proclamation has yet to be proved. It was no secret that nationalism in Slovakia was firmly entrenched, whether one liked this fact or
not. London responded to a Memorandum of February 10, 1943, issued
by a group in the Slovak underground.[80] The authors of this Memorandum were the persons in Slovakia closest to the pre-war centralist
policies, and like all elements in Slovakia's underground, this group
claimed to represent the entire local resistance. Beneš and others close
to his views were more than happy to respond, without analyzing the
degree of public support for the Memorandum's authors, without
predicting the effect of their broadcast in Slovakia. The Government in
Exile again supplied convenient ammunition to all its adversaries: to the
Slovak regime and to those supporting autonomy at home and abroad.

Gottwald in his broadcast of July 19, 1943, returned to the slogan
"equal with equal," and provided the exiled Communists with a con-
vincing argument in their debates.[81] There was no novelty in this slogan,
used frequently in Slovakia in the thirties by a variety of nationalists
and by the Communists. Since 1939, the Communists had, however,
abstained from using it. An authorative interpretation was missing; the
slogan implied that both Czechs and Slovaks were separate and equal
entities, which should treat each other with mutual respect. It was of the
constitutional, and not political side of the slogan which ruffled spirits.
Did it advocate a dualistic-national or dualistic-territorial structure of
the future state? (One should remember that both Bohemia and Moravia, although populated by Czechs, were separate historical units.) Or
did it intend to organize the Republic on a federative basis? There were
strong autonomistic tendencies in the pre-war CPCS. Can a nation be
autonomous in a bi-national state? Could such an autonomy be interpreted as the relations of "equal with equal"? Perhaps in reality the
autonomous entity enjoyed a privileged position. Or, on the contrary,
perhaps the autonomous unit could find itself in the situation of a lonely
ward, dealt with in paternalistic and contemptuous fashion. Could a
numerically inferior and economically and socially developing nation
take a stand of equality with another ethnic group, with double the
population and superior economic and social achievements? Possibly, if
the Slovak problems were to be solved, a standpoint of inequality and
positive discrimination should be adopted. Answers to these and many
similar questions could not be found in the Communist journalistic and
literary publications. One might say that the conditions of war were not
conducive to scholarly elaboration of the problem. True enough. But it
is a fact that the Slovak problem was dealt with pragmatically and in an

opportunistic way, at least until 1968. Moreover, Slovaks, whether
Communist or not, later charged the Czech Communists with national
discrimination and chauvinism.[82] The elaboration of the Slovak problem arouses suspicion that the CPCS leaders were not willing to commit
themselves to a definitive solution. As in the past, they saw in the
defense of the Slovak nationality above all a vehicle for gaining power.
It would be unjust to deny the Communist struggle against the hegemo-
nism and selfishness of certain circles around Beneš and the Government
in Exile. Often such battles were undertaken quite sincerely.[83] But
doubts emerge when we compare the present to the past and the future,
when we analyze not the Communist words but their actions. We will
return to this issue later.

London's Proclamation of June 30, 1943, had repercussions on the
structure of the Slovak underground as well. These were part of a
complicated process, to which we now turn.

## The National Front: The Slovak National Council

As recorded, the non-Communist underground was fragmented; and
the Communists labored in vain to unite the anti-Fascist front. In the
fall of 1943 conditions for such a front matured.

With the capitulation of Italy and the repeated beating of Germany
on all fronts, the results of the War were predictable, and preparations
had to be made. In Slovakia, the public reacted with restlessness to news
from abroad. An increasing number of citizens were willing to join the
resistance, in one way or another. They were not forced to do so by
objective reasons, as the living conditions in the country were fairly
good and pressures of governmental agencies—never excessively
harsh—had receded. The prickings of conscience, the need for alibis
and various pragmatic calculations led persons into anti-Fascist activity. Non-Communists and Communists sensed the upsurge and enjoyed
increased public support.

Without going into details of the non-Communist underground, a
brief description should be charted out. In very general terms three
components comprised this underground: elements from disbanded
parties—particularly younger Agrarians, Slovak Nationals, and right-
wing Social Democrats; a variety of dissatisfied patriots, including
numerous Czechs and their Slovak relatives and other family connections; and members of the armed forces.

Three resistance factors can be singled out as examples of the non-
Communist groups (which were amorphous bodies rather than well-

organized units). The so-called "Flora" group specified in intelligence
collection, and had no clear political backbone. Its imprint on the
political life of Slovakia remained marginal.

Around the veteran and well-known politician Dr. Vavro Srobár
concentrated a variety of personalities and friends from the former
Czechoslovakia and from the current Slovak State. While the amount
of practical anti-Fascist activity conducted by this group was slight, it
was the most active in preparation of political contingencies. Šrobár's
personality lent prestige to this group, and attracted considerable
support. Šrobár, similarly to the "Flora" group, believed in the
existence of a single, undivided, Czechoslovak nation.[84]

The "Agrarian-Slovak National" group combined political activity
with resistance. Centered around the veteran Agrarian leader, Ján
Ursíny and the younger Dr. Jozef Lettrich, members of this circle
represented the young generation of Slovak bourgeois democratic parties. They maintained close relations with the pilots of the Slovak
economy who were sympathetic to this group. While Ursíny, Lettrich,
and their friends were firm supporters and patriots of the Czechoslovak
Republic, they opposed the doctrine of a Czechoslovak nation. They
also adopted the slogan of "equal with equal;" and probably supported
the concept of the dualistic structure of the future Republic. Disclaim-
ing adherence to the October 1939 arrangement, they nevertheless
preferred a structure not dissimilar to that created in Žilina. In this
respect, the Ursíny-Lettrich circle clashed both with the London
government in exile and with the adherents of a single Czechoslovak
nation in Slovakia. And they regarded the young generation of Slovak
Communists, Husák, Novomeský, and the like, as allies.

In the past, Husák had already served as Communist liaison to
bourgeois circles. Husák differed from his Party superiors: a well-
educated intellectual, without a proletarian background, closely at-
tached to the *Dav* people (actually the head of the second generation of
*Dav*), he was unable to separate the goal of national liberation of his
people from the social aim. During Osoha's leadership, Husák had
moved into the Party's periphery; now with Šmidke he became a central
figure in Slovakian Communism. Learning the orders of Moscow,
Husák and Novomeský set out to organize a national front to combat
fascism. Firm believers in the slogan "equal with equal," the two naturally turned to their opposite numbers, Ursíny and Lettrich. They could
hardly reach understanding with the "Czechoslovakists," so the other
center was a natural choice. The Communists aspired to monopoly in
the resistance movement, and so did their partners. Consequently, other
underground movements were left out of the budding coalition. There

was a certain advantage for the Communists: they were in the position to choose and to play one group against the other. The bourgeois centers were forced to compete for Communist favors. The personal likes and dislikes and individual choices of Ursíny and Husák probably contributed to the exclusion of potential allies.[85] Above all, however, the desire to gain supremacy guided the Communist and non-Communist politicians.

For Husák and his friends it was important to exclude any force close to Beneš, such as Šrobár or "Flora." In his intense hatred for Beneš the man, Husák had much in common with the L'udáks.[86] The President, as the prime champion of the concept of a single Czechoslovak nation, aroused—and still arouses—intense ire in Hlinka's followers. Remarkably enough, Czech Communist historians—at least of the so-called "revisionist" brand—were talking much more thoughtfully and analytically of Beneš's concepts. They were willing to see the objective dangers awaiting both Czechs and Slovaks, dangers which had appeared very real at Munich, and continued to haunt Beneš the realist.[87] Nationalists of the type of Gustav Husák or Konstantín Čuleň, were not able to adopt the stand of *Audiatur at Altera Pars.*

Years later, when confronted with their comrades-inquisitors, at their "self-criticism" in 1950, Husák and Novomeský spoke of the profound impression which the "provocative" Proclamation of June 1943 and Beneš's plans on the Slovak question had left on their thoughts and actions.[88] Cooperation between Communists of the Husák and Novomeský category and bourgeois anti-Fascists of the type of Lettrich or Martin Kvetko (a leading young member of the Slovak National Party) appeared natural. There was no great gap between the nationalism of the two camps.[89]

It is interesting to examine the reasons why the bourgeois politicians sought cooperation with the Communists. The main answer appears self-evident: a sincere wish to create a united front against the enemy. Slovak politicians saw clearly the increase of Soviet influence in the region, and its effect on the popularity of the Communists. Dr. Lettrich had an additional explanation: the cooperation was also preconceived to force the Communists to collaborate with others, to give up the idea of attaching the country to the Soviet Union, and to accept the concept of reconstructed Czechoslovakia. Like so many allies of the Communists before and since, Lettrich and his friends believed that one can ride the tiger. They believed they could control the Party's activity, and prevent development of independent plans.[90]

Thus, after prolonged negotiations, two camps—the socialist and the democratic—agreed, on November 20, 1943, to form the so-called

Slovak National Council (SNC), with the aim of renewing Czechoslovakia.[91] The document is known as "The Christmas Agreement."

The signing of the Soviet-Czechoslovak Treay of Friendship in Moscow, on December 12, 1943, furthered the understanding between the two sides. The negotiators reached agreement readily on the formula for Czech-Slovak relationships ("the Czechs and the Slovaks constitute two nations that are most closely related"), and after more protracted negotiations, also on the restoration of Czechoslovakia with two nations living in equality.[92] Four years of rehashing the "Soviet Slovakia" slogan reached an end. In the manner of the Communists abroad, the home Party too formulated a new program more suitable for the given conditions.

One question remains open: was there a design to incorporate Slovakia into the Soviet Union? The possibility of Soviet annexation of pre-Munich territories increasingly troubled the Government in Exile, as the Red Army advanced toward the old borders. Already in 1943 the Soviets began reassuring the Czechoslovak partner of their good faith, renouncing any territorial demands, and denying intentions to interfere in the Republic's internal affairs. The Kremlin was guided by long-term calculations, and by the immediate problems raised by delicate negotiations with the Western Allies. Particularly painful was the Polish problem. Czechoslovak statesmen contemplated the future of Transcarpathian Ukraine and of Slovakia. Transcarpathian Ukraine had a long record of Soviet aspirations, as well as local Communist demands for incorporation into the Ukrainian Soviet Socialist Republic. The wartime Communist activity in Slovakia made its fate uncertain.[93] The topic surfaced during Beneš's visit with Stalin in December 1943. The Soviet host labored hard to convince the guest of his good faith and fair attitude toward Czechoslovakia. Stalin certainly impressed the susceptible Beneš.[94] The Soviet boss, who had little patience and understanding of Slovak problems, reassured the visiting President of his lack of designs on that country.[95] The President discussed the future national and political structure of the revived Republic with the Moscow-based Czechoslovak Communists. He was aware of a need for agreement with these partners, which objective condition forced on him. The Slovak problem was the hardest to settle. Beneš argued firmly for one, undivided, Czechoslovak nation, and his only concession was an awareness of different views. The "equal with equal" slogan, promoted by Gottwald and his companions, left Beneš unmoved. Consequently, the future administrative-national structure of the Republic was left open.[96]

The Communist historiography regards 1943 as the watershed in the activity of the Slovak resistance (and modern Slovakian history). This year was no less important for the metamorphosis of CPS. For the first time Communist leadership passed into the hands of men committed to the nationalistic goals of their people. Later events proved, however, that Husák did not neglect his movement's aims to attain supremacy in the country.


## The Encounter: 1944

In 1944 Slovak life underwent several major changes. The Communists both contributed to these changes and were influenced by them.

Although the Christmas Agreement had established a working coalition, the power struggle continued to rock the Slovak resistance movement. The Government in Exile contributed considerably to the struggle. As suggested earlier, significant elements among the exiles remained faithful to the doctrine of a single Czechoslovak nation. Beneš's modest concession to his adversaries was in granting everybody the right to choose his identity—Czech, Slovak, or Czechoslovak.[97] In contacts with Slovakia, London preferred those personalities who had remained faithful to the Czechoslovak nationality. In other words, Šrobár and his friends found considerble encouragement in Beneš's circle, while the Ursíny-Lettrich group sensed a certain coolness. As Moscow did not provide Šmidke with directives on how to relate to London, the Fifth CC hesitated as to which line to choose. It is not surprising, therefore, that London did not admire the SNC, and that this body reciprocated.

London wanted to advance Šrobár and to cement the mutual cooperation with Slovak's civil and military allies. The civil resistance groups recruited like-minded ranking Army officers. London seized at the opportunity, and the Ministry of National Defense in particular encouraged army resistance. The underground sections competed for the favors of the military. London had liaison officers in Slovakia, equipped with short-wave transmitters. The officers, and the frequent courier service through Switzerland and Turkey, provided London with the means of intervening in local affairs.

The Communists lacked means of contacting Moscow. Bacílek, whose task was to operate a transmitter relaying to Moscow, proved to be a failure. The only links left were Moscow's radio broadcasts. This one-way link was too general in content. The Communists could rely on their common sense and ideological preparation. Some information about their actions trickled through to Moscow via London and the Czechoslovak diplomatic mission in Russia. It is puzzling that the Soviet centers made no further efforts—to our knowledge—to establish a direct connection with the CPS. On the basis of their later behavior and activities, it seems that Russian-based agencies were not sufficiently informed about the developments in Slovakian resistance. The failure was a serious one: in Slovakia an armed uprising was brewing.

Today, reassessing the past, each of the groups and centers claims credit for preparation of the uprising. In Spring 1944 an army colonel, Ján Golian, accepted the nomination to head the conspiracy. SNC, Šrobár's group, and London, each separately, nominated Golian and demanded supremacy over the military. Šrobár's men, with London's blessing, toiled hard to gain the upper hand in the underground. They were in contact with others, including the Communists. Šrobár's followers organized so-called National Committees. They planned to cap them with a Central National Committee, to outbalance the SNC, and to take over the government in the country with the approval of the current masters. The Central National Committee would rule Slovakia on behalf of the Government in Exile. Šrobár recognized the validity of the Czechoslovak constitution, and the power invested in the hands of the President and his cabinet in London. He regarded them as guarantees of the legal continuity of the Republic. The conspiratorial work in the Slovak army was, therefore, to be aimed at the renewal of the Republic, and the officers were to be subordinate to the President in his constitutional rank of Supreme Commander. This conception was in accord with the plans prepared in London, particularly by the Ministry of National Defense. General Sergej Ingr dispatched detailed directives to Slovakia and negotiated—also on behalf of Slovakia's conspiracy—with the Allied military authorities in London and in Moscow.

The Czechoslovak authorities in London were interested in an armed uprising in Slovakia. They believed that such an uprising would serve as proof that Slovakia considered itself an inseparable part of Czechoslovakia. An uprising would wipe out the "treachery" of Fall 1938 and Spring 1939. It would present the Government in Exile as ruling part of its own country. The exiles hoped to neutralize the local "separatists" (i.e., members of the Hlinka Party *and* non-loyal anti-Fascists) by providing a "strong arm" government.[98] Finally, an uprising would not only strengthen the position of London exiles vis-à-vis the not always friendly Western powers, but, moreover, prevent liberation of the country by the Soviet Army.[99] The Ministry of National Defense's planning did not enjoy unilateral support of the British, was looked upon with suspicion by the Russians,[100] and clashed with the plans of the SNC. Golian's nomination by London, and the nurturing by the exiles of the Slovak Army as an independent center of resistance resembled certain

(Yugoslav) Mihailović-Chetnik contingencies. Neither the local non-Czechoslovak forces nor Moscow could remain indifferent to London's hopes and actions.

The proximity of views constituted the basis for establishment of the SNC. How far the body really represented the Slovak population, one may merely guess. Communists, in their later pretensions, naturally claimed for themselves the support of the Slovak nation, sovereignty in resistance, and credit for exclusive preparation of the uprising.[101] Popular support for the CPS, and in particular for the Soviet Union, increased in 1944. There is room for doubt, even on the basis of the available documentation,[102] as to whether the support was in fact overwhelming. Before Munich, the highest proportion of votes cast on behalf of CPCS in Slovakia was 13 percent.[103] In the only democratic elections held after the War, in May 1946, the Party gained about thirty percent of the ballot. The conditions in 1944 were very different from those of 1946, in both the advantages and disadvantages to the Communists. Nonetheless these elections can constitute a certain indicator of the popular strength of the CPS. Among the politically and intellectually active and articulate groups of the population, the Party enjoyed considerable support; but the faithful Catholic anti-Fascists gravitated to the non-Communists rather than to the Communists. Slovak Protestantism stood in opposition to the largely Catholic state and was well represented in the pro-Western resistance. Protestants had no particular reason to join the Communists. Support for the CPS in Slovakia's population in 1944 seemed to be considerable but far from overwhelming.

The Ursíny-Lettrich group was, as we have seen, only a fragment of the non-Communist (illegal) opposition in the Slovak State. Indeed, a contemporary historian, Jozef Jablonický, expressed profound skepticism as to the public strength of this group.[104] He thought it would be appropriate for the Communists to relate to other underground workers as well, above all to Šrobár, who would be willing to reach an understanding. Those of Ursíny's and Lettrich's associates living today in the West deny Jablonický's allegations about the public weakness of their group.[105] They claim that it was firmly entrenched in the Slovak economic and cultural elite. Protestants flocked to the group's flag, and so did many Catholics. Their nationalistic and non-Communist views reflected those of the majority of Slovakia's population. The greater part of the Slovakian political representation was, for a variety of reasons, never satisfactorily analyzed, being unable to detach itself from the Third Reich. Those groups who tried to blaze new paths were publicly weak, intellectually inconsistent, and lacked civil courage. They included the circle of Slovakia's Minister to the Holy See, Karol Sidor, and the pre-Munich democratic autonomists (like the Speaker of the Slovak Parliament, Dr. Martin Sokol).[106] Slovak emigrants in the West sympathetic to the Slovak State maintain that other segments of the local political and intellectual elite considered relations with the West. Their activities were confined to debates. Diplomats in neutral countries were either thoroughly committed to the idea of Slovak independence or had nobody in the official stratum to rely on, and therefore, did virtually nothing to assist their country to escape the Nazi embrace.[107] Some authors argue that Tiso and other elements in the Slovak political-military establishment were aware of the underground activity, and virtually shielded it.[108] The German Minister to Slovakia, Hans Elard Ludin, pointed out in 1941 (and his assumption remained unchanged to the bitter end) that Tiso—and with him most of the political establishment—had only two choices: either Bolshevism or Beneš's jail, or cooperation with the Nazis.[109] Tiso repeatedly proclaimed that he would remain faithful even to a defeated Germany.[110] In fact, he remained so. Joseph M. Kirschbaum, the Slovak Charge d'Affaires in Switzerland who met Tiso in August 1944, quotes him as saying, "Unfortunately, we cannot make a compromise with the Bolsheviks, and if the Americans let you know that the Slovaks had to accept Beneš and renounce their claim to independence, we have no choice. We cannot renounce the right to independence."[111]

These were pathetic words. Leaders of the Slovak State partially believed in the Nazi victory, partially hoped for a split in the anti-Nazi coalition or a similar miracle,[112] and left themselves to drift with the winds of the war. They could not make up their minds to choose a policy of "lesser evil" otherwise so popular with them and so often reached upon in order to explain deeds or misdeeds. The maximalist demands in the L'udák-Catholic camp to preserve the state's independence left the initiative entirely to the underground. SNC had knowledge of the existence of L'udák-Catholic circles willing to compromise and accept less than a complete independence. It is possible that SNC wanted to prevent these circles around Sidor and Sokol from taking the initiative, as Joseph Staško claims.[113] The Catholic personalities cultivated relations with the Šrobár circle, and to a lesser degree also with Ursíny and the former Agrarians. The contacts remained barren. Šrobár, after all, was close to Beneš, to whom Slovak autonomists were an anathema. It would be fair to say that Beneš's attitude spoiled the search for alternate solutions to the Slovak problem. Ursíny decided to go along with the Communists, and adapted himself to his partners.

The Communists were also willing to exploit the L'udák politicians to their advantage. Writers argue repeatedly that Communist and Soviet agents tried to enlist Tiso's cooperation, promising him the survival of the Slovak State. During the Uprising, Communists labored hard to secure the good will of the Catholic Church.[114] Outwardly, however, the Communists banned any open collaboration with personalities of the regime. Consequently, it was left to Ursíny, Lettrich, and their friends to represent Slovak democratic nationalism.

The strength of nationalism in Slovakia was considerable. Under certain conditons, it was willing to adjust itself to Czechoslovakia. These conditions included recognition of the Slovak nation's independ-ent selfhood *(svojbytnost')*, the separate existence, which would in the future enjoy territorial self-government. Confusion prevailed about details and ways and means of such self-government. A federal solution appeared most congenial to both sides, and was not dissimilar to the Žilina agreement.[115] The hyphen separating Czechs from Slovaks in Czecho-Slovakia attests to this.[116] The hyphen was common in the Republic's early days, and was reintroduced after the Žilina meeting. It symbolized a federative solution to Czech-Slovak relations, but Munich and Žilina discredited it for further use. The hyphenated Czecho-Slovakia in the "Christmas Agreement" demonstrated the SNC's predilection for a federative solution. In our argument, the hyphen signifies the Ursíny-Lettrich group as the faithful standard-bearer of Slovak non-Communist nationalism. The anti-Fascist coali-tion of non-Communist and Communist Slovak nationalists seemed natural and representative.

The clash between the "separate existence" nationalism of SNC and between London's Czechoslovakism was expressed in a letter sent to London by the end of July 1944.[117] This letter was to answer a message of of Dr. Prokop Drtina, a political adviser of Beneš, to the resistance groups at home. Drtina elaborated Beneš's views about the coming developments and liberation.[118] SNC's letter, an overture of the dispute to rage in the future, put the emphasis on the independence of the Slovak nation and requested recipients to leave the Slovaks alone to build their own life in reconstructed Czechoslovakia.

Ideas behind the prepared uprising recalled this letter. The SNC politicians geared for an independent action, aimed directly against the L'udák regime, but indirectly also against the personalities and concep-tions of the government in exile. The prepared uprising was to extend Slovak contribution to the Allied cause and introduce the liberation by local efforts. For the non-Communists, an uprising was a gesture directed also against their Communist partners.

**The Allies and Czechoslovakia**

As noted, the only known line of communication between Slovakia and Moscow led through London. The situation changed early in August, when organizers of Partisan troops parachuted into Central Slovakia. At that time the preparations for an armed uprising reached an advanced stage. Communists in Slovakia for the first time partici-pated in shaping the history of that country, a participation of which Moscow was unaware. The Central Committee of the CPCS could not boast of rapid changes in its way of thinking during the first half of 1944. The State's future organization remained undecided. Moscow Com-munists discussed the creation of territorial national committees—which had also been proposed by Beneš. The future national status of the Slo-vaks was as uncertain as before. Because of the lack of communications, the Party broadcasts to Slovakia were completely inappropriate.[119] As the Soviet Army advanced toward the Czechoslovak borders, the Party and the Soviet functionaries agreed to organize a Partisan movement.[120] News from Slovakia, which reached Moscow through the West, spurred Soviet activity. The military task of the Partisan movement was to assist the advancing Soviet troops. The political assignment was to organize a war of national liberation, with Communist preponderance. The Czechoslovak military units fighting together with the Soviet Army, as well as the Partisans, were expected to serve the Party in its contest for supremacy.[121] The Partisan High Command residing in Kiev directed the Partisan units, and the Czechoslovak authorities had no influence over them. Emissaries of the CC CPCS were instrumental in setting up the units to be parachuted in Slovakia. In a meeting with Czechoslovak ranking officers and politicians in Moscow, in Spring 1944, Soviet generals objected to plans for an uprising in Slovakia. Instead they advised encouragement of a Partisan movement. As will be seen later, the Partisan movement did not best serve the interests of the Slovak resistance. It answered well the Soviet needs in Slovakia.

An agreement, signed on May 8, 1944, for cooperation between the Soviet and Czechoslovak governments, also answered Moscow's needs.[122] This agreement designated the procedures for transfer of the liberated Czechoslovak territory into the hands of delegates of the Government in Exile. Neither of the contracting parties paid attention to the appearance of a representative body in Slovakia. The exiles, although better informed, ignored the Slovak aspirations. Moreover, London desired to establish its supremacy before any other claimants could appear. Therefore, the agreement seemed to be to the advantage of both signatories.

President Benes argued that the Soviets recognized the pre-Munich borders of Czechoslovakia[123] which included Bohemia, Moravia and Czech Silesia, Slovakia, and the Transcarpathian Ukraine. The Communists and the Comintern defined the Slavonic population of Transcarpathian Ukraine and of parts of Eastern Slovakia Ukrainians by nationality. The authorities of the First Republic and fractions of the population used the terms Russins (Ruthenes), Rusniaks, or even Russians.[124] By doing so, the speakers separated the local population from those living in the Soviet Union. During the War, the Czechoslovak Ukrainians fought in Czechoslovak units and were represented in the circles of the exiles and among the Communists in Moscow and London.[125] Communist speakers repeatedly referred to Transcarpathian Ukraine as a part of Czechoslovakia. They expected the region to enjoy special status in the Republic, not dissimilar to that of Slovakia. Propaganda for annexation of Eastern Slovakia by the Soviet Union was voiced among Ukrainians living in that district. Occasionally the "Soviet Slovakia" slogan took on a very special meaning in Eastern Slovakia.[126] Western observers reported the expectations and fears of the exile circles with regard to Eastern Slovakia and Transcarpathian Ukraine.[127] While visiting Stalin, Beneš offered the Transcarpathian Ukraine to the Soviet leaders, only to be promptly turned down.[128] Beneš probably wanted to probe the Soviet intentions, as well as to save Slovakia for his state.

Just as Slovakia served as a showcase for Hitler, so Czechoslovakia was to serve Stalin. Beneš's visit to Moscow coincided with the Teheran conference of the Big Three, in which the Allies coordinated their plans (November 1943–January 1944). The Supreme Commanders of the US and British armies habitually referred to Czechoslovakia as the Soviet operational sphere.[129] The Soviet supremacy in the region was obvious. Teheran had a definite impact on the Allies' thinking. The Poles momentarily presented the most urgent problem. The Yugoslavia problem was not so pressing, but documentation in the US National Archives and in the British Public Records Office clearly evoke the brewing tensions in the Balkans. The Soviet Army was approaching the gates of Rumania. The Kremlin used Beneš efficiently for window-dressing. The Czechoslovak President fulfilled the hopes pinned on him, by a repeated display of the different treatment accorded to (the friendly) Czechoslovakia and to (the hostile) Poland by the Soviet Union. Beneš also pronounced his faith in the statements of the Soviet dictator.[130] Was he trying to buy off the Russians, to hide his fears by parading ostensible understanding? Perhaps. But in the meantime he objectively played the role assigned to him by Stalin. The assurances given to Czechoslovak statesmen during 1944 concerning Slovakia seemed earnest. The impression is that the Soviet planners—insofar as they devoted time and thoughts to Slovakia—did not provide for an immediate annexation. In the short range Slovakia required due attention.

## Planning for the Uprising

In Summer 1944 the guerilla movement initiated by Moscow began to take form. This happened independently of, and possibly to the consternation of, the Fifth CC. Concomitantly, the SNC's preparations for an uprising reached the stage which was close to realization. The guerilla movement and the uprising were mutually contradictory, and possibly mutually exclusive.

As planning progressed and the Russian troops advanced, it became clear to the Slovak conspirators that they would have to coordinate their efforts with the Soviet Army. Planners suggested two alternatives for the uprising: an offensive, at the time when the Soviets reach the vicinity of Cracow; and a defensive campaign against the German troops occupying Slovakia.[131] For two Slovak Army divisions stationed in the Eastern part of the country, the planners prescribed an assault on the Carpathian mountains to clear the way for the Soviets. The planners, both civilian and military, assembled in the heart of Slovakia—the designated center of defense—basic commodities, military supplies, and money. All preparations were elaborated in close cooperation between the military and the civilians, including the Communists. Information, forwarded through London to Moscow, was received there with skepticism. The Slovak planners were ignorant of the Soviet moves, and decided to send a delegation to the USSR composed of a military and of a civilian (Communist) member. The Communists, suffering from the lack of communication with Moscow, were strongly interested in dispatching their man—the choice was Šmidke—to report and receive orders. After initial complications, the delegation departed for the Soviet Union on the personal aircraft of the Slovak Minister of National Defense, General Ferdinand Čatloš.

The General, previously a staff officer of the Czechoslovak Army, had deserted the flag becuase of disillusionment and the prospects of carving a career in the Slovak State. When the War turned to the German disadvantage, Čatloš sought possibilities of reaching an agreement with the Allies, and perhaps salvaging Slovak independent existence in one form or the other. We can assume that he acted in understanding with some Slovak functionaries, such as Mach and perhaps Tiso. The pragmatic mind of the Slovak Communists was receptive to Čatloš's advances. The delegation to the Soviet Union carried along a plan composed by Čatloš, which offered the Soviets the close cooperation of the Slovak authorities.[132] Čatloš's plans alarmed the Government in Exile. It awakened the suspicions of Soviet and Communist double dealing, and of separate designs for Slovakia. The suspicions were not entirely unfounded. London protested vehemently, through the Czechoslovak official agencies in Moscow, and possibly other channels as well. It also objected to "dealing with Quislings" or even to the so-called "Darlan strategy." The exiles, hostile in particular to Slovak politicians who had "betrayed Czechoslovakia," opposed any negotiations with Bratislava. London's alarm, in turn, increased the Soviet misgivings of "bourgeois" intentions in Slovakia. The Slovak delegation was kept for a long period in seclusion, the Communist Šmidke—incidentally a member of the Soviet Intelligence as well—being kept apart from the rest. Czechoslovak historians do not know the contents of the Soviet talks with Šmidke;[133] the non-Communists were left in suspense for some time, until they were by chance able to contact Czechoslovak agencies in Moscow. The non-Communist messenger was never given a serious opportunity to carry out his mission.[134]

The Soviet behavior raised many eyebrows. Why was the Slovak underground to be left in the dark, when every day which went by meant lost opportunities and increased dangers? (The underground anxieties grew with the unexpected appearance of the Partisans.) The curious treatment of the delegation contributed to the speculations of those who charged the Soviets with a hostile, or at least, nonchalant, approach to a Slovak uprising.

### Slovakia's Uprising

The Slovakian uprising occurred at an unopportune time; in fact it was initiated because of coercion by the Soviet-led guerillas. The Slovak officers, not exactly the most efficient and talented conspirators, were still in the closing stages of preparations. Nonetheless, much was still left to do. The greatest question was, naturally, the timing of the D-Day and the H-Hour, and this had to be decided in coordination with the Russians. Until then, the conspirators were careful not to awaken German suspicions, and not to provoke them to occupy the country. If Berlin decided on its own initiative, the D-Day would become a *vis major*. Such an occupation would force the Slovaks to adopt the defensive variation, and would prevent the opening of Slovakia before

Soviet troops. (Slovakia, a mountainous country, could provide the Germans with suitable terrain for a determined stand. Passage through friendly territory would bring the Soviet troops in a short period to the gates of Vienna and the heart of Europe.) By their activity, therefore, the guerillas provoked German occupation of Slovakia at an early date inopportune for the underground.[135]

The guerillas parachuted into Slovakia with orders issued in Kiev. Here they met a friendly population and cells of the underground. The Army, already in ferment, fraternized with the Soviet and Czechoslovak nationals among the guerillas. The Partisans enjoyed ever-increasing support and cabled enthusiastic wires to Kiev.[136] Their messages recalled the boastful fly from Aesop's fable of the plowing ox, since they ascribed to themselves all revolutionary achievements in Slovakia. When representatives of the underground begged the newcomers to delay their activities, they met with a stern response.[137] After a short interval the Partisans opened military actions. Not all CPS members agreed with the SNC tactics followed by the Fifth CC. There are signs that the radical elements were in sympathy with the Partisans, and were perhaps interested in compelling the SNC to act. Not heeding requests, the Partisans bombed routes vital to the future uprising, and virtually undermined its communications.[138] Kiev, taken aback by the news, first asked for further information about the situation in Slovakia. Later, probably under impact of the SNC delegation, Kiev ordered its men not to provoke an uprising, but permitted continuation of the guerilla warfare.[139] The Germans, who at just about the same time were preoccupied with the Warsaw Uprising and the Coup d'Etat in Rumania, decided to act. They were encouraged to do so by Bratislava. Facing the German invasion, the conspirators in the Army were forced to seize upon the defensive variant. The Slovak National Uprising began but not in the way foreseen by its initiators.

29 August 1944 is the date officially accepted as the first day of the Uprising. In retrospect, it was a somehow unhappy day. The conspirators would have preferred to delay it. For the guerillas it was insignificant. The Soviets looked upon the Uprising with suspicion. Although the exiles liked the idea of a battle on the Fatherland's soil, they sensed the problems posed by the reincarnated Slovak nationalism. This is the "End of the dream," commented the idealists among the elite of the Slovak State. The Germans were faced with a new front, sapping their dwindling reserves, and the Western allies were confronted with a new issue in the problematic cooperation with Moscow.

The conspirators themselves were caught by surprise. Most personalities resided in Bratislava and found it hard to reach Bánska Bystrica.

the center of the Uprising. Šrobár and his men convened an improvised assembly in Bánska Bystrica and almost snatched the leadership from SNC. Only with strenuous efforts did Husák, Lettrich, and the others hold on to the political command. A discreet power struggle, behind the scenes, marked the political history of the Uprising. It raged between the Communists and their allies, and among the variety of non-Communist participants.

The armed resistance operated under an unlucky star: the Germans quickly disarmed the two armed divisions in Eastern Slovakia. The Wehrmacht designated its maneuver with the code name "Potato Harvest," which was not very flattering to the Slovak martial spirit. Units of the Slovak Army could hardly withstand the superior fighting qualities of the German troops. Only on a few occasions, when commanded by gallant officers, did the soldiers prove a match for the Wehrmacht. The Army was short of weapons, ammunition, heavy machinery, air support, supplies, and other necessities. A longer period of preparation would certainly have solved at least a few of these and other problems. When the Uprising collapsed some two months later, its military command bore only a part of the responsibility for the failure. The contribution of the Partisan units to the uprising was debatable. Their commanders had too short a time to become acquainted with the country and did not adjust thier tactics to local conditions. Guerillas, by their very nature, could not effectively fight in the way a regular army does. Being under the direct command of Kiev, they were unmanageable by the (Czecho) Slovak Army command. Yet in their demands for weapons, ammunition, and above all for food, clothing and money, the guerillas were insatiable. Superior in fighting spirit to the regular soldiers, they were nonetheless inferior in discipline. We can conclude that once the Partisans provoked the Uprising, they left the soldiers to shoulder the brunt of the fighting. Communist historians and politicians later accused the Army commanders of negligence in preparing the Uprising. The soldiers and the civilians were blamed for initiating an Uprising, which would prevent a popular war of liberation.[140] The political objectives of the Partisan leadership did not escape the attention of the Army commanders. The soldiers were interested in cooperation with the Soviets, but fought for a Czechoslovakia without Communist supremacy.[141] The lack of discipline—and occasional atrocities—harmed the partisan reputation, and slighted Communism as well.[142]

In spite of the partisan escapades, it took the Soviet Union considerable time to make up its mind concerning the Uprising. Some of the reasons for its suspicisons were outlined earlier.[143] A Czechoslovak diplomat, Dr. Hubert Ripka, told his British counterpart that the Soviets disliked the Slovak efforts to liberate themselves by their own might, and suspected the hand of a Western leadership. The Soviets would have liked to see Slovakia exclusively grateful to its Eastern liberation.[144] Western personalities, whether military or political, made it clear that it was incumbent upon the Soviets to act in the region and that Moscow's stand required further clarification.[145] The Warsaw Uprising cast a shadow on the Slovak one. The dramatic act of the Polish patriots caused the Soviets to suspect the Slovaks as well. Moscow's suspicisons (and the role played by Communists in SNC) in turn influenced the Westerners in their hesitations as to whether to assist the fighting Slovaks. Calculations of global strategy and a possible need of Soviet assistance against Japan contributed to the Western reluctance to become involved in Slovakia.[146]

One may presume that Moscow distrusted the Fifth CC. Some of its members and their close friends were an unknown quantity, a home-bred contingent, which mounted the stage after familiar veterans vacated it. Only when the Moscow emissaries, Czechs Ján Šverma and Josef Slánský, and Slovaks Mark Čulen and Jozef Valo arrived at Bánska Bystrica, together with Soviet officers, did Moscow feel that the time had come to adjust itself. Records show the emissaries as having a hard time in dictating to the independent and proud Slovak comrades.[147] Even when the Soviet Union recognized the Uprising, her assistance remained measured. The adverse weather conditions, unfavorable for an air lift, serve to explain the Eastern parsimony. The Soviet pilots had to cross the Carpathians only in order to reach Slovakia. Western airfields were far behind the Alps. Still, Eastern historians habitually accuse the West of abandoning the Uprising.[148]

After dispatching limited help, the US Office of Strategic Services halted the transport.[149] The Soviet airborne support included a Czechoslovak brigade trained in Russia, a dozen fighter-intercepter planes, cargoes of light weapons and ammunition. A considerable part of the weapons dispatched went to the partisans. The Slovak request for heavy weapons, guns and armored vehicles, was disregarded. In spite of the early warning, conveyed by the SNC delegation, the Soviet Army made no alterations in its planning. Yet the Slovak Uprising held out the promises of saving lives of Soviet soldiers and perhaps bringing closer the end of the War. Such an opportunity should not be left unheeded. The Soviet command made changes only after the commander of the two disarmed divisions reached the nearest staff officers, and reported to them.

A Czechoslovak brigade, commanded initially by General Ludvík Svoboda, which was expected to attack the city of Ostrava in Moravia from the North, moved to the vicinity of Dukla pass in Eastern Slovakia and assaulted it. At this time, on September 5th, the Germans were ready. They beat back the assault, partly because of Soviet intrigues around the command of the Czechoslovak troops, and no other attempt was made to open a surface road to Slovakia at this time.

A summary of the Allied assistance would demonstrate that both sides could have done much more for the fighting, suffering Slovaks than they did.

President Beneš and his friends in London were overwhelmed by the Uprising. The event which they had labored for for so long, had taken place. They could present themselves to the Allies as a country fighting the enemy with its own means, on its own ground. The exiles regarded Slovakia as a nation absolving itself of the sins of the past, a prodigal son returning to the fold. The disappointment soon followed. When London set in motion activities to control and govern Slovakia—basing the claim also on the May 1944 agreement with the Soviets—it met with immediate opposition. The Slovak National Council, in cooperation with both major components, proclaimed itself ruler of the country. SNC confirmed the sovereignty of the Czechoslovak state and the primacy of London's government. But it requested recognition of the separate existence of the Slovak nation, which would live on terms of equality with the Czechs and the Carpathian Ukrainians in a common fatherland. The Council considered itself the supreme political and administrative institution of Slovakia. It was willing to cooperate with the central government, but not to submit.[150] Today the Communists claim exclusive credit for the SNC's record, arguing that it performed under their guidance and at their request.[151] Doubtless the nationalistic segments of CPS supported SNC.

Šmidke presented his Moscow hosts with a document prepared by the Party at home. The authors would have liked to see Slovakia as an autonomous republic in the Soviet Union. If this solution was impossible, then the best solution would be a federated Czechoslovakia in which Slovakia would enjoy self-rule.[152] The Communist opposition to London was well pronounced during the Uprising. A variety of sources claim that by the beginning of the Uprising, the rebels had proclaimed Soviet Republics in several locations.[153] Calls for Soviet annexation, or at least opposition to revival of Czechoslovakia, were frequent. A unification congress of the Communist and Social Democratic parties stated that if the future arrangements proved unsatisfactory, the Slo-

vaks would search for their own path.[154] In an editorial, Husák described his dream of a country without borders from Aš (the most
Western outpost of Bohemia) to Vladivostok (in the Eastern Soviet
Union).[155] The factional strife between the veteran doctrinaric Communists, and the younger nationalistic elements went on within the Party.
The younger could not easily reject the veteran opposition. A hard
uncompromising attitude towards London also reflected the intraparty
discussion. Moscow's intervention on behalf of Czechoslovakia probably silenced the opposition.[156] Three proclamations of the SNC, two
open and one secret, pronounced SNC's independence vis-à-vis
London.

The first, the declaration of September 1, 1944, has already been
mentioned.[157] This declaration did not refer, in so much as a word, to
the Government in Exile. After prolonged debates with London, and its
representatives in Bánska Bystrica, the Council convened secretly, on
September 29, 1944, and authoritatively declared its views.[158] Accordingly, the London Czechoslovak agencies represented the Republic in
international relations and preserved the legal continuity of the state. In
Slovakia, the SNC was sovereign. The future Republic would be established on the basis of the equality of the comprising Slavonic nationalities. Finally, on October 16, 1944, the SNC determined guidelines for
relations with the Delegate of the London government, who was dispatched to Slovakia to take over leadership of the country according to
the Czechoslovak-Soviet agreement of May 1944.[159] The Slovaks
decided to see in the delegate a liaison officer with the government in
exile, and an intermediary to the Soviet troops on Slovak territory.

Observers from abroad agreed that both parts of the SNC were
equally determined to defend Slovakia's status in the Republic.[160] An
observer described the Communists of the SNC as "Red Ludaks,"[161] a
nickname to be repeated frequently later. Their words often had an
"anti-Prague," and perhaps anti-Czech, sting. When it became obvious
that the misunderstandings were too profound, the SNC dispatched
negotiators to London.

There were three participants in the delegation. Ján Ursíny represented the non-Communists, Laco Novemeský the Communists, and
Colonel Mirko Vesel the Army. The pronouncements of the delegation
were often confusing. In negotiations with Czechoslovak authorities, it
followed the orders received in Bánska Bystrica. When meeting Allied
representatives and the press, the delegates spoke about a decentralized
yet unified Republic, and did not raise particular Slovak demands.[162] In
fact, even ranking American and British officers gained the impression
that the Slovak-Czech problem was predominantly an administrative

one. Explanation of the ambiguity may perhaps be found in Novomeský's reminiscences. He tells that in the West the delegation learned
about the urgent need to convince the foreign public of Slovakia's desire
to stay within the re-established Republic.[163] Once he was in Moscow,
Novomeský's statements lacked the ambiguity which had marked them
in London.[164] Regarding the stand of the Slovak political—yet anti-
Fascist—elite, it would be wrong to speak about an "End to the dream."
These personalities, while devoid of the obscurantist tinge of the L'udák-
type nationalism, were nevertheless similarly determined to defend the
independent existence of the Slovak people. As far as authoritarian
designs go, the Communists had no reason to feel inferior to the
L'udáks.

## The Uprising in Perspective

In our view, the Slovak National Uprising saved Slovak nationalism,
albeit after a metamorphosis. Croatia can serve as a convenient illustration. The Ustasha rule in that country discredited nationalism. Today
any national aspirations of the Croatian people are easily rejected by
labelling them "Ustashism." By putting themselves on the side of the
Allies, the Slovaks purged themselves of suspicion of collaborating with
the Nazis. As long as the Nazis dominated Europe, the L'udáks were the
rightful defenders of Slovak nationalism. When the Third Reich suc-
cumbed, Slovak nationalism had to rid itself of these benefactors, in
order to survive. From a distance of thirty years, one must admit that
the Uprising was an act of ingratitude toward the Hlinka Party. But it
was a necessary act, if Slovak nationalism was to live. Moreover,
non-Communist politicians could hardly provide Slovak nationalism
with the leadership it needed in the post-War world. The outstanding
non-Communist personalities belonged to the ancient—but decaying—
Slovak elite, the Lutherans. The Žilina Agreement terminated forever
Lutheran dominance of Slovakia's public life, and even the seemingly
successful comeback in SNC was doomed to failure. Absurd as it may
seem, the Communist leadership represented the Catholic majority of
Slovakia. The minute the Hlinka Party lost, Slovak Catholic masses
were bound to look for new torchbearers. Since non-Communist parties were doomed, in post-War Eastern Europe, Slovak Catholics found
the path to the Marxist party and eventually made it the representative
of local nationalism. Without the Uprising, Slovak nationalism would
have had a much more difficult time.

For these reasons it is hard to accept claims of the L'udák exiles (and
others) that the Uprising was a Lutheran-Communist undertaking.[165]

There were many Catholics among the non-Communist civilians, and
the Army was predominantly Catholic. But, above all, the Communists
now represented the interests of Slovak Catholic nationalism.

By these means, the Uprising shielded Slovak nationalism from the
aggressive Czech nationalism—and even from the Slovak Protestant
allies of Czech nationalism. The London government, with a majority
of Czechs in key positions, lost in the Uprising not only the ideological
justification for placing a stigma on the Slovaks; it also forfeited the
administrative means to do so. During the Uprising, new independent
institutions came into existence, which erased the last vestiges of the
Habsburg Empire heritage. Although the Communists later confined
the new institutions in authoritarian fetters, now for the first time
elected committees, rather than appointed officers, would manage local
affairs. The centralistic rule of Prague, and later of Bratislava, was at
least temporarily broken.

So, also for the first time, the Slovaks had acted for themselves,
without waiting for assistance from abroad. In World War II their
contribution to the liberation of Czechoslovakia greatly exceeded their
part in the First War. There were those who reminded the public of
Slovak resistance activity and Czech passivity during the War. Such an
observation is hardly acceptable. One fact is definitive: Slovakia did not
owe its liberation to the Czechs. Pro-L'udák writers in the West and
Czechoslovak Communists agree; the Slovaks destroyed their own state
for the sake of Czechoslovakia.[166] This is the heritage of the Uprising;
and therein also lies the Communist contribution to Slovak
nationalism.

Superior German forces conquered Bánska Bystrica on October 27,
and spelled the end of the Uprising. Political activity of anti-Nazi forces
in the territory of conquered Slovakia amounted to almost nil. At the
same time it increased in London and above all in Moscow. In London,
the SNC delegation made it clear to everybody willing to listen—and
there were many unwilling to do so—that the new Czechoslovakia
should be a state based on equality of the indigenous nations. Novomeský took a more radical nationalist stand than Ursíny.[167] Results of
the negotiations were recorded in documents prepared by both negotiating sides and by a resolution of the government of October 23,
1944.[168] The importance of these documents lies in its testimony to the
impact the negotiations had on the exiles' thought. This was demonstrated by President Beneš, who for the first time was willing to admit
publicly a separate Slovak nationhood.[169] The importance of these
documents was scarcely lasting, however.

More influential were the talks taking place in Moscow, which lasted until the departure to Czechoslovakia of the various diverse participants. The most dramatic period in the history of Czechoslovakia started with talks in Munich, and terminated with talks in Moscow. No citizens of Czechoslovakia participated in the former talks; in the latter we only know of Czechoslovak participants. The War ended and the future was clouded.

## Chapter 4

# THE THIRD CZECHOSLOVAK REPUBLIC

After the Fall of 1944, the Republic underwent gradual Soviet occupation. The process lasted about six months, and the conquered lands were supposed to be transferred to the Czechoslovak authorities. The Republic's resurrection took a lengthy course. The first stop of the Soviet soldiers was the Transcarpathian Ukraine. Here the Czechoslovak citizens—including the Communists—encountered their first major surprise. Notwithstanding the past promises, the Soviet authorities initiated the region's decision to act for the Ukrainian Soviet Socialist Republic. The political Commissar of the Fourth Ukrainian Front, Major General Lev Zakharovich Mekhlis presided and coordinated the action. The CPCS delegated three of its members, including the veteran Czech Communist Josef Krosnař and two native-born Ukrainians, to the region. Upon his arrival, local authorities ordered Krosnař out of the country within twenty four hours.[1] The official Czechoslovak representation fared no better. Suspicions that Slovakia was next in line disturbed the Czechoslovak officials.[2] There were, indeed, some disquieting signs of a movement in that direction.[3] Most pressing was the fear for the fate of Eastern Slovakia.[4]

The American diplomat, George F. Kennan, writing from Moscow on November 11, 1944, expressed the view that the Soviets were not interested in annexing Slovakia, but rather in using it as a lever to influence the Prague government.[5] Stalin's letter to Beneš, of January 23, 1945—on the eve of Yalta—finally dispelled the fears.[6] Thoughts of opting for the Soviet Union were alive also among the Communist groups inside the partisan units.[7] The negotiations in Moscow put an end to subversive plans, and the Third Czechoslovak Republic came into existence.

## The Moscow Talks

The SNC delegation arrived in Moscow from London on November 14, 1944, after some Soviet hesitations as to whether it should be admitted. The Soviets wanted to prevent suspicions of double deal.[8] Several Slovak politicians, evacuated from Bánska Bystrica before the collapse of the Uprising, were already staying in the city. Husák arrived in Moscow for three weeks on the last day of January 1945. On March 17, 1945, the Czechoslovak Ambassador Zdenek Fierlinger greeted President Beneš and other leading exiles at the Moscow airport. Five days earlier an expanded delegation of the SNC also flew in. The final talks about the future arrangements in Czechoslovakia were about to start.

The Communists had concluded their parleys earlier. One of the decisive preparatory talks, with the participation of the leader of the disbanded CI, Georgij Dimitrov, Gottwald, Novomeský, and three others, took place on December 6, 1944. The Bulgarian Communist advised against immediate Sovietization of Czechoslovakia, and against separation of the Slovaks from the Czechs, and proposed a federal structure for the Republic.[9] Moscow-based Communists prepared a document detailing their proposals for the regime in Czechoslovakia. This document served as the platform for the round table between the Muscovites and the Londonites.[10]

A SNC Declaration of March 2, 1945, summarized the Slovak views. This declaration, the outcome of conversations in the Council and with other personalities, resembled a resolution of the Working Conference of CPS (Košice, February 28–March 1, 1945).

Husák opened the Working Conference with a key address, which reflected his discussions in Moscow. The address, and likewise the concluding resolution, demanded federalization of the Republic, on the basis of equality of the nations within it. The Conference proposed independent legislative bodies for each constituting nationality and central government and parliament. The state should be undivided and common to both nations, and until the new constitution was accepted, the SNC would rule Slovakia and promulgate laws.[11] The SNC resolution added to the above-listed stipulations requests for Slovak units in the Army and recognition of Slovakia for a limited period as a separate economic, custom, and monetary unit.[12] The resolution expressed the wishes of the population. Some parts of the Declaration, like that concerning the Army, already mirrored the Communist aspirations to dominate the Republic.

In Moscow, the SNC Declaration met with the almost uniform opposition of the Czech non-Communist parties. Before the round-table talks began, Gottwald pressured first the Slovak Communists, and then the entire Slovak delegation, to shelve the Declaration. He convinced the Slovaks to base their proposals on Chapter VI of the CC

CPCS document.[13] This document recognized the independent existence of the Czechs and of the Slovaks, based on the principle of "equal with equal." It advised the Republic to recognize the SNC as the legislative body of the Slovak nation, and the executive organ in Slovakia. Besides a law-giving council, a separate board of commissioners was to be entrusted with the task of day-to-day governing. The Czechoslovak Army would include Slovak national units.[14]

In accepting the Communist proposals, the Slovaks in fact gave up their own plans for federalization of the Republic. They cleared the way for the so-called "assymetric structure," which established the Slovak national constitutional inferiority in the Republic for some twenty-three years. Once realized in the liberated state, the "assymetric structure" provided for Slovak national institutions, without a parallel on the Czech side. Slovak ministers sat in the Central government and ruled Bohemia and Moravia, although they—and their Czech colleagues—had little to say in the rest of the Republic. Other results of this lame compromise were the continuous disputes over the SNC's rights and responsibilities, the central government's authority, and an endless list of lesser issues.

As will be demonstrated below, the struggle over assymetry was to constitute the central problem of Slovak nationalism for the years to come. Although the Slovak nation achieved theoretical equality with the Czech counterpart, the legal status of Slovakia was not equal to that of Bohemia and Moravia. The arrangement provided neither for "mechanic" equality nor for a "sophisticated" brand. The outcome was neither dualism of the *Ausgleich* type, nor a federation which would provide a measure of self-government to each part, nor autonomy and complete self-government for Slovakia. The "assymetric structure" institutionalized and perpetuated the difference in treatment of both sides of the Republic. The Slovaks were not satisfied with the rights and freedoms they were granted under the new conditions. They complained against the decisive influence of Prague in the entire state. The Czechs grumbled against the alleged preferential treatment of the Slovaks. Therefore the solution was neither fish nor fowl, and delayed the natural course of development.

In their considerations, the Communists were influenced by the Soviet model,[15] which combined regional cultural autonomy with rigid political centralization. Autonomous regions inside the Russian Soviet Federative Socialist Republic provided the working examples. The Czech Communist Václav Kopecký, equating his people with the Russians, has seen in the Czechs the "leading nationality" in the Republic. Later, already in the Summer of 1945 (during the common meetings of the CC of CPCS and CPS on July 17 and 18), Kopecký and other Czech Communists proposed the abolition of Slovak national institutions, and establishment of a territorial national committee *(Zemský Národný Výbor)* for a Slovakia similar to that of Bohemia and Moravia.[16] The Slovaks, on the other hand, once they gained *via facti* their own institutions, were not willing to give them up. When the Slovak representative concluded that federalization had too few chances, they grasped at the "assymetric structure" as the second best solution. Thus, with the assistance of the Communists (and with the Soviet Union looming behind), the Slovak non-Communists imagined that they were acting to their own advantage. Or, as Josef Korbel put it, they had "the tragically happy conviction that they had struck a good bargain in matters of Slovak autonomy."[17]

At the Moscow negotiations (March 22–24, 1945), the non-Communist Czechs took a hard line on the Slovak question. They were evidently in an inferior position. The liberation of the Republic started in the East, and advanced westward, and Soviet soldiers were doing the fighting. Consequently, the non-Communists were at the mercy of the Russians. They craved returning home badly, yet the only way led through Moscow. The "Lublin model"[18] was a threatening omen. The exiles also believed that they would be able to regain influence, once established securely at home. They concluded that a compromise with the Communists was a necessity, and they were ready to haggle over the terms. The Communists too were in need of such a compromise.

The prevailing opinion among the Communists was that Slovakia was in their pocket, but the Czech attitude was not known. Suspicions of rampant anti-Communism forced Gottwald and his friends to be cautious. In wishing to use Slovakia as a trump, they ran the risk of negative Czech reaction.

The Moscow Communists recognized the Czech hostility toward the Slovaks, because of their alleged treason, and were bound to calculate how Slovakia's prerogatives would affect the Communist standing in Bohemia and Moravia. There existed, besides the so-called "Slovak Question" also a "Czech Question." In plain words, it amounted to the survival of the Czech island in the center of a German sea, closing in on it from three sides—with only Slovakia keeping the gates open to the Slavonic masses. The Nazis were cognizant of the "Czech Question," and labored to lure to their side, with a not insignificant success, at least parts of the "Protectorate" population. By disassociating the Czechs from their ethnic brothers, and by gradual Germanization or extermination, the Nazis would eliminate "the finger pointing to the heart of Germany," to use Otto von Bismarck's expression.

In this respect, Slovakia's association with the Third Reich meant not only treason to Czechoslovakia; it was a stab in the back of Czech nationalism. Many intellectuals were enraged over Slovak deeds. How would these people, questioned the Moscow Communists, react to an expansion of Slovakia's rights, an act equivalent to giving a reward for hideous wartime conduct. Therefore concessions to Slovaks were to be limited, but still extensive enough to convince that nation of the advantages of Communism. The Soviet Union cautioned its comrades, since the Polish occurrences demanded prudence. Western statesmen were already alarmed, and Stalin could not risk an exacerbation of the Czechoslovak situation. The Republic again became a pawn in the game for much higher stakes. For such reasons, the assymetric structure appeared a suitable solution for all parties involved, although the Czech non-Communists fought back nail and tooth.

The Czechs were reluctant to admit now the existence of an independent Slovak nation and grant it its own institutions. Instead, they proposed to leave the issue to the decision of the democratically-elected representatives of the liberated population. They had a point: the Slovak delegates did not fail to emphasize that they came from the territory of the Republic and knew the moods there. While the argument had certain advantages, it actually served the other side as well. The Czech moods at home were a cipher. Only when Gottwald staged a threatening appearance, with the backing of the Slovak delegation, did the Czechoslovak politicians submit.[19] It should be mentioned that the negotiating sides abstained from inviting the Slovak delegation to participate. Only when immediate Slovak matters were on the agenda, did the SNC delegation take its place at the round table. This was curious: after all, most of the matters discussed reflected on Slovakia's fate as well. In other words, the Czechs, whether Communists or not, saw the Slovaks as sort of junior partners in their own home—a stand not too promising for the future.

### The Košice Program

The Moscow negotiations resulted in a document, which in turn constituted the basis for the so-called Košice Program of the Third Republic's First Government, promulgated on April 5, 1945. Read by Gottwald at a festive session of the SNC, the Slovak paragraphs of the document are known as "The Magna Charta of the Slovak Nation."[20] This definition was questionable. The text was the result of a compromise, to the disadvantage of the Slovaks. The original Magna Charta was a set of privileges *granted* by a sovereign: was the Slovak position to be that of a vassal? The program was a Slovak achievement and not a gift. Despite the reservations, the document was, nevertheless, a breakthrough in Czech-Slovak relations. It was the first statement of a legal Czechoslovak government, given on the home territory, which officially acknowledged the existence of the independent Slovak nation and entitled it to its own national institutions.

Slovak Communists at home had little or no knowledge of the Moscow talks. In the anarchic conditions after the liberation, the Communists, drunk with success and relying on Soviet support, tried to force their will on the defenseless population. Excesses, later dubbed in Czechoslovak literature as "sectarianism" bore a witness to the radicalism of a long-time frustrated minority—in particular in Eastern Slovakia.[21]

Communist historians wrote that in 1945 Slovakia was ripe for a social revolution, but was forced to abstain from action because of the less-advanced Czech lands. We are here touching on the discussion about the alleged backwardness of Slovakia in revolutionary achievement. During the entire period, from 1945 to 1948, Slovakia had to adjust itself to the Czechs: whether it was behind or ahead, it was not free to act on its own. The Czech and the Slovak Communists followed their own revolutionary aims and not the local needs. This way of operation caused internal changes in CPS. As we have seen, the Fifth CC managed the Slovak Communists during the last stages of World War Two. The veteran leaders, above all Široký and Ďuriš, spent this time behind bars. An attempt to free them during the uprising failed badly. German occupation authorities deported the Communist prisoners to the concentration camp Mathausen. Several inmates died on the way to the camp or during their stay there. Those who survived, including Široký and Ďuriš, emerged bitter and vindictive toward the members of the Fifth CC because its alleged negligence during the liberation attempt. This vindictiveness would have a certain role in the future misfortune of Husák, Novomeský, and their entourage. Once free, Široký and Ďuriš were quickly coopted by the incoming comrades from Moscow, and placed in positions of control.

Members of the Fifth CC, later dubbed "bourgeois nationalists," vigorously defended Slovak national rights. Without being outright anti-Czech, Husák and friends were well aware of the need for assistance from the Czech Communists, especially as they found that there was no "revolutionary Slovakia." The Communist Party in Bohemia-Moravia turned out to be more powerful than that of Slovakia; it maintained important positions in the central government. Without the assitance of the Czech comrades, the Slovak Communists had little hope of preserving and expanding their influence at home. Unluckily, the Moscovites did not trust the "home-grown" Uprising generation. Its strength and prestige sprouted in independent actions during the War. In feelings, they were closer to the patriots of their country, and could more easily find a common language with the non-Communist elite. Široký and other wartime prisoners were unable to develop any positive actions during the years behind bars; the gulf between them and the population was wide, and they fell into oblivion. Some adversaries recalled the Magyarized and/or Jewish background of Široký and several of his friends. Such a background resulted allegedly in insensitivity toward the Slovak feelings. Only the Moscovites inspired Široký, Ďuriš, and their circle with fresh energy. The result was a struggle for power with the Uprising generation on the losing side.

Ironically enough, Husák and friends could draw certain support from their non-Communist partners, organized in the Democratic Party (DP). While opposing the Communist supremacy in the country, Lettrich and company defended the national achievements of the Uprising. And since nationalistic slogans were and remained popular in the country, Husák and Novomeský were better suited to face Lettrich and Ursíny than were Široký and Ďuriš. Consequently,the Democrats not only guarded, directly and indirectly, the Slovak national institutions, but also Husák's and Novomeský's personal positions.[22]

The activity of the DP dispelled any illusions of quick Sovietization the radicals might have cherished. Excesses of Soviet soldiers toward the civil population and the international situation were among the important factors which adversely affected Communist plans. Above all, the available documentation would have us believe that the Communists were under orders of Moscow to delay any immediate importune actions.[23]

The danger of an immediate Communist takeover decreased. The need to set up a workable condition for the state administration grew stronger. Observers believed that Moscow was interested in a Slovakia rich in prerogatives, because of Bratislava's ability to pressure Prague in the future. American intelligence claimed that the NKVD was also recruited to assist the Slovak nationalists.[24]

### The First Prague Agreement

The Košice program established the framework of future arrangements, details to be further elaborated. Talks within the political elite, not always serious and thorough, resulted in the so-called First Prague Agreement between the Central Government and SNC. The Slovaks advised the Czechs to create institutions similar to their own.[25] The Czech partners, including the Communists, turned down the Slovak proposals.[26] Instead,they agreed to the broad legislative and administrative prerogatives of SNC, in addition to its representative role. The long detailed list of rights and prohibitions could be seen as a Slovak achievement.[27] The Slovak Democratic and Communist parties contributed toward the positive conclusion of the negotiations, on June 1, 1945.

The cooperation of Slovak parties angered the Czech Communists. Supported by Široký and Ďuriš, the Prague Central Committee labored for curtailment of the relative independence of CPS. The "Uprising Generation" came under fire. The Czech comrades accused it of a nationalistic and anti-Czech trend, and forced the Slovaks to agree to Prague CC supremacy.[28] During a CPS conference (Žilina, July 17 and 18, 1945), the Moscovites captured the leadership. The "Uprising Generation," veteran Communists at home, and exiles who had spent the war in the West were demoted to less important positions in the Party. The deposed leadership, and the Slovak nationalism, suffered a heavy beating. Gottwald was particularly vociferous, yet Široký, Ďuriš, and others were not idle either.[29] The Czech leader argued that in Czechoslovakia, primarily in Bohemia and Moravia, the working class was at the helm. The Communists had pledged to preserve Slovakia's achievements, and there was no room for fear. Therefore the Slovaks should concentrate on solving internal problems, instead of fighting Prague.[30] Miroslav Kropilák, one of the leading contemporary Slovak historians, admitted that the Žilina conference had introduced non-democratic norms into Party life, and created the platform for persecution of the "Uprising Generation," the so-called "bourgeois nationalism."[31]

With the reduction in the home Communists' influence on Party life, the heat in the Slovak political arena increased. The defense of the local interests gradually became the task of the DP alone.

The democratic "Uprising Generation" also forfeited much of its integrity. Under conditions of political polarization, given the need to gather quantitative strength and guided by opportunism, the Democratic Party increasingly became the refuge for dubious elements. Members of the outlawed Hlinka Party transferred allegiance to the Democrats. To a contemporary reader, Čas, the organ of DP, appears as a disseminator of anti-Semitism. The daily never tired of castigating Jews for all sorts of alleged and real crimes, in a country permeated with racial hatred and not free of pogroms. Other sensitive fields were similarly attacked, and the Communists easily found vulnerble Democratic spots open to onslaught. The Communists cleverly enlisted the support of Czech parties which, due to nationalistic shortsightedness, willingly assisted the CPCS against the Democrats.[32] While Gottwald and comrades presented themselves as fighters against Slovak nationalism, they actually toiled to undermine anti-Communist forces in Slovakia. They did so consecutively with CPS efforts to recruit local nationalism to its own advantage. The CPS attitude to the Magyar and German minorities, to give an example, demonstrated the opportunistic line.[33] The aggressive nationalism, displayed so frequently, did not prevent the CPS's gradual deterioration.

In Slovakia, where the majority of the population still lived in villages and worked in agriculture, the agrarian question was most important. Land reform was the issue of the day in the villages. The mostly poor peasants with small lots hoped for an egalitarian division of estates belonging to the richer and the rich, to the Church, and to the national minorities. Indeed, in the spring of 1945, and also later, CPS considered a land reform. Such a reform constituted an important element in the Communist plan of social reconstruction and a major supplement to the national policies. The Slovak Communists were obliged to defer their plans, however, under the pressure of the Czech comrades. Gottwald and his friends feared an adverse reaction on the Czech countryside one radical steps were taken in the Slovak agriculture. Thus the field was left wide open to Democratic activity. The Democratic Commissioner of Agriculture Martin Kvetko, who labored to expropriate land belonging to the minorities, gained considerable popularity. Through their agricultural policies the Democrats were gathering strength. The Communists, left with unfulfilled promises, watched with anger and despair their adversaries' success.

Elections to Worker Committees and to (municipal) National Committees showed a decrease in Party popularity and CPS speakers talked about "stagnation."[34] In reality, the factual strength of the Party emerged with the evanescence of the post-war atmosphere. The Communists had undoubtedly gained many members and followers since 1938, and increased in popularity, but the numbers were still considerably smaller than the party-activists believed. The CPS's expansion suffered. The misconduct of Soviet soldiers, fear of the Soviet Union, and suspicions of Communism harmed the Party's prospects.[35] Many a follower was afraid of annexation by the Soviets, if the Communists showed themselves excessively popular, and preferred to leave the ranks. Above all, the conservative-religious outlook of a considerable part of the population made itself felt. Only a short while ago, Slovak Communists had been forced to dampen their revolutionary zeal because of the uncertain situation in Bohemia and Moravia. Now the strategists began to regard

Slovakia as retarding the revolutionary tempo of the entire Republic. Prague leaders asked the Slovak Communists to renounce revolutionary-nationalistic demands. Small wonder that CPS members started to question why in every case Slovakia's demands were sacrificed. As before, Slovakia's nationalistic politics were regarded as a threat to progress.

The central institutions such as the government and the Provisional National Assembly (PNA) singled out for criticism the Slovak Board of Commissioners—the executive arm of the SNC. Prague charged the Commissioners with a failure to enforce laws and decrees enacted in the Capital, and with promulgating their own norms to which there was no Bohemian-Moravian equivalent.[36] Although there was more than a grain of truth in Prague's charges, one may still wonder whether it was not the very existence of independent Slovak institutions, rather than their inconsistencies, which provoked Czech criticism.[37] Most typical of the attitude of Czech parties was the speech of Dr. Petr Zenkl,the Chairman of the National Socialist Party (previously the party of Dr. Beneš), in the National Assembly. Zenkl stated that he and his party would not accept responsibility for acts and developments in Slovakia after August 29, 1944.[38] The Czech pronouncements could not but fan the flame of Slovak nationalism—which anyway did not need much assistance in order to stay alive. There were frequent exchanges in the National Assembly, in the press, at public meetings, and on the platforms between Czech and Slovak spokesmen, including the Communists. The CPS competed with the DP in real and alleged defense of Slovak national interests.

An important element in the acrimonious debate was the problem of the industrialization of Slovakia. Faithful to the Marxist doctrine, the Communists believed that the economic retardation of Slovakia was responsible for its shrill nationalism. Czech Communists and their Slovak followers were the chief proponents of this doctrine, although others did not lag far behind. It should be noted that the Communists believed in the elixir of industrialization before the War as well. Non-Communist Slovaks were also aware of the economic maladies of their country, and were anxious to cure them. Slovakia accrued much good will on the Czech side, where its needs were well known. Czech speakers repeatedly confessed to the desire to assist their more backward brethren. When it became necessary to translate words into deeds, a debate ensued: where, how, who should do what, who should stay in charge? The Slovaks demanded to be left alone to manage their own affairs, and asked the Czechs to content themselves with providing assistance.

Czechs, and particularly the non-Communists, replied that Slovaks lacked the know-how to run firms and introduce new industries. The Slovaks in turn complained that Prague wished to control their country by means of economy management. Both sides offered proof for their charges. Factories to be transferred from the Sudeten region served as an illustration. While Czech workers rebelled against the transfers, the Slovaks charged Prague with procrastination. In Slovakia there were few specialists to operate the new plants. The Slovaks suspected the incoming Czech instructors of intending to exploit the country as they had been accused of doing during the First Republic. And again, Slovak Communists took part in this debate, accusing the Czech bourgeoisie of scheming to keep the Republic's Eastern half underdeveloped. Nor could the Communists act differently, if they did not want to lop off the branch on which they were perched. The alleged and real backwardness of Slovakia gained increasing importance in the Communist thinking. In the hands of the Široký-Ďuriš group it assumed major proportions. By promoting industrialization, the two men explained and justified their political line, and subsequently promoted personal ambitions. The politics of industrialization became an important tool in manipulation of the life of the Party and nation. The need to assist the "weaker Slovak working class" came to vindicate the outside intervention in the life of the CPS and the Slovak body politic.[39] In 1947 Slovakia was accused of delaying the revolutionary progress of the Republic. Only the country's industrialization could propel its revolutionary spirit. The Marxist doctrine, being in a position to analyze Slovakia's conditions, served the Communists as a pragmatic, nay opportunistic, tool in their efforts to dominate Czechoslovakia.[40]

## The Second Prague Agreement

The Republic underwent a gradual consolidation during 1945. The fears of Communist ascendancy waned. Russian soldiers left the territory, the political scenery was more tranquil. Yet sensitive observers noticed developments, which were soon to reach menacing proportions. An American diplomat reported on June 13, 1945, "Reaction of people ... is that at Munich, Czechoslovakia was sold to Germany, and at Yalta to Russia. While the former was temporary, they fear the latter will last."[41]

Would it be right to say that the political life in Czechoslovakia of 1946 had returned to routine, to "business as usual"? Perhaps. Taking into account the various and complicated results of the war, a return to parliamentary-institutional political activity may indeed appear as a return to "business as usual." Small wonder that outside observers saw Czechoslovak political life in 1946 in this light.[42] Only at a distance of dozens of years can we analyze the unusual conditions: the advantageous position of the Communists in the struggle for supremacy, the unique international situation revolving around the Cold War axis, and the deep changes wrought by Nazi domination.

Today it appears that the non-Communists in Czechoslovakia at that time had little hope of survival. Their struggle, under conditions of "normalcy," their "democratic" election of 1946, their attempts to guard the civil rights, can all be denoted futile. It is illuminating to reconstruct the months, weeks, and days before the final tragedy of February 1948, so as to examine Communist strategy and tactics, and responses of the other side.

The Communists allotted nationalism a place of honor, and the Czech comrades used it superbly not only against the non-Communists but also against the Slovak fellow party-members. In almost "Machiavellian" fashion, arguments of nationalism were used to disarm the CPS and overpower the non-Communist Czech and Slovak parties. In retrospect, the bourgeois parties demonstrated poor judgment and played into the hands of their adversaries. The Communist strategy was to keep Czech and Slovak anti-Communists divided. By looking for immediate benefits,they neglected to watch their principal enemy. From a determinist angle, the Czech and Slovak non-Communists were bound to clash and thus to further the CSCP struggle for supremacy. In any case, the bitter disputes among the exiles in the West were pointless. Both the Slovak Democrats and the Czech non-Communists represented a short-sighted viewpoint in face of the mortal danger. Instead of cooperating for the sake of freedom, they defended narrow-minded nationalistic aims, and only too willingly fell into the traps continuously prepared by the Communists.

The new Czechoslovak constitution and the legal position of Slovakia were the major political issues of 1946. They were discussed hotly among the politicians and in the press.

Czech parties, including the CPCS, were not satisfied with the arrangements concerning Slovakia for many reasons. These included suspicions and fears of the future developments, political considerations and calculations, hidden anger and malice, and nationalistic designs. The Slovak side was no less discontented. The local people dreaded alleged Czech domineering spirit. Nationalistic hatred, and long-term political planning also troubled the waters. In the last analysis, the causes of dissatisfaction on both sides were quite similar, and involved emotional, irrational issues. The formal arrangements left much to desire; new problems, legal and pragmatic, kept appearing. In two main spheres a speedy solution was required: relations between the SNC and the central government (including relations between central ministers and Slovak commissioners), and the extent of the President's prerogatives. Much attention was given to provisions for elections, discussed in the Provisional National Assembly. This discussion involved questions of relations between the Assembly and the SNC. To settle the problems, the central government entered into formal negotiations with the SNC (April 9-11, 1946).

The negotiations were neither easy nor pleasant. In the confrontation, the Communist and non-Communist Czech parties faced the DP delegates. Slovak Communists stood aside. They could not oppose their Czech comrades, and did not wish to do so. They neither wished nor dared to harm the cause of Slovak nationalism. And they remembered the approaching general elections. Therefore, the brunt of the negotiations was left to the Democrats. The Czech Communists again drew up a reckoning of "progress" and "reaction." Slovakia seemed reactionary, and held out the threat of danger to the democratic order in the state. Separatism allegedly influenced Slovak politicians, and the strength of non-Communist forces threatened the future domination of the pro-Soviet phalanx.[43] Therefore, the Czech Communists aspired to increase control of the Prague center over Slovak matters, and reduce the rights and privileges of Bratislava's national institutions. The non-Communists believed that an increase of Prague's authority in Slovakia would strengthen their position as well. In the face of stubborn Democratic defense, the Czech achievements were not too extensive. The so-called Second Agreement of Prague of April 11, 1946, clarified and extended the President's prerogatives in Slovakia, and further defined the mutual relations between Prague's and Bratislava's institutions and ranking officials. In practice, the Second Agreement curtailed and unfavorably interpreted the provisions of the First Agreement as far as Slovakia was concerned.[44]

The PNA negotiations were more to the Slovak advantage, probably because of the common front of the Slovak deputies. As a Democratic deputy put it: "when the Slovaks appear unified, the Czechs retreat."[45] The status and the rights of Slovakia were enhanced by law in the way advocated by the Slovaks. The voting regulations also guarded Slovak interests.[46] The major disadvantage, and direct result of Slovak Communist passivity, was the small number of seats allotted to Slovakia in the future Constitutional Assembly. Originally, the Slovaks had hoped to receive a third of the three hundred seats. They negotiated for eighty seats, and had to acquiesce to only sixty-nine. The Communists were not interested in an increase of Slovak representatives in the Parliament, which would necessarily mean a larger non-Communist delegation.

The issue involved the structure of the Republic. The Czech Communists objected to a federation which would prevent Prague's intervention in Bratislava. For similar reasons they opposed dualism—after all just another form of federation. Dualism was a cursed word: every party and politician labored hard to prove its devotion to the cause of unity. And unity seemed to be the antithesis of dualism. Defending the "unity" meant eating one's cake and having it too. Politicians habitually alleged that the proposed laws and reforms were intended to strengthen the unity of the Republic. Nonetheless, Slovak and Czech particularism remained very real. New legislation signified further erosion of Slovakia's stand in direction of centralization. The Communists, instead of retarding the process as might have been expected, initiated it or contributed significantly to its acceleration. Those of the Slovaks who desired to stop the erosion had no weapons left. With the Cold War raging among various states, the trend in Europe was toward centralization. Moscow was cementing its domination over the client states. Regions, little nations, and small states were losing their bargaining ability. Slovakia, without foreign contacts, without military power, and without economic importance, could not hope to catch the eye of great powers. Furthermore, because of their affiliations during the War, the Slovaks were dubbed "reactionary," and had little chance of competing with the victims of appeasement, the "progressive" Czechs. Naturally, neither the West nor the East would comfort "reactionaries."

The disappearance of the united front of the "Uprising Generation" sealed Slovakia's fate. Slovak Communists, by assisting in the emasculation of their country, were preparing their own downfall. Instead of playing an independent role in the state's politics, they became CPCS lackeys. In other words, Gottwald's group in Prague sold out Šmidke, Husák, Novomeský and the others to Široký and Ďuriš. The latter two faithfully executed the policy of the CC CPCS, which was indifferent to the Slovak national emotions. The Democrats were left alone to defend local interests. The CPS continued to use nationalism to mobilize the masses behind the Party. When decisions were to be taken, the Communists sacrificed Slovakia's interests to the needs of "progress and revolution."[47] The Communists fought for the "domination of the working class," and under this cloak renounced the achievements of the Slovak National Uprising.

## The General Elections

The general elections of May 26, 1946, confirmed the relative failure of Communism in Slovakia. In these elections the CPS got 30.37 percent of the votes cast, while the DP polled 62 percent.[48] In comparison to the last general elections of the First Republic in 1935, the Communists almost tripled their vote.[49] And while in 1935 a definitive part of the votes came from the regions populated densely by Magyars and Germans, the ballot was now almost solely Slovak. It would be hard, therefore, to speak of an absolute failure. The Communists fell far short of their expectations. And in the wake of the failure, they lost the fifty percent representation in municipal and country institutions which they had held ever since the Christmas Agreement.

Years later Dr. Husák claimed that Dr. Lettrich had proposed to Široký a single list of the Uprising parties, with a fifty-fifty distribution of deputies. Široký allegedly balked at the proposal. Dr. Martin Kvetko denied that such a proposal was ever made.[50] Lettrich believed that four reasons brought about the Communist advancement in Slovakia after 1935: the liberation by the Soviet Union; the regime of the Slovak State, which caused radicalization of the population; the fact that the Social Democrats—who previously constituted a considerable force—voted at this time for the Communists; and the moderate socially-extremist national platform of the Communists.[51] Achievements of the Uprising, postwar nationalization and agrarian reform, and lowering of the voting age may also have contributed to the Communist gain in strength. After all, the postwar European population was marked by political radicalization.

No less interesting is the question of why the Communist gain was not much larger. It is almost a truism to say that fear of Communism in general and of the Soviet Union in particular was the main reason. In the First Republic, political radicalism increased as one moved eastward. The year 1946 demonstrated the very opposite phenomenon: the Communists were strongest in Bohemia, and weakest in Slovakia. Moreover, in Western and Central Slovakia their standing was relatively better than in the Eastern part of the country, immediately adjacent to the Soviet Union.[52] The Democratic Party also developed and changed sufficiently to serve as a home to all kinds of elements which would scarcely have followed it in September-October 1944. The Party accommodated non-Communists under the condition of the virtually bi-party system of Slovakia.[53] The non-Communist "Uprising Generation" included members who could hardly be described as liberal or democratic-minded. Some of them were outspoken anti-social and authoritarian personalities, chauvinists, and racists. Others were progressive, democratic-minded, and fair. The major problem was the kind of representation the Party could offer the Slovak masses.

The majority of Slovak voters were Catholics. The Communists, even while obscuring their atheism, were aware of the difficulties involved in capturing this vote. Therefore, they set a lesser aim, to draw the Catholic vote away from the Democratic coffers. This could be done, so they believed, by the creation of a Catholic party which would split DP's ranks and offer an independent representation for people of the Roman faith. The Communist planning coincided with a fermentation in the midst of the nationalistic Catholic intelligentsia, and of the Episcopate. Segments of the Catholic population felt discriminated against in the new Czechoslovakia, with no political representation to defend their interests. They distrusted the DP because of the Uprising heritage, and because of the significant Protestant and Agrarian leadership. The Catholics engaged in political activity ("political Catholicism") and accused the Democrats of neglecting and harming the interests of their faith and their people and cooperation with the Communists at the expense of Catholicism.

Certain Catholic personalities, inside the DP and outside of it, hoped to gain political significance in Slovakia beyond their actual role. They banded together with other Catholic activists, contacted the Episcopate, and set upon a path leading to the creation of a Catholic blend. Consequently,the Communist design and the Catholic fermentation coincided. Others, including Šrobár and additional anti-Ľudák Slovaks, joined the initiative. The Communists were willing to support an anti-Democratic body and to assist in its political planning, disregarding potential dangers for the "Uprising heritage." The result was the foundation of the so-called "Party of Liberty." The Democrats understood perfectly well the Communist scheming and its threats to their electoral strength, and, in a clever move, emasculated the new party from the outset.

As noticed, there were Catholics and Protestants in the DP leadership. The public following of the Catholic personalities was, however, uncertain. If the Party wanted to capture Slovakia, as the case was, it needed a massive Catholic vote. To secure such a vote, the DP signed, on March 30, 1946, a document which became known as the April Agreement. The other signatories were an amorphous group of the Catholic clergy and laymen, backed by the Episcopate. The document specified the conditions for Catholic cooperation with the DP. The April Agreement secured political representation for parts of the

Catholic masses, a representation they lost with the disappearance of the Hlinka Party. Catholics again directly influenced Slovakia's political fate.[54] Leaders of the Democratic Party were forced more than ever to pay attention to dubious elements and pressures. Although the Democrats gained considerable public support, the Agreement provided their adversaries with excuses to attack the Party and accuse it of destructive and nefarious activities.

## The Third Prague Agreement

The Democratic victory alarmed the Communists. The DP majority in Slovak institutions could place obstacles in the path of further advancement of Communism in that country; moreover, it could cause adverse influence in Bohemia and Moravia. As the Communists put it, the reaction would misuse Slovak institutions and prevent extension of brotherly assistance of the Czech working class. The Slovak toiling people were in danger.

The two euphemisms "Slovak toiling people" and "brotherly help" repeated themselves in the Communist parlance, and meant in fact "CPCS designs" and "enforcement of CPCS designs." (In 1968, the expression "brotherly help" meant occupation of Czechoslovakia by forces of the Warsaw Pact.)

As usual, Czech Communist and non-Communist attacks on the DP concealed an assault on the CPS[55] and the Slovak national institutions. An offensive against the Democratic Party followed. Again, the Czech Communists used the non-Communist parties, and those—blinded by the antipathy toward Slovak nationalism—let themselves be used to their own disadvantage. The stage chosen at this time was the so-called National Front of Czechs and Slovaks (NFCS). This was a cumbersome body formed in Moscow with the aim of providing a platform for informal negotiations, before issues went to formal institutions. According to the official interpretation, the NFCS expressed the national unity of anti-Fascist forces, and guided the political activities for the sake of the Republic.

In reality the NFCS acted as the coordinating and clearing body of the coalition government, and was therefore a convenient place for CPCS action. A parallel NF also existed in Slovakia. Now Gottwald submitted to the NFCS a proposal to shape Czech-Slovak relations on a new basis. The proposed reforms would tighten Prague's control over Bratislava. The non-Communist parties seized upon the Communist initiative, and the Democrats were left with no support. Husák

explained to the Democratic delegate, Dr. Samuel Belluš, that the
heavy pressure of the Czech Communists and of Široký prevented the
Slovak Communists from defending Slovak national institutions.[56] For
Široký, Ďuriš, and perhaps even for their intraparty adversaries, the
Czech pressure was a welcome assistance against the victorious Democrats. For fear of the Democrats the Slovak Communists took refuge in
the bosom of the CPCS. In NFCS the Democratic Party was intimi-
dated by exclusion from the governmental coalition, and by the remote
threat of being dispersed. Security agents privately blackmailed certain
Democratic leaders. The Democrats had no choice but to surrender.
The Third Prague Agreement of June 24, 1946, at that time no longer
maintained between the government and SNC but among the political
bodies represented in the National Front, castrated the Slovak institutions. The more important specifications included a requirement to
submit SNC laws to the central government for approval, partial extension of the ministerial authority to Slovakia, and Prague's budgetary
control over the entire Republic.[57] For the DP the May 1946 elections
meant defeat in victory; for the CPS they were a total defeat.

After the elections and until the Communist coup d'etat of February
1948, the question of industrialization and the new constitution preoccupied Slovak nationalists. Behind them loomed the cardinal issue of
the Republic: the Communist efforts to attain supremacy.

The dispute over the constitution was a continuation of the everlast-
ing debates concerning Slovakia's position in the Republic. The main
issue to be determined in the constitution included: the formal status of
Slovakia and the Slovaks, relations between Bratislava and Prague
institutions, and voting procedures over laws affecting Slovakia. A
planning body of the National Socialist Party, the chief promoter of
Czech nationalism after World War II, proposed, in July 1946, various
ways of assimilating Slovaks.[58] The Communists were more modest,
and merely elaborated a program for subduing the Democratic Party,
and for pacifying the "Uprising Generation."[59] There were elements of
horror in the Communist talks. A short time after the election defeat,
Široký addressed an internal assembly with the following words:[60]

"I think that all the comrades who were in Bánska Bystrica (i.e., in the
Uprising) will agree with me. We are today paying the bill for our weakness,
our false humanity, and for not staying on a basis similar to that of the
Yugoslav War of Liberation—the most human mission of this revolution
was to beat down the Fascists without mercy, and to exterminate physically
the representatives of Fascism and bourgeoisie."

Široký's words conveyed his personal hostility to the "Uprising Generation," and his bitterness at being left in prison. But the central content is

unmistakably brutal. Široký regretted the failure of his comrades to perform mass extermination of certain parts of the Slovak people. One may agree with Široký that such exterminations would for a time considerably weaken the anti-Communist resistance of the local nationalists.

The same Široký guided his comrades in political activity:

"For us, the Communists, it is not a question of principle, of how our mutual relations [with the Czechs] will be arranged. Whether it should be a federation or an autonomy, is not a matter of principle. The basic question is whether we want to lead our nation on the road to progress . . . socialism. . . ."[61]

Years later Husák accused Široký of being lukewarm toward Slovak problems. Široký, of Magyarized parentage, talked Slovak with a heavy Magyar accent, not unsimilarly to the notorious L'udák leader Dr. Vojtech Tuka.[62]

Much of the material quoted or considered in this study was little known or completely unknown during the period discussed here. Nevertheless, those active and alert were aware of the problems the constitution was raising. Today, in retrospect, we know that the Communists were considerably responsible for encroachment on Slovak achievements in the prepared constitution. In February 1948, the document was still disputed and unfinished. Yet for a long time it attracted domestic and foreign attention, and acted as a catalyst of public opinion. Such was its importance.

Another topic of importance with far more effective results, was the proposed economic advancement of Slovakia. As shown,[63] the Communists saw industrialization as the miracle cure for Slovakia's illnesses. The platform of Gottwald's first government included generous economic plans for Slovakia. The Two Year Plan of Economic Reconstruction of the Republic emphasized Slovakia's industrialization. The attention paid to the country's problems was encouraging. Soon, however, the Democrats discovered that the reins of economic activity were surely kept in Prague, in the hands of the Communist ministers. In a flood of invective, the Communists charged their adversaries with neglecting Slovakia's needs.[64] The Democrats pointed rightly to the increasing centralization, a result of Gottwald's government activity.[65] The Democratic Čas commented:

"We do not see in an economic plan and its fulfillment sufficient safeguard of Slovak interests. A nation lacking the opportunity to manage its own fate through political means cannot manage its own economic and social development either."[66]

Communist writers confirmed the Democratic thesis, though almost twenty years too late.[67] Attempts of the SNC and the Board of Commissioners to stop, or at least to delay, the erosion of their powers could hardly succeed. Sabotaged by the local Communists and facing a united front in Prague, the actions of the Slovak institution had little hope of success.[68]

The Communist success was—as usual—a result of their relative strength in the West of the Republic, of efficient manipulation of non-Communist Czech parties, and of increasing weakness of the Democrats. Today it seems that the Third Prague Agreement sapped the DP's stamina. Though cooperation with the Catholics added to the strength of parliamentary representation, it undermined the Party's unity. The Communists found it easy to find soft spots in the Party personage and line. The DP was leaning toward neo-L'udák activities and ideology. The "Uprising Generation" leadership's grip on the fragmented body was weakening. The Catholic partners were disappointed when Lettrich and company failed to save the life of Dr. Tiso, thus violating the spirit of the April Agreement. All the efforts of the Democrats to prevent the execution of the Slovak state's President failed. He was sentenced to death by the National Tribunal and hanged on April 18, 1947.[69] Clever Communist maneuvers destroyed Protestant-Catholic cohabitation in the Democratic Party. As before, the decrease in DP abilities had repercussions within the Communist "Uprising Generation." The Prague-based Central Committee lacked the finesse to attend to Slovak particularities. Though officially on an equal footing with the Czechs, the CPS suffered overt and effective discrimination. The mechanistic and bureaucratic conduct of Party affairs frustrated the Slovaks. Prague Communists felt that only direct intervention, "brotherly help," could save the retarded Slovaks from the clutches of the L'udáks and their Democratic heirs. The theory of Czech-Slovak equal progress toward socialism showed itself detrimental to Slovakia and its Communists.

## The Weak Link

In 1947, the Communists discovered that Slovakia, and particularly the DP, were the "weak link" in the Czechoslovak system. Playing a somehow risky game, the Czech Communists encourged nationalism in Slovakia. In these years of turbulence, the task was not too difficult. On the other hand, even if elusive, the external effects of nationalism were not unmanageable. Anti-Semitic demonstrations, a sure barometer of the pressure of public feelings, erupted fairly frequently. It was safer to attack the Jews than the authorities. While security services were much under Communist control, little was done to prevent the outbursts. Participation of the Communist-led partisans, party-members, policemen, and soldiers in the pogroms was not infrequent. This is how the outspoken Kopecký outlined the Communist strategy:[70]

> Asserting that Slovakia was the key to the Czechoslovak problem, Kopecký suggested that the fomenting of anti-Communist activities was part of the Communist strategy of bringing an end to the prevailing political situation in the Republic: 'When we are successful in getting Slovakia to secede, it will be easy to liquidate (political opposition) in Bohemia-Moravia'.

Extra-parliamentary activity, anti-Czech, anti-Czechoslovakia, anti-Communist, and anti-Jewish demonstrations and riots were grist to the Communist mill. It may well be that some of the outrages were Communist initiated. Nationalist and pro-Fascist elements assisted unconsciously in the Communist surge.

Having the *corpus delicti* in hand, it was not too hard for CPS to go to the Czech parties and to threaten them with problems in Slovakia. Yet, in summer and fall, non-Communist parties showed signs of comprehension of the Czech Communist tactics. As the non-Communists started to close ranks, the pressure on them increased. The Democratic toleration and even limited support of the Ľudáks, encumbered the Czech non-Communist overtures. Ultimately, however, the threat of danger bridged the differences.[71] Seeing this, the Communists— dialectically—desired cooperation with the Democrats, thus putting a wedge between the bourgeois Slovak and Czech parties.[72] Among the variety of tactics, so skillfully used by the Communists, that of a concentrated attack on the Democrats finally prevailed.[73] During the last part of 1947, the DP was on defense. Its adversaries displayed boundless vigor and ingenuity. The February coup centered on Bohemia and Moravia—there was little need for it in Slovakia.

Important events in 1947 included remarks of President Beneš to the Slovak delegation of the "Czechoslovak Society," a body promoting Czech-Slovak cooperation. Beneš reacted to the statement of the Slovak Archbishop Dr. Karol Kmeťko at Tiso's trial. Kmeťko stated that the Czechoslovak Republic was the second best choice of his nation. The President retorted sharply that Slovakia was not in the position to constitute a part of the Republic conditionally. The Czechs, encircled as they were by the Germans, needed direct borders with the Russians. A further attempt at Slovak independence must either be supressed or the country would have to become a part of the Soviet Union.[74] Beneš' words, pronounced against the background of steady

haggling over the new constitution, caused a shudder in Slovakia. The
Democrats, Protestants, and Catholics responded in multiple ways.

All reiterated their allegiance to and faith in the Republic, and
determination to secure its existence.[75] Slovak Communists held aloof.
They did not feel particularly affected by Beneš' remarks. Communist
spokesmen often reminded the public, with veiled threats, that the
Soviet Union was the immediate neighbor of Slovakia. Slovakia was
also conscious of being encircled by Soviet troops; Bohemia and Moravia had the advantage of bordering on Western military zones in
Austria and Germany. Once more the chief speaker of Czech nationalism played into the Communist hands. By presenting the survival of the
Czech nation as the main objective of the common Republic, he rein-
forced the arguments of Slovak nationalists against his people. He also
indirectly helped the Communists, and confirmed that the Soviet Union
was the only substitute for the Czechoslovak state.[76] The President
intervened in the dispute over the future structure of the Republic,
siding, in fact if not in theory, with the centralists. In the Czech territories the centralist front included the National Socialists, the (Catholic)
People Party, the Social Democrats, and the Communists. On the
Slovak side, only Široký and his wing of the CPS talked about "the need
for Slovak institutions to create equally positive conditions for the
Slovak nation in the spirit of the popular-democratic principles of our
state policies and not a tool for the increase of differences in economic
and social structure."[77] The perpetual debate over the constitution
revolved around the extent of Slovak national privileges and institutions, and creation of a similar arrangement on the Czech side.[78]

The Slovaks argued that they did not want autonomy, since they were
not a minority.[79] The Czechs answered that creation of political-
administrative institutions for Bohemia and Moravia would mean federalization and encouragement of the separatists in Slovakia. Široký
charged the Slovak oppositionists of centralism with resistance to the
people's democracy.[80] Using the habitual euphemistic expression, Široký actually admitted that Democrats prevented Communists from
usurping power in Slovakia. It should be reiterated that both Siroký
and Husák wished to become sole rulers of the country. Husák resisted
the democratic decision of the majority of the Slovaks against his Party.
Or, as he put it, "twenty village grannies, who voted according to the
instructions of a priest, cannot equate the position of a politically
conscious factory worker."[81] One may assume that the debate inside the
CPS at least partially expressed difference of opinion as to the most
convenient way to gain the upper hand in Slovakia. The result was
increased pressure on the Democrats.

Široký tended to transfer issues to Prague, where the anti-DP forces were stronger. The Democrats resented the search for solutions in Prague and preferred to keep it in their own hands or pass it on to Bratislava and to institutions under their control. Yet they were not consistent, as demonstrated by the request of amnesty for Tiso. Instead of pardoning him in Bratislava, the Democrats left the inconvenience to the Czechs. Naturally, Czech politicians could not overlook the significance of this step or refrain from seeing in it a precedent.[82] Later, when the weight of the Third Prague Agreement was made felt, Democrats protested in vain. Prague efficiently hampered the work of Slovak national institutions, and the Democrat defense was powerless.[83] In hindsight, however, it is hard to charge or to praise. The developments in Slovakia seemed to parallel occurrences in other countries under Soviet domination. The Summer of 1947 witnessed the termination of the Communist take-over in Hungary and Bulgaria. The pro-Communist regimes in Poland and Rumania outlawed the parties of opposition, and neutralized their leaders. Czechoslovakia was the last of the countries liberated by the Soviets which still enjoyed a degree of democracy and civil liberties. The situation was in a process of change. Moscow forced Czechoslovakia to turn down the invitation to participate in the Marshall Plan. It prescribed to Prague the Treaty of Friendship with Poland. It created the Cominform, where CPCS was represented by a single delegation. The threatening omens increased.[84]

The onslaught against the Democrats resembled in some ways the tactics used against the Hungarian Smallholders and the Polish Peasant Party. A steady stream of accusations defamed the Democrats in the eyes of the public and disturbed their routine work. The Communists lent support to an adversary party and attempted to cause a split within the DP. They effectively employed police terror and violence, as well as mass organizations under Communist influence. The Communists hoped to undermine and splinter the DP, to break their resistance to force them to vacate the field.[85] CPCS led the offensive. As in the past, Slovak Communists were aware of the dangers to local institutions inherent in the attack on the Democrats, but because of the "class struggle" façade of the action, they kept their silence. They tried to alleviate the personal situation, and Šmidke called directly on Soviet diplomat, but to no avail. This was a further episode in the same old story.

"Only because the Slovak Comrades turned wise, subdued their feelings, did not oppose us the way they have done in the past, (did we succeed), but they will have to turn even wiser, and should some eggshells be broken, they should not protest that the Slovaks are under attack, because this is necessary,"

exhorted Gottwald.[86]

The crisis in Slovakia culminated in the discovery of a conspircy, allegedly led by Ludak exiles in the West. Evidence in our hands is too meager to enable us to compile a clear picture of the conspiracy. Some of the alleged conspirators were members of the Democratic Party, or close to it. In a small country like Slovakia, with a limited amount of qualified manpower, it was impossible to neglect or reject competent persons despite their contaminated past. The Communists employed them, and so did the Democrats. The Democrats were unfortunate in that the police were more apt to search in their files. And perhaps somehow less sensitive to one's record. Discovery of renegade Democrats, some of them placed in the centers of power, threw the Party into a state of crisis.

The Communists waged a public campaign, designed to force the Democrats to renounce several implicated members, including deputies. They shrewdly utilized the presence in Slovakia of Ukrainian ("Bandera") nationalist guerilas to claim relations between the conspiracy and the bands. The authorities armed veterans of Second World War partisan units, and sent them against the Ukrainians. The Association of Slovak Partisans, a mushrooming organization with thousands of real and newly-minted partisans, was under Communist control. Undisciplined in war and in peace, the partisans harbored in their ranks numerous radical Communists of the Osoha brand. Equally, they hid hooligans with a L'udák past and organizers of post-war anti-Jewish pogroms. Now the Communists directed the Association, many of its members armed, against the lawful institutions, and used them as a pressure group to force a change in the existing political order in Slovakia. The weakened Democratic Party could no longer resist, and accepted the Communist dictate. Slovak central institutions were reorganized in such a way that the DP lost its plurality, some of the most important offices, and its former influence. Heavy internal crisis—and fear—paralyzed the Party's movements. The dismissals deprived it of some of its most talented and creative personalities.[87]

In this sequence of extraparliamentary and parliamentary steps, the Communist "Uprising Generation" took the lead, yet in close cooperation with Široký. As a couple of Slovak historians wrote later, the "aim of the campaign was to alter the entire political structure of Slovakia."[88] These objectives were achieved. Slovakia returned to leadership of a social revolution.[89] Slovak Communists, the Uprising Generation, seemingly improved its position. The Democratic Party, which in the words of American Ambassador Lawrence A. Steinhardt, "has been badly in need of a housecleaning for a long time," caused a weakening of the anti-Communist front in Czechoslovakia.[90] In Slovakia, in spite of the electoral defeat of May 1946, the Communists were in the driver's seat in November 1947. It is ironical that they succeeded thanks to continuous undermining of the nationalistic policies of the Democratic Party. The shrewd Communist tactics (and the ruthless use of force) deprived the Democrats of the trust and support of non-Communist Czechs and left them alone to defend themselves.

### "The February Victory of the Working People"

Once the Communists were victorious in Bratislava, the center of activity shifted again to Prague. The sand in the hourglass of Czechoslovak liberties was running out. Paradoxically, at this time signs pointed to considerable weakening of Communism in the Czech lands. Public support was weakening, among the working class as well. Gottwald's collaborators in the Social Democracy, who drove the Party toward cooperation with the Communists, were losing power. National Socialists and even the Populists resisted with increasing determination the Communist encroachment of the state's authorities. Again, we are wise in retrospect: the anti-Communists had very few chances, if any. In February 1948 they were devastated. Available documentation does not provide unimpeachable answers: Were the threads pulled entirely in Moscow, or did Prague Communists show ingenuity? What role did Gottwald and Slánsky play? Was the faulty strategy of the anti-Communists responsible for granting the chance to the enemies, or did Moscow set the machine in motion? The role of President Beneš is still a matter of controversy. Whatever happened, occurred in Prague. In Slovakia, the Communist steamroller encountered even less resistance than in Bohemia and Moravia. We know that in Slovakia, the Communist-managed security services had the coup prepared in detail, up to sealed envelopes, which had to be opened on the D-Day. Did Slovak weakness condition Czech infirmity? The Democrats tailed the Czech partners, and gave them little comfort.

After reorganization of the Board of Commissioners, in Fall 1947, the Democratic Party witnessed a wave of desertion of the ranks. The Communists encouraged splits in the Democratic Party, and initiated Catholic counter-parties. It is amazing how successfully the Communists, so outspokenly anti-religious, used the unsolved Catholic problem against the Protestant-led DP. Catholics, without a genuine political representation, were the convenient tool of the atheists. The

Protestant leaders of the Democratic Party made small allowances to the population's majority. They zealously guarded the positions gained during the resistance period. This situation was exploited for an adroit double game: the Communist press attacked the Democrats for alleged cooperation with the L'udáks. At the same time Communist personalities busied themselves drawing Catholic support, and setting up competing Catholic parties. Several Catholics, of somewhat clouded past, were afraid of the Communists and accepted their hints. Others, out of political blindness or even of religious hatred and perverted vengeance toward the Democratic "Uprising Generation," agreed to cooperation with the Marxists. Some of the Catholic functionaries of the DP were planted agents of the CPCS. Once more the Communists manipulated the very specific Slovak Catholic nationalism for their particular ends.[91]

Nonchalantly, Široký continued to brandish the "reactionary danger" in Slovakia against his party adversaries. He easily recruited the CPCS leadership in which Stalinist centralism was already prevailing. He also pointed, without difficulties, to the nationalism of the Slovak comrades. And there was no shortage of examples. In the years of the Prague trials, the Party spokesmen often recalled Husák words, written in February 1948 and directed against the Czech nationalists: "The Slovaks can bite each other for whatever reason, but their views and stands about national existence are united and firm."[92] Not without interest were Karol Šmidke's words addressed to Slovaks in Hungary: "Although I am a Communist, above all I am a Slovak, and as such I am working for our common interest in the Czechoslovak Republic."[93] Husák and Šmidke did not distinguish between Slovak rich and poor, Democrats and Communists, when the national existence was in danger. For Široký, such words were a proof of "bourgeois nationalism" of the "Uprising Generation." During February 1948 Husák served as Chairman of the Board of Commissioners. After the resignation of the non-Communist ministers in Prague on February 20, Husák simply dismissed the Democratic Commissioners.[94] The Communists easily smashed the Democratic Party, and created in its stead a new body staffed by fellow travelers. Some of the Catholics who cooperated with the Communists against the Protestant Democrats were among the leaders of the new-old party.[95] In Slovakia, the Communists won easily and quickly and members of the "Uprising Generation" were the prime movers behind the victory.

Despite the fast victory in Slovakia, Slánsky did not hesitate to repeat the old maxim: "The Slovaks should reach the recognition that today danger does not emanate from Prague, but from the separatist reactionary elements in Slovakia, which are scheming against the Czechs."[96] The mass media and Communists' speakers announced time and again that a new period in Slovak national life had begun.[97] The legislative conditions in Slovakia worsened, however. The new Constitution of May 9, 1948, put the Board of Commissioners under a direct supervision of the Prague government, and severed its close ties with the Slovak National Council. Consequently, this Council lost the ability to directly influence Slovak life.[98] The Council itself was subordinated to the government and its head.[99] Several years later a jurist interpreted the position of Slovakia in the Constitution. He explained that Slovak bourgeoisie was interested in federalization of the Republic. A federalization would lead to lessening of industrialization of Slovakia and would prevent the Czech working class from assisting the local proletariat. Strengthening of the Slovak bourgeoisie would lead to growth of the power of the Czech bourgeoisie. There was a necessity to secure maximum influence of the Czech working class and of CPCS in Slovakia if the dangers threatening the working class and the people democracy were to be averted.[100] The Constitution of May 9 introduced to Slovakia political conditions worse than those prevailing before Munich. In the intensity of its centralism, the new regime was superior to the First Republic. In contrary to the past, the citizen now lacked the formal protection of law. Many of the old rulers of Prague, above all Professor Thomas G. Masaryk, were committed to democracy and humanism and guarded the rights of the individual. This could not be said after the February coup. The new norms soon made themselves felt.


### Epilogue


For all practical purposes, our story thus reached its end. The Communists ruled Slovakia. In the struggle for power, they repeatedly used nationalism as a vehicle to advance their particular aims. Once in power, they paid lip-service to Slovak needs and clapped down a sort of centralism of unparallelled severity.

Yet there was a double epilogue: the CPCS swallowed up its Slovak sister, and during the session of the CC CPS of September 27–29, 1948, Široký for the first time publicly attacked the bourgeois nationalists. The men who dared to combine nationalism and Communism became the victims of Moscow's servants:[101] the mills of "socialist justice" started to grind the Communist members of the "Uprising Generation," the past members of the *Dav* group, and Slovak Communists who lived during the war in the West.

The Stalinist leadership of CPCS, in which Široký, Ďuriš, Bacílek, and other Slovaks played prominent roles, differentiated between "socialist patriots"—modestly ascribed to themselves—and the others. Foes presented the "bourgois nationalists" as anti-party and anti-governmental fraction, which endangered the state's well-being. The wave of persecutions in the 'fifties hit mercilessly. Vlado Clementis, the outstanding Davist who opposed the Ribbentrop-Molotov Treaty and spent the War in London, was hanged. The jailed ones included among others Novomeský and Husák, Ladislav (Laco) Holdoš—a veteran of the Spanish civil war and the French Maquis, and Dr. Anton Rašla, the ranking left-wing Social Democrat, who allied himself with the Communists. Only Šmidke was lucky to escape: he died in time, in 1952.

True enough, numerous victims of the persections were indeed convinced nationalists. Their past record and present suffering lent credence to their beliefs and respectability to the resurrected Slovak nationalism.[102] Behind the façade of demands of justice and protest against the crimes of the "cult of personality," Slovak nationalism gathered strength. It erupted time and again, significantly in the midst of the *literati*—the writers, the journalists, the students, and the members of humanistic professions. More often than not they were card-carrying party members, and belonged to Catholic families. The Czechoslovak post-Stalinism blundered frequently, and in particular the economic failures provided ammunition for criticism. The curtailed Slovak liberties, the chauvinistic outbreaks of President Antonín Novotný, the emasculated CPS, all embittered and plagued the new crop of home grown patriots. The Communist domination was challenged on many accounts.

Little wonder, then, that Slovak Communists lead the assault on Novotný's regime in 1967-1968. During the "Czechoslovak Spring," the Slovak body politic split three ways. Those interested in true democratization and liberalization of the Republic were weak and unsignificant. Not much better waged the orthodox Communists, the ones who believed in discipline and in the Soviet Union. The real victors, the force to carry behind the majority of the nation, were the nationalists, as personified by Husák and Novomeský. The only tangible remnants of the "Spring" is federalization of Czechoslovakia—a fruit of nationalistic efforts. With creation of Czech and of Slovak Socialist Republics, the asymetric structure passed away. Moscow willingly accepted the innovations, as long as they played in her hands. Today Slovak intellectuals share only modestly the human rights activities—initiated by Czech liberals, like Charta 77. Apparently nationalism still leads in Slovakia, and dwarfs other fields of public interests.

## Chapter 5

# SLOVAK COMMUNISTS AND THE MINORITIES

The Slovak question cannot serve as the only criterion for judgment of Communism in the Eastern half of Czechoslovakia. In the preceding chapters we mentioned frequently the Magyars, the Germans, the Ukrainians, and the Jews. Although minorities, they were not treated much differently from other nationalities in the CPCS. The Communists tapped the grievances of nationalities for political aims. Eventually, during the late thirties, nationalist parties drew the support of the Magyars and the Germans, and years of Communist efforts were lost. After 1938, the minority problem completely changed its nature, and therefore justified separate treatment.

In the years following Munich, the minorities raised particular problems, and forced the CPS to consider each of them. During the War, Germans and Magyars mostly offered allegiance to foreign states. The Germans, in considerable numbers, placed their faith in Hitler. Hungary, on the other hand, annexed southern parts of Slovakia, including the hundreds of thousands of Magyars living there. The vaunted internationalism of the Communists faced heavy tests during the entire period. The Slovak regime had seen in the Jews a separate group, and the Communists had to clarify their stand. Persecution of the Jews and rampant anti-Semitism required response. Finally, Soviet annexation of the Transcarpathian Ukraine intensified the ethnic conscience of the Ruthenes in Eastern Slovakia, transformed them into Ukrainians, and aggravated the Communists problems.

While the policy toward individual ethnic groups was very much a matter of local trial and error, the general policy was determined abroad—mainly in London and Moscow. The exiles made up their mind to have a Slavonic state after the War, a state of Czechs and Slovaks, (and Ukrainians). No minority rights were to be given to ethnic groups; and moreover, Germans and Magyars were to be expelled. One should add that the London exiles accepted the Zionist solution of the so-called "Jewish Question."[1] The Communists adopted a neo-Panslavic line,[2] which though disguised by euphemisms, in fact signified attachment to the Soviet and pro-Soviet group of states in Eastern Europe. Another meaning of the new policy was a life under the protection of the Soviet Union and a fear of resurrected German militarism. Therefore neo-Panslavism blended in well with heated Czech and Slovak nationalism, and the Czechoslovak desire to have a nation-state. Consequently, the plan for the expulsion of non-Slavs (who, moreover, were branded traitors in the First Republic) was easily accepted by the indigenous politicians, including the Communists. Expulsion was not in the CPS's books before January 1945,[3] but it quickly became pioneer advocate of the demand. The period of 1945–1948 was one of the most xenophobic in the annals of Slovakia.

## The Jews

The Jews were about the first subject on the Communist agenda. Two Jews, Alexander Markuš (Markus) and Vojtech Kohn, active in the Communist ranks, were sensitive to the position of their ethnic group. Both had seen in anti-Semitism a phenomenon typical of capitalist society.[4] Therefore, they argued, disappearance of that system would lead to solution of the "Jewish Question" as well. In other words, they supported the inflexible Stalinist concept. For doctrinaire reasons, Slovak Communists were unable to see the Jewish tragedy developing before their eyes. Moreover, they preferred to observe the minority of Jewish capitalists and not the majority of Jews, who were paupers. Adopting veiled anti-Semitic tenets and equating Jewry with capitalism, Communists in Slovakia regarded persecution of the Jews as a minor evil. After all, in "Aryanizing" and in liquidating Jewish undertakings and property, the authorities were only damaging and distributing the property of bourgeoisie.[5] In Spring 1940, during the Nazi attack on the Low Countries, a Communist leaflet went to the absurd lengths of charging Germany with preserving the Judeo-barons *(Židobaroni)*. The leaflet argued that Germany had gone the way of Hungary, Belgium, and the Netherlands.[6] It is easy to see that in order to gain sympathy, the Slovak Communists had recourse to anti-Semitism. Similarly to nationalism, this was another attempt to compete with the L'udák regime by employing its own weapons. During the deportations to extermination camps, the Communists abstained from assisting those left-wing Zionists who contemplated armed resistance.[7] The Party had no opinion as to what the Jews should do, and in a few cases young Communists went "where the masses are going." Assistance to deported Jews was on a personal basis, and not a matter of policy. The

conscience of Jews in the ranks—and there were many of them—
protested, however. An example was the underground journal *Zprávy
KTK* (News of the Communist Press Agency), edited by Markuš and
other Jews, which repeatedly attacked the deportations.[8]

Although a Communist historian claims that the CPS encouraged
the Jews to resist, there is little proof of this.[9] It is true, however, that the
first Communist guerila groups in Slovakia included numerous Jews in
their ranks.[10] The Slovak underground generally preferred to exclude
Jews, ostensibly because they were more vulnerable to governmental
agencies. Therefore, the individual assistance to Jews included help in
hiding, in forging identification papers, and similar aids. Despite their
cool reception, hundreds of Jews found their way into the Communist
and non-Communist underground, and fought in the Uprising and in
the partisan units.[11] The treatment they received was not innocent of
enmity and the Fifth CC of the CPS was also somewhat hostile.[12] As for
the exiled Communists, those living in Moscow denounced the persecution,[13] while in London, Clementis (then outside the Party) broadcasted
home words of anger and chastisement.[14]

The Uprising authorities cancelled all anti-Jewish laws.[15] The SNC
imposed forced supervision on the Jewish "Aryanized" property, but
did not consider turning it over to the surviving original owners. The
Uprising *Pravda* (an organ of CPS) raised the demand of nationalization of this property.[16] A Jewish official, serving with the Government in
Exile in London, sent to the Jewish Agency in Jerusalem statements
allegedly made by the SNC delegates visiting England. According to
these, the Uprising authorities had refused to return to Jews all civil
rights and property, thus following the wishes of the masses.[17] Even if
we take the report with a grain of salt, there was little doubt that both
partners in the anti-Fascist struggle coveted the Jewish property. Much
of the hatred and anti-humanism disseminated by the Nazis was
absorbed by their opponents. For the Communists, expropriation of
the property of ("rich") Jews meant the beginning of the social revolution. Such was the spirit of Gottwald's words, written to his London
comrades on Decmeber 21, 1943.[18] After the liberation *Pravda* (Košice)
expressed the view that Aryanized Jewish land should never be returned
to previous owners.[14] At the CPS Working Conference of February 28,
1945, Husák stated that property should be returned only to the poor
among the Jews. "We have no interest in returning the property to these
rich men, who never had any understanding of the case of the Slovak
people, who put their private interests above the interests of the
nation."[20] The meaning of these words was unmistakable. This
remained the policy of the CPS until the wholesale nationalization after

February 1948. There was then a certain aggravation of the situation—as the CPS accepted a somehow passive role in the policy of restitution of Jewish property. The Party was careful not to anger its voters, many of whom acquired Jewish goods and assets. After considerable procrastination, the PNA passed laws of restitution, and the Communists voted in favor of them. The laws were not generous, and red tape impeded their execution. Nevertheless, despite the proclaimed policy, the Communists eventually did not block the restitution.

The Communist coldness did not discourage numerous Jews from acting on behalf of and even joining the illegal Party.[21] When liberation of the country was near, Gottwald warned his Slovak comrades to screen the Jewish membership of the Party. Such a warning was superfluous for Husák.[22] Years later he charged Slánsky and Široký with having relied on Jews during the power struggle after 1945.[23] Nevertheless, after the War, the CPS admitted many Jews into its ranks. They possessed professional skills, and served the Party well. Sometimes conviction and an opportunism and carrierism impelled them. They were exposed to the hostility of the anti-Semitic public, and guarded by the good will of the leaders. To Jews, choosing between the Communists and the Democrats, the former seemed to be the lesser evil. The Democrats, fond of repeating the cliché of the need to preserve the "Christian tradition of the Slovak people," did not appeal to the oversensitive Jewish mind. The Democrats had a reputation for defending the L'udáks, and even promoting anti-Semitism.[24] Therefore, the Communists, with the halo of anti-Fascist activity, could more easily attract the Jews. Needless to say, neither the Communists nor the Democrats were composed of one stock. Jews had friends and enemies in both camps.

Although individual Jews encountered Communist good-will, the Jewish community faced hard struggles. The authorities abolished the Jewish nationality,which had been recognized in the First Republic. They also turned down a Jewish demand to be represented in the National Assembly and in SNC.[25] The Jews were expected, even requested, to assimilate into the population, and those desiring to emigrate could do so easily. The wish to make Czechoslovakia a nation-state explained the official attitude toward the Jewish collective entity. There was little difference between Communists and others in this respect. In fact, Communist authorities continued to be friendly to the Zionist organization even after February 1948.[26] The overall Communist policies toward Palestine had much to do with the CPCS line. Nevertheless, the wish to solve the "Jewish Question" once and for all was of considerable importance. The representative of the Jewish

Agency for Palestine in Prague was told in no uncertain terms: Jews will be permitted to emigrate, on condition that they do so fast.[27] Three major factors seemed to influence the Communist policies toward the Jews: the desire to eliminate minorities, anti-Semitism with an anti-capitalist corollary, and an anti-Fascist-internationalist policy which could be combined with the need for Jewish hands and brains.

### The Magyars

If the position of the Jews was partially a result of an anti-Magyar and anti-German policy, the Hungarians' fate was a direct product of the expulsion of the Teutons. There was little noticeably Communist interest in the Magyars during the War. Germany and its local collaborators of whatever nationality were the principal enemy. The Viennese arbitration of Fall 1938, which awarded Southern Slovakia to Hungary, seemed somehow less bothersome to the Communists. A few Communist publications addressed the Magyars, others mentioned Hungary and its ruling class.[28] Among available Communist material, publications addressed to Germans or to the Ukrainians seemed to be more numerous.

Nevertheless, Slovak nationalism considered Hungary and the Magyars as the traditional enemy. Magyar nationalism and not Germany had threatened Slovak national survival in the past and even during the Second World War. Hungary held territories considered to be Slovak. When nationalists gained the upper hand in CPS, the party was bound to direct attention to Hungary and the Magyars.

The creation of the Fifth CC was accompanied by increased Communist interest in Southern Slovakia. The Uprising authorities closed the Magyar-speaking schools.[29] *Pravda* indulged in anti-Magyar invectives.[30] The Office of the Commissioner for Internal Affairs, headed by Husák, banned Germans, Magyars and members of the Hlinka Guard and Hlinka Party from membership in National Committees.[31] The equation of Magyars, Germans, and incriminated Slovaks became a permanent definition. Actually, the position of the incriminated Slovaks improved, and the CPS opened its gates to "honest members of the Hlinka Party."[32] For Germans and Magyars the standards for initiation remained nationalist. It was not until Fall 1948 that the CPS was again willing to initiate Magyar members. A party, which in the past had prided itself of an internationalism and multi-national membership, now openly discriminated on ethnic grounds. The CPS was not only unwilling to introduce new members, but also froze the membership of those inside, and withdrew protection from its Magyar folowers.[33] Such veterans as the Deputy Istvan Major, once the darling of the CPCS, were now denied public roles.[34]

Magyar schools, outlawed during the Uprising, and opened for a short spell in Winter of 1944-1945, were closed again.[35] Although Novomeský, the first Commissioner of Education in liberated Slovakia, toyed with the thought of changing the rigid line, Magyar children received schooling in their mother tongue again only after 1948.[36]

This above-described policy was repeated, in a more stringent version, with regard to the exclusion of Magyars from National Committees. Magyar Communists, with long records of political activity and suffering, could at best become members of advisory committees to Slovak Commissars assigned to administer locations with predominantly Hungarian population. The authorities dispersed Committees created spontaneously by Magyar anti-Fascists.[37] Only if there were no choice did Magyars keep administrative and political positions. A dispute between the Slovak and Hungarian Communist Parties provided an interesting intermezzo in the complicated situation. Communists in Hungary tried to establish Committees and local branches on Southern Slovakian territory, and did not hesitate to distribute membership cards. Slovak Communists were disturbed, suspecting their Hungarian comrades of irridentistic aspirations towards territory regarded to belong to Czechoslovakia.[38]

Inclusion of a huge Magyar minority in Trianon Czechoslovakia greatly troubled not only the Communists,[39] but also authorities of the First Republic. When discussing the future borders of recreated Czechoslovakia during the War, President Beneš recognized the necessity for certain territorial adjustments in favor of Hungary.[40] Then and later Czech politicians did not dare to pronounce such thoughts in public and kept them for private discussion.[41]

Now, however, the Communists closed ranks with the more extremist Slovak nationalists. Husák established the tone on February 28, 1945, at a CPS Conference in Košice:[42]

"The Magyars should understand that no territory will be relinquished to Hungary, and we shall not even discuss the topic with anybody. The Slovak peasant and worker, who was shoved out from the rich counties and for centuries forced into mountainous corners, must again return to those ancient Slovak territories, and gain an opportunity for a suitable life."

Husak's words included a great deal of fiction. Communist speakers repeatedly returned to this made-to-order version of history.[43]

And if the territory was Slovak from the immemorial, and foreigners had seized it from the rightful owners, then the time was ripe to regain Southern Slovakia.[44] The foreigners should be sent back from whence they came. Slovak Communists, who until February 1945 had talked at most of punishing the transgressor Magyars, now accepted the line of the exiles.[45] The Czechs demanded expulsion of the Germans, and the Magyar case was measured by the same yardstick. They, too, were accused of stabbing Czechoslovakia in the back in the Fall of 1938. Indiscriminately, the authorities charged the whole Hungarian minority with a collective sin, and demanded collective punishment. Expulsion to Hungary would, therefore, render historical justice to the Slovaks and the Magyars. It would also secure peace in the Danube basin.[46] Communists and Democrats voiced the same arguments, and showed the same vigor in persecuting the hapless minority.[47] Years later, the shamefaced Communists tried to put the blame on the Democrats, on President Beneš and, in fact, on everybody but themselves.[48]

When the peace negotiations took place in Paris, the Czechoslovak delegation labored to persuade the reluctant Great Powers to agree to the expulsion. The delegation was convinced of Soviet, and specifically Stalin's, compliance.[49] Communist spokesmen did not miss a single opportunity to emphasize Soviet support.[50] The reality was considerably different. The Czechoslovak mass media strongly attacked the Western Powers for siding with Hungary, and the Soviet Union quietly supported Budapest. The Soviet support was cautious: it would not back Hungarian demands for Slovak territory, however justified they were. But Moscow remembered the Hungarian loss of Transylvania and Vojvodina, limited Hungarian resources, and above all its own long-term design and that of the Hungarian Communist Party. Hungarian Communists were struggling for power no less than Czechoslovak Communists. In comparison to the CPCS with its backing at home, they were an insignificant minority in their own country. Hungarian Communists could not afford to allow undermining of Magyar nationalism, not to say the vital interests of the Magyar state. The Russians understood this well.

Czechoslovak Communists knew the situation of the Communist Party of Hungary, but had their own script, and were ready to sacrifice the Magyar minority to the "social revolution."[51] In other words, the Magyars were also to serve as oil to the wheels of Sovietization of Czechoslovakia. If one adds the clash between Slovak and Magyar nationalism, as personified by the home Communists, like Husák and László Rajk, sources of Prague-Budapest divergences seem to be clear. By no mere chance, the leading pretenders of Budapest, the Moscovites

Matyas Rákosi and Mihály-Farkas, tried repeatedly to settle the
Czechoslovak-Magyar dispute; and on the opposite side, Husák and
Clementis promoted the (disturbing) Slovak interests.[52] Therefore, the
Magyar nationals regarded the Husák-Novomeský group as the chief
instigators of the anti-minority campaign.[53] Sovietization of both Hungary and Czechoslovakia put an end to official persecution of Magyars
in Slovakia.[54]

The Paris Peace Conference refused to force Hungary to accept
Magyars residing in Slovakia and advised both countries to arrange for
population exchange on a voluntary basis.[55] Only those of the Magyars
who settled on Czechoslovak territory after Viennese arbitration and
who belonged to Fascist and/or nationalist Magyar political movements[56] (altogether 68,407 souls) were expelled or resettled.[57] In
exchange, there arrived from Hungary 73,273 individuals, who proclaimed themselves Slovaks, and automatically received Czechoslovak
citizenship.[58] The expulsion had, incidentally, an anti-Jewish tinge.
Under the pretext that they were Magyars, Bratislava authorites tried to
eject to Hungary South Slovakian Jews who had just returned from
Nazi concentration camps.[59] The whole campaign was occasionally
conducted in a brutal way and it was evident that the brutalization of
human relations introduced by the Nazis was an accepted standard for
the victims as well.

Once it became clear that the Great Powers would not permit "reset-
tlement" of the Magyars, Slovak authorities tried another trick, called
"Reslovakization." Manipulating history again, the politicians
explained that inhabitants of Southern Slovakia were forced to accept
Magyar culture and nationality. Now the nation was willing to welcome
its lost sons and take them to its bosom.[60] The conditions for return
were proclamation of Slovak nationality and acquaintance with the
Slovak language and culture. The "Slovak League," a chauvinistic
organization, which during the War busied itself with forceful "Slovakization" of Ukrainians and Poles, was in charge of "Reslovakization."
The League had the blessing and active support of the Communists, and
of Husák personally.[61] Czechoslovak legislation cancelled the citizenship of Germans and Magyars.[62] Hence the Magyars struggled to rescue
their livelihood and property by means of "Reslovakization." Some
325,000 of them subscribed to Slovak nationality.[63] An American
report, entitled "Reslovakization—blind men's bluff," (sic!) described
the unhappy fate of those who opted for Slovakization: ostracism by
both Slovaks and Magyars, insufficient legal defense, lack of security of
the property, etc. Another aspect was the forced recruitment of the
powerless Magyars to political parties, and particularly to CPS.[64]

The Communists fostered expropriation of Magyar land and its distribution among Slovak settlers. They also compelled Magyars to move to territories in Bohemia vacated by the expelled Germans. In 1925 Istvan Major protested against national persecution of the Magyar minority and expropriation of land for Czech and Slovak colonization.[65] Twenty years later the CPS raised the slogan of colonization of "those ancient Slovak territories."[66] Indiscriminating in their methods, Communists in Czechoslovakia took a nationalist stand toward the Hungarian minority, and furthered their own ends at the expense of the Magyars.[67]

## The Germans

Slovak nationalists regarded Magyars as the historical enemy of their people. The insignificant German minority in Slovakia scarcely aroused similar passions. During the War, not all German-populated regions were equally afflicted by the Nazi plague.

The CPS had numerous German members and several cells in Bratislava and other regions and towns like Spiš (Zips), Handlová, and Kremnica.[68] Holdings of the SS *Sicherheitdienst* included many German-language Communist leaflets.[69] These leaflets repeatedly described Slovaks and Germans as two brotherly folks, Slovakia as a common fatherland, and Nazism as enemy of all.[70] The Bratislava branch of CPS published a German-language underground journal *Der Hammer* (The Hammer). The German Paul Tonhauzer held a ranking position in the underground Party, and a unit (Thaelmann company),[71] staffed with ethnic Germans, fought in the ranks of the Slovak partisans. One may presume a moderate, or perhaps friendly and internationalist attitude toward the ethnic Germans. CPS policies did not testify to strong hostility to ethnic Germans. Strong feelings became evident with the appearance of the partisans, particularly during the Uprising. Legislation against the ethnic Magyars was equally aimed at the ethnic Germans. More serious was the killing of German civilians.[72] One may regard it as a spill-over of the Russian hatred of the German invaders.

After the War, Slovak authorities organized the expulsion of the ethnic Germans. Here again we meet application of the principle of collective responsibility; furthermore, the expulsion was a by-product of the action carried out in the Czech lands. Communists were frequently in charge of the operations and brutalities were no rarity. The Germans were denied citizenship similarly to the Magyars,[73] but were able to recover it.[74] The expulsion from Slovakia was not as extensive as that from Bohemia and Moravia, and only about 50 percent of the Germans were scheduled to leave the country.[75] The authorities divided the vacated land among Slovak settlers. The Communist agricultural functionary Michal Falt'an defined the expropriation in these words: " . . . finally you are on this piece of land of your forefathers."[76] Evidently, the Party line toward the ethnic Germans had changed since the days of the War.

## The Poles

Although national conflicts with Poland were not of comparable intensity to clashes with Magyars or Ukrainians, there were nevertheless disputes in the regions of Orava and Spiš. Parts of these regions had been a bone of contention ever since the creation of the Czechoslovak and Polish states after World War I. After the conquest of Poland in 1939, the Germans awarded the villages claimed by Bratislava to their Slovak allies. The Poles reclaimed these few wretched locations after the War, and persecuted those inhabitants who demonstrated Slovak zeal. This Polish activity aroused anger in Slovakia, and the Communists Clementis, Edo Friš, and others added their voices to the protests. The Soviet Union eventually suppressed this Polish-Czechoslovak friction.[77] Slovak and Polish Communists continued to display their conflicting nationalistic passion, until the Pax Sovietica stifled both.

## The Ukrainians

In dealing with national minorities, the CPS faced the most difficult situation in Eastern Slovakia, namely: the Ukrainian problem. Here Slovak Communists were confronted with an equally aggresive and nationalistic minority. Ukrainian nationalists counted on Soviet support, which was indeed forthcoming. For three years, Czechoslovakia and the CPS steered a careful course, and the problem found a (provisional?) solution only after February 1948.

During the War, the Ukrainians in Slovakia were in a confused situation. The official authorities regarded them as a disturbing and unreliable element, which because of its Slavic ethnicity was endangering the national unity of the country. The German Nazis looked upon them as a potential ally. Internally, they were split into feuding groups which identified themselves as: Russins (Ruthenes), Ukrainians, Russians (and Slovaks). Some Ukrainians held the view that none of the East Slovakian Greek Catholics (Uniates) were Slovaks, others affirmed the Slovakhood of all non-Roman followers of the Pope. The Communists fished in the troubled waters; exploiting the proximity of Soviet borders after September 1939, they incited the "Russians" to join "Socialist Russia." Without mentioning the Ukraine at all, they promoted Soviet annexation of about one third of Slovakia (to the city of Poprad).[78] The Soviet Union had a considerable pulling power, as both the Nazis and the Communists were aware.[79] Communist and pro-Communist writers suggest early dates (end of 1943 and beginning of 1944) for the creation of the "National Liberation" organization of the Ukrainians.[80] Whether this is true or not, there is no dispute about the Soviet contribution to the formulation of Ukrainian independent institutions much later on.[81]

After arranging for the annexation of the Transcarpathian Ukraine, Communist and pro-Communist officials, to a certain degree under Soviet auspices, devised a similar trick in Eastern Slovakia. Here they met with the resistance not only of the non-Communist Slovak and Ukrainian population and of officials of the Government in Exile, but also of Slovak Communists.[82] On March 1st, 1945, in the city of Prešov an array of Ukrainian public figures founded the Ukrainian National Council of Prjaševščina (UNCP).[83] In its manifesto, the UNCP virtually ignored the SNC and Czechoslovak authorities. While not saying so unequivocally, the Council aimed at annexation of "Prjaševščina" to the Transcarpathian Ukraine, i.e., to the Soviet Union.[84] In a SOS cable to the CC CPCS in Moscow, the Slovak Communists urged comrades to guard their country's interests.[85] The Czechoslovak authorities were scared. They had already experienced Ukrainian nationalism and Soviet intrigues, and wondered if additional territories were in danger.

Amputation of a part of Czechoslovak territory proper, on the basis of an alleged or real ethnic argument, could serve as a precedent for other Slovak counties populated by aliens, for the Duchy of Tešin demanded by the Poles, and even for the "Sudeten" regions. In other words, Beneš was afraid of a confirmation of the Munich agreement and of further loss of territory.[86]

The Ukrainians in Prešov and the Communists in Košice convened at the same time. The Slovak Communists, after alerting their Moscow comrades, paid immediate attention to the problems raising in the East. First Husák, and then the conference as a whole reiterated the civil equality of all Slavonic people living in Slovakia: the Czechs, the Ukrainians, the Russians and others—with the Slovaks. National and cultural rights would be safeguarded. The Ukrainians in the Eastern

Slovakia, said the conference, who were then developing a sense of belonging to the Ukrainian nation, should have all their political and cultural rights assured.[87] Hence, the Communists were not willing to consider the Ukrainians as a nationality on equal footing with Czechs or Slovaks. The Ukrainians were a mere (Slavonic) minority, with the rights according to such. They had been promised minority rights because of being Slavonic. The Communists were not willing to consider division of their country, and to transfer soils to the Soviet Union.[88] They, together with Slovak non-Communists, clashed with Ukrainian Soviet-sympathisers, and opposed the covert moves of the UNCP. On later dates, various writers blamed the Democrats for inciting Ukrainian nationalism. Although one might expect the Democrats to seek collaboration with anti-Communist elements among the Ukrainians, it is hard to believe that the DP would have promoted separatism in Eastern Slovakia.[89] The UNCP was barked by certain Soviet ambitions and the escalated nationalism of the local population, which shortly before had witnessed the changes in Transcarpathian Ukraine.

There are signs that, eventually, intervention of Soviet authorities silenced the Ukrainian separatists.[90] The UNCP accepted the primacy of the SNC in Slovakia and that of the Prague government in the entire Republic.[91] The term "Prjaševščina" was quietly dropped.[92] Two issues deserve our attention in this period (approximately 1945). The Russins (Ruthenes) failed to clarify their ethnic affinity and regularly described themselves by a double name "Ukrainians (Russians)."[93] Second, although they recognized the prerogatives of central Slovak and Czechoslovak institutions, the Ukrainians demanded extensive minority rights (not unsimilar to those of the Nazified German minority in the Slovak State).[94] According to the policies agreed upon, the Ukrainians received extensive rights, especially in the field of education and culture. They gained representation in the SNC and the PNA, a representation based on ethnic rather than political affiliation. The Republic facilitated emigration of those Ukrainians, who preferred to live in the Soviet Union. The exact number of the emigrants is hard to determine.[95] The emigration had an adverse effect on the strength of the minority: people were afraid to opt for Ukrainian nationality because the of danger of being expelled to the Soviet Union. Some Slovak Communist officials indeed considered forced emigration, but dropped the plans.[96]

The zealous Ukrainian patriots continued to create problems not only for the Slovak authorities, but even more for the Russin population at large. The demands for virtual autonomy of the Ukrainian-population region, or the wish to Ukrainize the indigenous culture of the Slovak Russins, could only disturb the life of that minority.[97] It is, therefore, not without interest that the events of February 1948 forced the Ukrainians to bow to the discipline of the CPCS.[98]

The Ukrainian minority created a confusing problem. Jews, Germans, Magyars, (and gypsies) could easily be mistreated and denied minority rights. The Communists, who appeared or posed as defenders of Slovak national interests adopted and applied slogans of local nationalism. The Ukrainians constituted a real danger. Backed by elements in the Soviet Union and their own Slavonic ethnicity, they were in the position to advance objectives of Ukrainian nationalism— not necessarily identical with the wishes of the population—without fear of punishment by Slovak nationalism. The clash between two conflicting nationalisms, though partly concealed by Communist window-dressing, was nonetheless clearly apparent.

The minority issue created another front of the Slovak Communists. An observer concludes that it was first pragmatism and opportunism; second nationalistic arguments, and only third, internationalist considerations which guided the Communists in their actions.

## Chapter 6

# SUMMARY AND CONCLUSIONS

Communism in Slovakia dates its beginning from the commune of 1919. After its passing, the Communists turned to organizational activity. As happened frequently in the extreme left, it was not ideology but questions of organization which exposed some of the vital problems of the movement. Creation of one, unified and centralized Communist Party of Czechoslovakia intensified the national sensitivities of members of diverse origin. The "internationalist" structure also provided good opportunities for ambitious and gifted leaders of whatever nationality. Separated emotionally from the majority of the population and from the leading nation, leaders of non-Slovak descent steered the Party in barren and sterile directions. The Slovak nation, which had only recently achieved national self-awareness, was not yet prepared for the lofty ideas of internationalism, particularly since the independent Slovak identity was questioned by members of the numerically, socially, and economically stronger Czech people. Communists in Slovakia had no clear solutions and answers for the Slovaks, who were searching for emancipation. Instead, the Party toiled to advance the social liberation of all citizens, without distinction of nationality.

Such efforts, as noble as they may have been, left the Slovak masses unmoved. With growing national consciousness, Slovaks in increasing numbers pledged their allegiance to Hlinka's Slovak People's Party. That movement, parochial and obscurantist, and even somehow blind to social ills, could offer simpler and less sophisticated solutions. Both the CPCS and the HSPP were extremist, demagogic, and stubborn. Yet the HSPP's message was easily comprehensible, and its prophets spoke the language of the population. In the race between the two parties, the Communists were left behind.

In 1929, Gottwald replaced Šmeral as head of the Party. The new Central Committee adopted arrogant and obstinate tactics. Communist national policies became further removed from the emotional needs of the Slovak people. It was evident that for the CPCS the national question was no more than a vehicle for promoting its chances in the country. The Communists labored to attain power first and only from a position of primacy would they begin solving the diverse problems according to the doctrine.

The last years of the thirties forced the CPCS to alter its tactics, to move closer to the population and the state, and to respond to their voices. The Party sought to listen to the Slovaks as well, but to no avail. More than ever HSPP radicalism was capturing the mind of numerous Slovaks. The Hlinka Party exploited Hitler's pressures on Czechoslovakia to advance its own nationalistic designs. The CPCS, which now regarded the defense of the Republic as a necessity, possessed only limited space for maneuvering. The Communist failure to exploit the goodwill of at least a considerable fraction of the Slovak people became evident after Fall 1938: the Party was easily outlawed and beaten. Its only hope for the future seemed to be in aping the L'udáks and in promoting Slovak separatism.

During the first years of Slovak independence, the Communists advocated replacement of the Nazi protectorate over the state by Soviet patronage. They seemed to be uninterested in the fate of Czechoslovakia, and instead, concentrated their efforts on influencing the existing state. Acting among nationally-fulfilled people, the Slovak Communists accepted the *fait accompli* of March 1939. Social, and not national, problems were the focus of attention. Those tactics remained unchanged even after the Reich's invasion of the Soviet Union. Only when a new crop of Slovak Communists took the helm did the Party respond to up-to-date needs. During a short period, which lasted perhaps two years (from 1943 to 1945), the tactics and the feelings of CPS leaders were identical. Nationalism became the Party's official policy, and not merely a tool for measured use. Husák and his colleagues genuinely desired the Party's supremacy in Slovakia, but no less genuinely defended the national interests of their people. Small wonder that in these two years the Party gained the widest public support in the thirty years surveyed here (and possibly in its entire history).

Once the nationalists were removed and replaced by bureaucrats faithful to Prague, the Party forfeited its previous standing among the public. Now manipulations and force preserved the CPS in the positions secured in the past. Any further advancement was a result of intrigues and a power-game, initiated mostly in Prague's CC CPCS. The extent of the nationalists' success was proved by the May 1946 elections, in which for the first time in history of the country the Communists won a considerable share of the votes. Yet a decline in public support had been evident for some time. That development was a result of many factors—no less complicated than the earlier Communist upsurge. Changes in CPS leadership, however, undoubtedly contributed considerably to the decline.

The Democratic Party exploited the Communist retreat, and consolidated its public standing. Now Slovak Communists felt that their own strength—as reflected in popular support and activities of front organizations (such as the Association of Slovak Partisans, Association of Slovak Farmers, the Revolutionary Trade Unions, etc.)—was slackening. Afraid of the future, the CPS had to rely on the (overwhelming Czech) CPCS. Consequently, the CPS was trapped in a vicious circle: Slovak Communists paid for Czech assistance with national prerogatives, arduously acquired in the past. With each loss of prerogatives, the distance between the Party and the population grew, and the need for Czech tutelage became greater. Eventually, the victory of Communism in Slovakia was no longer a victory for Slovak nationalism. Although nationalism continued to play an active role in Communist moves, it again adopted the role of a vehicle for alien aims. Naturally, the genuine Communist nationalists became the victims of February 1948.

The very specific conditions of the closing months of the War and the immediate post-War period advanced the national Communists. They easily adapted themselves to the unprecedented conditions. Once the conditions improved, the atmosphere changed, and a return to normalcy became the slogan of the day, the need for exceptional, new elites diminished. Subsequently, Czech Communists and their Slovak allies took up the reins of power in the CPS (and in Slovakia). The situation was not unsimilar to that of the First Republic, when Czech Agrarians and National Socialists, and their Slovak allies managed Slovak affairs. During that period, the Communists followed the non-Communist model. Prague's CC and its henchmen in Slovakia led the Party between wars. (This work does not deal with the question of the reasons for Czech supremacy in the country, a supremacy marked by positive and negative aspects.) Slovak national Communists, the *Dav* group, shared only a fraction of power in the Party.

Another Communist trend disappeared after Spring 1945: the radicals who would have liked to see Slovakia a part of the Soviet Union. We encountered them in the early thirties, during the War, and immediately after the Soviet occupation of the country. In the new situation, with the arrival of the Moscow exiles and the return to normalcy, each shade of opinion had to adjust to the new reality. The "Soviet Slovakia" school was in a different position. The aspiration to see Moscow as the capital could not but clash with the wishes to cement Prague's supremacy. When the Moscovite (mostly Czech) Communists succeeded to the leadership, there was no longer room for admirers of "Soviet

Slovakia." Although this school of thought was closer to the national Communists than to the "internationalist" Moscovites the two forces did not cooperate. Eventually both were forced to vacate the field. Moscow had made its choice. It helped the "internationalists" (or perhaps "Czechoslovaks") to power, and ordered out the others. At least for the time being, Moscow had no need either of Husák and his friends, or of the heirs to Osoha.

Only once did all three trends make a joint public appearance, and even cooperate to a certain degree: in the Uprising. The radicals then caused considerable trouble both to Husák and Šmidke, and to Šverma and Slánsky. The three-cornered battle lasted until the Spring of 1945. Yet while the fighting against the Germans lasted, Communists of whatever persuasion participated actively in the Party work and helped to promote its aims.

Nevertheless, the Uprising was above all an achievement of the national Communists (and naturally, their non-Communist partners). The SNC people elevated the Slovaks from the ranks of defeated nations, and thus made the major contribution to Slovakia's future. (The efforts of the Government in Exile in London secured and preserved Slovakia's place among the victors, in spite of Bratislava's active and willing cooperation with the Nazis.)

At a conference in Prague, marking the fiftieth anniversary of the establishment of the Czechoslovak Republic, a Czech historian said:

> It seems that the Communist movement has always suffered the malady of being willing any time to claim the heritage of the passing generations and epochs, and to abandon it just as quickly."[1]

This statement epitomized the Communist strategy in Czechoslovakia. The foremost task was to attain power. If nationalism could advance this end, it was used. However, Czechoslovak Communists did not recognize the real national grievances and emotions, and paid little attention to their needs. If socialism were bound eventually to provide a magic panacea to all ills, why bother now with provisional solutions. The lust for power and not the love of their nation guided the Communists in Slovakia in their long uphill battle.

# NOTES

## Chapter 1

1. Paul Reimann, *Dejiny komunistickéj strany Československa,* Prague 1931, p. 89, Hereafter, Reimann.

2. According to the first Czechoslovak census of 1921, of 3,000,870 inhabitants of Slovakia, 650,547 were Magyars, 145,844 were Germans, 88,970 were Ruthenians, and 73,628 were Jews. Method Bella, "The Minorities in Slovakia," in R.W. Seton-Watson, ed., *Slovakia Then and Now,* London, 1931, p. 337. The ethnic identity of the Slavonic population of Subcarpathian Ukraine and parts of Eastern Slovakia was often disputed, and it was termed in a variety of names.

3. See text of the law in Samo Falt'an, *Slovenská otázka v Československu,* Bratislava 1968, Appendix No. 8, p. 285, (Hereafter Falt'an, *Slovenská otázka*)

4. The dispute around this topic covers countless pages. For some older views, see Jozef L'udovit Holúby "Slováci a Česi" and Karel Kálal "Čechové a Slováci" in Ján Kabelík, ed., *Slovenská čítanka,* Prague 1925, pp. 331–342; Josef Jirásek, "Československá otázka na Slovensku," *Delnická osvěta,* XII, 1 (January 1926), pp. 31–34 and XIII, 2 (February 1927), pp. 264–266; L'udovit Novák, *Jazykovedné glosy k československéj otázke,* Turčianský Sv. Martin 1935. For a doctrinaire Marxist study, see Vladimír Kulíšek, "Úloha čechoslovakismu ve vztazích Čechů a Slovaků, (1918–1938)," *Historický Časopis (HČ),* XII, 1 (1964), pp. 50–74. (Hereafter, Kulíšek.) For a contemporary analysis, see Falt'an. This sample by no means represents the whole gamut of opinions.

5. Tibor Sule, *Socialdemokratie in Ungarn,* Cologne—Graz 1967, pp. 171, 192; Cf. *Istoriia vengerskogo revoliutsionogo rabochego dvizheniia,* Moscow 1970, p. 64; *Prehl'ad dejín KSČ na Slovensku,* Bratislava 1971, p. 60, (hereafter, *Prehl'ad*); Miloš Gosiorovský, *Dejiny slovenského robotníckeho hnutia (1848-1918),* Bratislava 1956, pp. 185, 196, (hereafter, Gosiorovský).

6. *Prehl'ad,* pp. 63, 64; Gosiorovský, pp. 177–80.

7. See the text of the resolution in Gosiorovský, pp. 347–48. For a perceptive evaluation, see Ján Mlynárik, "První kríze slovenského Slovanství," *L* (Prague), 2 (13), Nov. 14, 1968.

8. "Vzpomínky dr. Ivána Dérera," *L* (Prague), 2 (13), Nov. 14, 1968.

9. The major work on the Slovak Soviet Republic is Martin Vietor, *Slovenská sovietská republika r. 1919,* Bratislava 1955. See also Peter A. Toma,

126                                        THE LUST FOR POWER

"The Slovak Soviet Republic of 1919," *The American Slavic and East European Review (ASEER),* XVII, 17, 2 (April 1958), pp. 203–15; Eva S. Balogh, "Nationality Problems of the Hungarian Soviet Republic," in Ivan Volgyes, ed., *Hungary in Revolution, 1918–1919,* Lincoln, Nebraska 1971, pp. 112–20, (hereafter, Balogh); Martin Vietor, "K tridsiatemu piatemu výročiu Slovenskéj republiky rád," *HČ,* II, 2 (1954), pp. 161–90, (hereafter, Vietor).

10. *Rudé Právo (RP),* (Prague), May 31, 1935; Rudolf L. Tokes, *Bela Kun and the Hungarian Soviet Republic,* New York 1967, p. 191; Balogh, *op. cit.;* Vietor, p. 189. Cf. L'ubomír Lipták, *Slovensko v 20. storočí,* pp. 85–91, (hereafter, Lipták).

11. Balogh, *op.cit.;* Vietor, pp. 161, 170, 172; *Dejiny KSČ, Študijná príručka,* Prague 1967, p. 142, (hereafter *Dejiny KSČ*).

12. For Communist historians, see Falt'an, *Slovenská otázka,* pp. 43, 53, and Lipták, pp. 88, 89. For right-wing nationalists, see František Vnuk, *Kapitoly z dejín Komunistickéj Strany Slovenska,* Middletown, Pa. 1968, pp. 11–15, (hereafter Vnuk, and Ctibor Pokorný, "Der Kommunismus und die Slowaken," *Der Slowakei als mitteleuropaisches Problem in Geschichte und Gegenwart,* Munich 1965, pp. 181–83. See also Reimann, pp. 97–100.

13. Wolfgang Jankovec, "Nové Slovensko," *Delnická osvěta,* 9–10 (1938), p. 323.

14. L'udovít Holotík, "Ohlas velkéj oktobrovéj socialistickéj revolucie na Slovensku od konca roku 1917 do vzniku ČSR," *HČ,* V, 4 (1957), p. 438, and "Oktobrová revolucia a revolučné hnutie na Slovensku koncom roku 1918," *HČ,* XV, 4 (1967), pp. 425–50

15. Ján Mlynarík, "Robotnícke hnutie na Slovensku roku 1920, (Od parlamentných volieb do decembrového generalného štrajku.)," *HČ,* VIII, 1 (1960), pp. 42, 46, (hereafter, Mlynárik, "Robotnícke hnutie"); Reimann, p. 103.

16. *RP,* Aug. 19, 1920; parliament session No. 6 of Dec. 12, 1925, and No. 5 of Nov. 30, 1927. *(Stenographische Protokolle des Abgeordnetenhauses. Prag.)*

17. Zdenka Holotíková, "Niektoré problémy slovenskéj politiky v rokoch 1921–1925," *HČ,* XIV, 3 (1966), p. 446, (hereafter, Holotiková "Niektoré problémy"); "The Slovak Question and Czechoslovak Communist Party in the pre-Munich Czechoslovakia," *Studia Historica Slovaca,* IV (1966), p. 149, (hereafter, Holotiková, "The Slovak Question"); Ján Mlynárik, "O hlavnom nebezpečí," *Reporter,* IV, 8 (Feb. 27, 1969), p. 12, (hereafter, Mlynárik "O hlavnom"); Viliam Plevza "K niektorým otázkam vývinu komunistického hnutia za predmnichovskéj ČSR," *HČ,* XIII, 4 (1965), (hereafter, Plevza, "K niektorým"). Cf. the nationalist Vnuk (pp. 43–50), who accused the Communist Party of being Magyar-ridden. In order to prove it was "un-Slovak" he mentioned also the Jewish and Czech leaders.

18. *RP,* June 14, 1921.

19. *Thesen und Resolutionen des V. Weltkongresses der kommunistischen Internationale, Moskau, von 17. Juni bis 8. Juli 1924,* Hamburg 1924, p. 133, (hereafter, *V. Weltkongress*).

20. During the Convention of the CPCS on May 16, 1921, the leading Slovak leftist Julius Verčík proclaimed: "The opinion of several Magyar com-

rades that Slovakia is the Ukraine of Hungary, is false. The Slovak proletariat will never accept serfdom and the yoke from the hands of other people. (Stormy applause.)" *Rudé Právo Večerník (RPV),* (Prague), May 18, 1921.

21. Czech worker units participated in the defense of Slovakia against the Magyar Communists. *Dejiny KSČ,* p. 49.

22. Ferdinand Peroutka, *Budovaní státu,* Prague 1934, Vol. I, p. 304.

23. Václav Král, ed., *Cesta k Leninismu. Praměny k dejinám KSČ v letech 1921-1929,* Prague 1971, p. 17, (Hereafter, Král); Miroslav Klír, "Úloha B. Šmerala pri vypracovaní strategicko-taktické orientace KSČ," *Prispěvky k dejinám KSČ (PDKSČ),* V, 1 (1965), p. 17, (hereafter, Klír, "Úloha Šmerala").

24. Klír, "Úloha Šmerala," pp. 32, 33.

25. Ladislav Lipscher, *K vývoju politickéj správy na* 1918-1938, Bratislava 1966 (hereafter, Lipscher).

26. Konštantín Čuleň, *Boj Slovákov o slobodu,* Bratis

27. For the full text, see Falt'an, *Slovenská otázka,* app

28. Peroutka, Vol. II, part 2, pp. 1218-40, gives a fine p Slovakia in 1919.

29. Viliam Plevza, *KSČ a revolučné hnutie na Slovensk* lava 1965, p. 19; Juraj Purgát, *Od Trianonu po Košice,* Br *RPV,* Aug. 1, 1920, May 10, 1921.

30. Mlynárik, "Robotnické hnutie," p. 30, and "Vývoj na strednom Slovensku v rokoch 1918-1920," *HČ,* IV, 3 (1 ter, Mlynárik, "Vývoj").

31. Deputies from Slovakia attacked cultural and pol against Slovaks. See parliament session No. 150 of June 2 of June 26, 1922.

32. For Šmeral's views on the national question in Slo p. 72; *RP,* Aug. 1, 1920, July 14, 1921; Miroslav Klír, "Di *PDKSČ,* V, 6 (1965), pp. 930-39, (hereafter, Kiír, "Šm Šmerala," pp. 28-33; Ján Mlynárik, "Dr. Bohumír Smera nostná otázka v počiatkoch komunistického hnutia," *Čes historický (ČČH),* XV (1967), pp. 653-66, (hereafter, Mlyn last essay particularly is important for understanding Šmer early years of the Republic. Mlynárik argues forcefully tha views was detrimental to the further development of the Party. See also Jan Mlynárik, "Kdo má tedy pravdu," *LL,* 25, Aug. 15, 1968, (hereafter, Mlynárik, "Kdo má"); Vladimír Dubský, "Utvarení politické linie KSČ v období Šmeralová vedení," *PDKSČ,* VII, (1967), pp. 645-68, 803-38.

33. For an English description of the founding of CPCS, see H. Gordon Skilling, "The Formation of Communist Party in Czechoslovakia," *ASEER,* XIV (1955), pp. 346-58. See also Josef Korbel, *The Communist Subversion of Czechoslovakia 1938-1948,* Princeton 1959, pp. 17-26, (hereafter, Korbel, *The Communist).*

34. There participated 149 delegates, including 88 Slovaks, 36 Magyars, 15 Germans, 6 Ruthenians, and 4 Jews (although there were many more delegates of Jewish origin, only four members of the Poale Zion Party identified them-

selves as Jews by nationality). Josef Husár, ed. *Zjazd v Lubochni 1921, Doku-menty*, Bratislava 1969, p. 57 (hereafter, Husár). See also Ľudovít Holotík, "Sjazd socialnodemokratickéj strany (ľavice) na Slovensku v januári 1921," *HC*, XI, 3 (1963), (hereafter, Holotik, "Sjazd"), pp. 337-65; Heinrich Kuhn, *Der Kommunismus in der Tschechoslowakei*, Cologne 1965, pp. 24-25, (hereafter, Kuhn).

35. Husár, p. 60.

36. Husár, pp. 34, 40, 57, 60, 61, 122.

37. Husár, p. 38. Cf. *RPV*, Dec. 2, 1920.

38. Husár, p. 125. We have few details on this debate. The police dispersed the meeting, and the participants did not finish the agenda.

39. Husár, pp. 158, 160.

40. *Prehľad dejín*, p. 116.

41. Reimann, p. 93; *RPV*, May 18, 1921. In an editorial of May 10, 1921, the paper admitted the existence of the Czechoslovak language.

42. Mlynárik, "Šmeral," pp. 658, 659. For previously unknown details on founding of the CPCS, see Karel Gorovský, "O založení KSČ—dražďanská konference v dubnu 1921," *Revue dejín socialismu*, 3 (1968). See also H. Gordon Skilling, "The Comintern and the Czechoslovak Communism," *ASSER*, V (1960), pp. 234-47.

43. *Die Tätigkeit der Exekutive des Prasidiums des EK der kommunisti-schen Internationale vom 13. Juli 1921 bis 7. Februar 1922*, Petrograd 1922, p. 40, (hereafter, *Die Tätigkeit*); Král Document No. 6, p. 68, and No. 8, p. 71.

44. Plevza, "K niektorým," p. 496; Kuhn, p. 21; Holotíková, "Niektoré problémy," p. 448; Mlynárik, "Šmeral," p. 665.

45. Juraj Krámer and Ján Mlynárik, "Revolučné hnutie a národnostná otázka na Slovensku v dvadsiatých rokoch," *HČ*, XIII, 3 (1965), p. 430, (hereaf-ter, Kramer & Mlynárik). An outstanding leader of Slovak Communists, Jozef Schiffel, emigrated in disappointment to the United States.

46. Lipták, p. 104.

47. *Pravda Chudoby (PCH)*, Oct. 4, 1923.

48. Lipták, p. 104.

49. Král, Document No. 22, p. 101; *Rudé Právo*, May 9, 1922, Nov. 23, 1922; *PCH*, Jan. 2 and 9, 1923.

50. Die Tätigkeit, p. 43; *RP*, Oct. 8, 1921; Miloš Hájek, *Jednotná fronta. K politické orientací Komunistické internacionaly v letech 1921-1935*, Prague 1969, p. 51, (hereafter, Hájek).

51. Parliament session No. 150 of June 21, 1922; *PCH*, Jan. 2, 1923.

52. *RP*, May 30, 1922, Nov. 23, 1922; parliament session No. 151 of June 22, 1922; *PCH*, Jan. 2, 1923. Of particular interest is the article "Cesta Hlinková" (Hlinka's Way) in *PCH* of Jan. 16, 1923. The anonymous writer explained that one cannot oppose a demand of national autonomy, as every people has the right for self-government. But Slovakia is not self-sufficient enough to stay on her own feet. Economic crises strike not only Slovakia, but the entire world, and only doing away with capitalism will solve the country's problems.

53. *RP*, July 18, 1924, and Feb. 12, 1929.

54. Cf. *Bericht über den IV. Kongress der kommunistischen Internationale. Petrograd-Moskau vom 5. November bis 5. December 1922*, Hamburg 1923, p. 60.

55. Klír, "Úloha Šmerala," p. 33; Plevza, "K niektorým," p. 506.

56. *PCH*, Máy 29 and 31, July 31, Dec. 8, 13 and 18, 1923; Zdenka Holotíková, "Bolševizačný proces KSČ v rokoch 1924–1929," *HČ*, V, 2 (1957), p. 208, (hereafter, Holotíková, "Bolševizačný"); Plevza, "K niektorým," p. 497; Miloš Gosiorovský, "Slovensko a V. sjazd KSČ," *CCH*, I, 1 (1954), p. 9, (hereafter, Gosiorovský, "Slovensko"); *Protokoll der Konferenz der Erweiterten Exekutive der kommunistischen Internationale, Moskau 12.-23. Juni 1923*, Hamburg 1923, p. 199.

57. Parliament sessions Nos. 150 and 151 of June 22, 1922, and No. 156 of June 26, 1922.

58. *PCH*, Jan. 16 and 23, Feb. 2, Mar. 10 and 22, Sept. 18, and Oct. 9, 1923.

59. *RP*, Jan. 14, 1926; Mlynárik, "Šmeral," p. 662; Gosiorovský, "Slovensko," pp. 8–11.

60. Holotíková, "Niektoré problémy," p. 433.

61. *PCH*, Mar. 10, Apr. 14 and 29, May 12, Aug. 12, Sept. 4, 1923.

62. The Lubochňa meeting disbanded the Jewish faction, Husár, pp. 67, 68, 125. Cf. *Protokol VII sjezdu Komunistické strany Československa 11.-14. dubna 1936*, Prague 1967, pp. 137, 138; Holotik, "Sjazd," p. 355.

63. Parliament session No. 172 of Nov. 23, 1922.

64. Hájek, p. 98.

65. Král, p. 31, Document No. 25, p. 108. Cf. *V. Weltkongress*, pp. 124–31.

66. *V. Weltkongress*, p. 131.

67. Reimann, p. 151; Plevza, "K niektorým," p. 506.

68. *RP*, Sept. 23, 1924.

69. Karel Kreibich, "Národnostná otázka v Československu," *Komunisticheskii internatsional*, 3–4 (May–June 1924), pp. 96–103, quoted by Plevza, "K niektorým," p. 498; *RP*, July 5 and Aug. 18, 1924; Parliament session No. 295 of Aug. 30, 1924.

70. *Pondelní noviny*, Prague, Sept. 13 and 22, 1924.

71. Král, Document No. 32, p. 124; *RP*, Sept. 3 and 4, 1924.

72. *PCH*, July 30, 1924.

73. *RP*, Aug. 22, 1924.

74. Miloš Gosiorovský, "K niektorým otázkam vzťahu Čechov a Slovákov v politike Komunistickéj strany Československa," *ČČH*, XVI, 3 (1968), p. 362, (hereafter, Gosiorovský, "K niektorým"); Vojtech Mencl, "K historií II. sjezdu KSČ," *ČČH*, III (1955), (hereafter Mencl, "K historií"), p. 586; Purgat, pp. 76, 77; Plevza, "K niektorým," pp. 506, 507.

75. *RP*, Nov. 7, 1924.

76. The "national bolsheviks" later came to be called "bourgeois nationalists." Cf. Kulíšek, p. 69.

77. The address by Manuilsky is in *RP*, Nov. 5, 1924.

78. *RP*, Sept. 4, 1924.

79. It should be noted that Verčík himself deserted the line and requested the

breakup of Czechoslovakia and independence for Slovakia. Mencl, "K historii," p. 586.

80. Mlynárik, "Šmeral," p. 665. The Party's inconsistency in dealing with Slovakia was criticized not only by the men of the "Czechoslovak Spring" but also by the orthodox such as Miloš Gosiorovský and Bohuslav Graca, and by the opportunist such as Viliam Plevza and Zdenka and Ľudovít Holotíks. The historiography of the history of nationalism in Slovakia and the Communists is an amusing story, worthy of an essay by itself.

81. Holotíková, "The Slovak Question," p. 154.

82. For an interpretation of the Party's weakness among the Slovaks, see Holotíková, "The Slovak Question," pp. 148–51.

83. For *Dav* and its contributors, see Viliam Plevza, *Davisti v revolučnom hnutí,* Bratislava 1965; *DAV. Spomienky a štúdie,* Bratislava 1965; Štefan Drug, *DAV a davisti,* Bratislava 1965.

84. Plevza, "K niektorým," p. 508; Král, Document No. 49, p. 197; Holotíková, "Bolševizačný proces," p. 213.

85. Plevza, "K niektorým," p. 508; Král, Document No. 63, p. 249. Even Zinoviev branded the Slovaks as ultra-left. See *RP,* June 18, 1925.

86. *Protokol erweiterte Exekutive der kommunistischen Internationale,* Moskau, 2. Marz–6. April 1925, Hamburg 1925, p. 73; *RP,* Apr. 15, 1925. See also Stalin's participation in the Czechoslovak committee of CI, Král, Document No. 53, p. 202.

87. *RP,* Jan. 24, Sept. 19, and Oct. 29, 1925; parliament session No. 368 of Oct. 1, 1925 and No. 3 of Dec. 18, 1925.

88. *RPV,* July 13, 1925; *RP,* Oct. 29, 1925.

89. *Protokol III. řadného sjezdu Komunistické strany Československa,* Prague 1967, p. 262.

90. *Szakszervezeti Munkas* (Prague), III, 11 (November 1925). For the crisis and the rightist coalition, see Vera Olivová, *The Doomed Democracy,* London 1972, pp. 157–60, (hereafter, Olivová).

91. *RP,* Jan. 10, 1926, carried the text of the communique. See also the editorial and the commentaries.

92. *RP,* Jan. 13, 1926.

93. *RPV,* Jan. 12, 1926; *RP,* Jan. 14 and 20, 1926.

94. RP, Jan. 20, 1926.

95. Parliament session No. 10 of Feb. 19, 1926.

96. Parliament session No. 36 of June 19, 1926.

97. *PCH* of July 29, 1929, carried the text of the proclamation.

98. Krámer & Mlynárik, pp. 431, 437–39; Plevza, "K niektorým," p. 510; Mlynárik, "Kdo má"; Mlynárik, "Šmeral," p. 661; Holotíková, "The Slovak Question," pp. 155, 156; Gosiorovský, "Slovensko," pp. 8, 9.

99. Reimann, p. 172; Mlynárik, "Kdo má"; Krámer & Mlynárik, p. 439. See the harsh attack on Verčík in Gosiorovský, "Slovensko," pp. 8, 9.

100. See examples in *RP,* Jan. 18, 1927; parliament session No. 93 of July 1, 1927. Cf. Viliam Plevza, *Československá štátnosť a slovenská otázka v politike KSČ,* Bratislava 1971, pp. 111, 112 (hereafter, Plevza, *Československá štátnosť').*

101. Lipscher, pp. 157–59. Parliament session No. 93 of July 1, 1927.

102. Parliament sessions Nos. 61 of Jan. 15, 1927 and No. 90 of July 20, 1927; *RP*, July 20, 1927.

103. *RP*, March 24, 26 and 27, 1927. Cf. Gosiorovský, "K niektorým," p. 364, and *Za bolševickou orientaci KSČ, Sborník dokumentů k I. svazku spisů Klementa Gottwalda*, Prague 1953, p. 68.

104. *RP*, Mar. 8, 11, and 12, and June 18, 1927.

105. Václav Kopecký, *ČSR a KSČ*, Prague 1960, p. 227, (hereafter Kopecký). Karlin is a quarter of the city of Prague.

106. Ján Mlynárik, "O hlavnom nebezpěčí," *Reporter*, IV, 8 (Feb. 2, 1969), pp. 12, 13; Mlynárik, "Kdo má," Zdenek Hradilák, "Místo v dejinách. Čtyricet let od V. sjezdu KSČ," *Reporter*, IV, 7 (Feb. 20, 1969), pp. 14–16, (hereafter, Hradilák, "Místo"). During the "Czechoslovak Spring" historians argued that the Fifth Congress rerouted the CPCS away from the wise guidance of Šmeral and opened the door to the "cult of personality." For an attack on the "revisionist" historians, and a defense of the Gottwald group, see Michal Štefanák's introduction to *Protokol V. řádného sjezdu Komunistické strany Československa, 18–23. února 1929*, Prague 1971, esp. p. 7, (hereafter, *V. Sjezd*). Cf. Plevza, *Československá štátnost*; pp. 116–22.

107. Viliam Plevza, "Príspevok o činnosti davistov v revolučnom hnutí za predmnichovskéj ČSR," *HČ*, XII, 1 (1964), pp. 7–9, (hereafter, Plevza, "Príspevok"); Holotíková, "Bolševizačny proces," pp. 217, 218; Gosiorovský, "Slovensko," pp. 12–14; Bohuslav Graca, "O vzniku a boji KSČ za predmnichovskéj ČSR," *HČ*, IX, 2 (1961), p. 197.

108. *Sechster Weltkongress der kommunistischen Internationale, Moskau, 17. Juli–1. September, 1928*, Hamburg–Berlin 1928, p. 341; Král, Document No. 80, pp. 302–9.

109. Vladimír Dubský, "Historický význam V. sjezdu KSČ," *ČČH*, VII (1959), p. 22.

110. *V. Sjezd*, pp. 50, 51; Klement Gottwald, *Výbor z díla*, Prague 1971, pp. 59, 60, 70, 71.

111. *V. Sjezd*, pp. 76–79, 90–92, 121–23, 147–49, 197–99, etc. Cf. *RP*, Feb. 12, 1929; Miroslav Klír, "Karel Kreibich," *PDKČS*, VII, 1 (1967), p. 85.

112. *V. Sjezd*, pp. 449–53.

113. Mlynárik, "Šmeral," p. 656; Krámer & Mlynárik, p. 432.

# Chapter 2

1. "K národnostný otazce," *RP*, Feb. 12 and 13, 1929; Klement Gottwald, *Výbor z díla*, Prague 1971, Vol. I, pp. 128, 174, etc., (hereafter, Gottwald, *Výbor*).

2. *RP*, Nov. 3, 1929; *Pravda* (Ostrava), July 13, 1930; Viliam Plezva, *KSČ a revolučné hnutie na Slovensku, 1929–1938*, Bratislava 1965, p. 121. (hereafter, Plevza, *KSČ*).

3. *RP*, Oct. 6, 1929; *Protokol VI. řádného sjezdu KSČ konaného v Praze ve dnech 7. az 11. brezna 1931, Prague 1931 (?), p. 58, (hereafter VI, Sjezd)*;

Zdenka Holotíková, "Bolševizačny proces KSČ v rokoch 1924-29," *HČ*, V, 2 (1957), p. 215, (hereafter Holotíková, "Bolševizačný proces,"); Ján Mlynárik, "Vyvrcholenie hnutia nezamestaných na Slovensku v rokoch 1929-1933," *HČ*, XIV, 1 (1966), p. 40, (hereafter Mlynárik, "Vyvrcholenie"); Oto Krajňák, *Komunisti bratislavskéj oblasti v boji proti fašizmu v rokoch 1938-1942*, Bratislava 1959, p. 14, (hereafter Krajňák, *Komunisti*); Viliam Plevza, "Vytvorenie celoslovenského kraja KSČ a revolučné hnutie na Slovensku na začiatku tridsiatých rokov," *HC*, X, 2 (1962), pp. 166, 167, 170, (hereafter Plevza, "Vytvorenie").

4. Kermit E. McKenzie, *Comintern and World Revolution*, London and New York, 1964, pp. 130-35. Cf. "Narustajíci světová hospodarská kríse, masová nezamenstnanost' a stávkové boje. These prijatá na zasedaní rozšireného predsednictva Výkonního výboru Komunistické internacionaly, konanem ve dnech 8.-28. února 1930," in *Za chléb, práci, púdu a svobodu, Sborník dokumentů k II., III., IV. a V. svazků spisů Klementa Gottwalda*, Prague 1954, pp. 7-23, (hereafter *Za chléb*).

5. Ján Mlynárik, "O hlavním nebezpečí," *Reporter*, IV, 8. Feb. 2, 1969, p. 12; Holotíková, "The Slovak Question," p. 149.

6. Plevza, "Vytvorenie," p. 175; Holotíková, "Bolševizačný proces," p. 217. On Feb. 22, 1936, the Communist regional leadership in Slovakia called for the first time for Slovakization of the movement, and criticized the inadequate preparation of Slovak "cadres." Viliam Plevza, ed., *Prehľad dejín KSČ na Slovensku*, Bratislava 1971, p. 226, (hereafter Plevza, *Prehľad dejín*).

7. Vladimir Clementis, *Vzduch naších čias*, Bratislava 1967, vol. II, pp. 136-42, (hereafter, Clementis, *Vzduch*); Plevza, "Príspevok," p. 15; Plevza, *KSČ*, pp. 138-40, 232, 308-14; Holotíková, "The Slovak Question," p. 157. For a later condemnation of the *Dav* group, see Kopecký, p. 190.

8. Holotíková, "Niektoré problemy," p. 453; Faltán, *Slovenská otázka*, p. 86; Juraj Zvara, *Maďarská menšina na Slovensku po roku 1945*, Bratislava 1969, pp. 31-32, (hereafter Zvara, *Maďarská menšina*); Holotíková, "The Slovak Question," pp. 148-51; Plevza, "Vytvorenie," p. 187.

9. Hradilák, "Místo," p. 15; Holotíková, "Bolševizačný proces," p. 215; Plevza, *Prehľad dejín*, p. 172, "Vytvorenie," p. 170, *KSC*, p. 57; *Materialy z vedecké konference věnované 50. výročí Československé Republiky*, Prague 1968, Vol. 1, p. 129, (hereafter *Materialy*).

10. Plevza, "Vytvorenie," pp. 165-97; Ján Mlynárik, "K niektorým otázkam revolučného hnutia Československu v rokoch 1918-1938," *ČČH*, XII, 2 (1964), pp. 209, 216; Krámer & Mlynárik, p. 430; Mlynárik, "Vyvrcholenie," p. 40; Gosiorovský, "Slovensko," pp. 14, 15; Plevza, *KSČ*, pp. 68-75.

11. For example *RP*, Sep. 5, 1929; Parliament Session No. 88, Nov.8, 1930; Gottwald, *Výbor*, pp. 306, 307, 309.

12. *RP*, Sep. 5, 1929, Speech of Dimitry Z. Manuilskij; *Materialy*, Vol. II, p. 207.

13. For differing views on Slovakia between the years 1918-1938, see Eugen Steiner, *The Slovak Dilemma*, Cambridge 1973, pp. 27-33; Lipták, *Slovensko*, pp. 95-174. Further Jörg K. Hoensch, *Die Slowakei und Hitlers Ostpolitik*,

Cologne-Graz 1965, pp. 1–115; Jozef Lettrich, *History of Modern Slovakia*, London 1956, pp. 43–109, (hereafter Lettrich). Still further Joseph A. Mikus, *Slovakia, A Political History 1918–1950*, Milwaukee, Wisc., 1963, pp. 1–65,(hereafter, Mikus); František Vnuk, "Slovakia in pre-Munich Czecho-Slovakia," in Joseph M. Kirschbaum, ed., *Slovakia in the 19th & 20th Centuries*, Toronto 1973, pp. 97–119.

14. On the life of the Magyar minority and on the Magyar Communists there, see Juraj Purgat, *Od Trianonu po Košice*, Bratislava 1970, pp. 11–126, (hereafter Purgat, *Od Trianonu*); Dezider Czizmadia, "K problematike vzťahov československých a maďarských pokrokových síl medzi dvoma svetovými vojnami (1918–1938)," *HČ*, XVIII, 1 (1970), pp. 406–426.

15. B. Much, "Slovensko v ohni útoku," *RP*, Apr. 23, 1930; Vladimír Dubský, "Historický význam V. sjezdu KSČ," *ČČH*, VI, 1 (1959), p. 22; Plevza, *KSČ*, p. 225.

16. František Janáček, "O čechoslovakismu a československství (1918–1968)," *Reporter*, IV, 7 (Feb. 20, 1969), p. VI, (hereafter Janáček, "O čechoslovakismu"); Plevza, *KSČ*, p. 72; *Materialy*, Vol. I, p. 131.

17. Miloš Gosiorovský, "Leninismus a riešenie slovenskéj otázky," *Nová Mysl*, XXIV, 5 (1970), p. 726. Gottwald ended his maiden speech in the Parliament on Dec. 21, 1929, with a toast to the Czechoslovak Socialist Soviet Federative Republic. This toast is missing from the text of the speech in Gottwald's collected works, published in 1971 (Gottwald, *Výbor*, p. 134).

18. *Rudý Večerník* (Prague), Aug. 28, and Sep. 18, 1929; *RP*, Oct. 10, 1929, Feb. 4, 1931; Laco Novomeský, *Publicistika 1924–1932*, Four vols., Bratislava 1967–72, vol. I, p. 229, (hereafter Novomeský, *Publicistika*); Clementis, *Vzduch*, vol. I, p. 381, vol. II, p. 46.

19. Parliament session No. 10 of June 21, 1922; *Pravda Chudoby* (Žilina), Jan. 2, 1923.

20. Jàn Ušiak, "Boj KSČ s Hlinkovou Slovenskou Ľudovou Stranou o vlyv na masy v období nástupu fasizmu," *PDKSČ*, III, 5 (1963), p. 711, (hereafter Ušiak, "Boj KSČ"); Parliament session No. 75 of Dec. 17, 1936.

21. *VI. Sjezd*, p. 291; Cf. Klement Gottwald, *Vojenská politika KSČ*, Prague 1972, p. 62; Parliament session No. 266 of Apr. 27, 1933.

22. *VI. Sjezd*, p. 135.

23. *VI. Sjezd*, p. 300. The historian Gosiorovsky claims that the term "autonomy" was substituted for "federation," which would have been erased by the censor. Gosiorovský, "K niektorým," p. 365.

24. *VI. Sjezd*, pp. 300–02, 309–310.

25. *Ibid.*, p. 144.

26. František Hrbata, Ladislav Niklíček, "Na ceste k VII kongresu Kominterny," *ČČH*, XIII, 5 (1965), pp. 665–74, (hereafter, Hrbata & Niklíček, "Na ceste"). For other interpretations see Franz Borkenau, *Der europaische Kommunismus, Seine Geschichte von 1917 bis zur Gegenwart*, Munich, 1952, pp. 61–71; Hájek, pp. 194–254.

27. Plevza, "K niektorým," pp. 503, 504; "Vytvorenie," pp. 175, 176, "Príspevok," p. 20, *KSČ*, p. 362. Viliam Plevza, director of the Historical Institute of

the Communist Party of Slovakia, is the leading Slovak expert on the period discussed here. Unfortunately, many of his works use the same material—and even wording—under different headings.

28. *RP,* Aug. 14, 1931; Ján Mlynárik, "K otázkam všeľudového protikapitalistického hnutia na Slovensku v rokoch 1931–1933," *ČČH,* X, 3 (1962), pp. 365, 366; Krajňák, *Komunisti,* pp. 20, 21, 27.

27. *RP,* Apr. 23, 1930; Plevza, *KSČ,* p. 264.

30. Mlynárik, "Kdo má," Lipták, *Slovensko,* p. 145; Hrbata & Niklíček, "Na ceste," p. 671.

31. Ferdiš Juriga, *Blahozvest' kriesenia slovenského národa a slovenskéj krajiny,* Trnava 1937 (?), pp. 238–44; Ivan Derer, *Slovenský vývoj a ľudacká zrada,* Prague 1946, pp. 134–40; Konštantín Čuleň, *Boj Slovákov o slobodu,* Bratislava 1944, pp. 175–78.

32. *RP,* July 8 and 9, 1932; Clementis, *Vzduch,* Vol. I, pp. 74–76.

33. Tido J. Gašpar, "Triedenie duchov," *Slovenské Pohľady, XLVIII, 7–8 (July–Aug. 1932), pp. 496–502,* "Z pamätí," *LXXXIV, 6 (June 1968), pp. 91–99; Prager Rundschau,* II, 6 (June 1932), p. 345; František Dithger, "Duchcov a Trenčianské Teplice," *RP,* July 9, 1932; Kopecký, p. 190. "Bourgeois nationalism" is an expression both ambigious and enigmatic. It is used occasionally *inside* the Communist movement against fellow members. Although an exact definition is not available, the expression denotes the egoistic and exclusivistic nationalism, which allegedly characterizes the bourgeois. "Proletarian nationalism," in contrast, is regarded as altruistic and internationalist in spirit.

34. Pavel Reimann, "Jak vestí boj za narodní osvobození?," *RP,* July 15, 1932; *Materialy,* vol. II, p. 209. Cf. Novomeský, *Publicistika 1924–1932,* vol. I, pp. 315–328.

35. Clementis, *Vzduch,* vol. I, pp. 328–339, 393–399.

36. *RP,* May 31, June 3 and 7, 1936; Clementis, *Vzduch,* vol. II, pp. 193–195.

37. The Slovak Party boss opposed Clementis' candidacy for Parliament in the elections of 1935. During 1951–1954, Clementis, Nŏvomeský and other Davists were among the chief victims of the Slovak purges.

38. "Ne Masaryk, ale Lenin! Všem pracujicím lidu Československa!" *Za chleb,* pp. 401–403.

39. "Proti pracovnímu souručenství s buržoazii—za bojové socialistické souručenství. Usnesení X. pléna Ustredního výboru KSČ z listopadu 1934, prijaté k referatu Jána Švermy." *Na obranu republiky proti fašizmu a válce, Sborník dokumentů k dejinám KSČ v letech 1934–1938 a k VI., VII. a VIII. svazků spisů Klementa Gottwalda,* Prague 1955, pp. 15–36, (hereafter *Na obranu); Materialy,* vol. I, pp. 135, 136.

40. František Hrbata, Ladislav Niklíček, "Nádeje a skutečnost'. Bezprostrední vliv VII. kongresu Kominterny v mezinarodním delnickém hnutí," *ČČH,* XV, pp. 674–681, 687–688; Gottwald, *Výbor,* pp. 361–387.

41. Lipták, *Slovensko,* p. 146; *Materialy,* vol. I, p. 136; Olivová, pp. 192–193, 196.

42. *RP*, Feb. 5, Mar. 21, and 22, and Apr. 14, 1935; Clementis, *Vzduch*, vol. I, p. 26, vol. II, pp. 60–68; Parliament session No. 4 of June 24,1935; "Jak bránit republiku proti Hitlerovi. Diskusní prispěvek Jána Švermy na VII. kongresu Komunistické internacionaly dne 15. srpna 1935," *Na obranu*, pp. 136–148.

43. *Materialy*, vol. I, p. 134, vol. II, pp. 212, 213, 216; Gosiorovský, "K niektorým otázkam," p. 366; Plevza, *KSČ*, pp. 452–54, 465; Plevza, *Československá státnost*, p. 140; Filo, *Boj KSČ*, p. 59.

44. Ušiak, "Boj KSČ," p. 725; Gosiorovský, "K niektorým otázkam," pp. 366, 367; *Pravda* (Moscow), July 29, 1935. Cf. "Za levicový režim—za lidový rozpočet. Reč Jaromíra Dolanského v rozpočtověm výboru poslanecké snemovny dne 5. listopadu 1936," *Na obranu*, p. 210.

45. *RP*, Jan. 23, 1936; Zvara, *Maďarská menšina*, p. 65; Purgat, *Od Trianonu*, pp. 107, 108; Plevza, *KSČ*, pp. 361, 403.

46. Kulíšek, p. 71.

47. *Protokol VII. sjezdu Komunistické strany Československa 11.-14 dubna 1936*, Prague 1967, pp. 480–482, 511, 518, 519.

48. Plezva, *Prehl'ad dejín*, p. 226; Holotíková, "The Slovak Question," pp. 157, 158; Filo, *Boj KSČ, p. 59. Cf. Materialy*, vol. I, p. 137, vol. II, p. 213; Klír, "Kreibich," p. 85.

49 *Materialy*, vol. II, p. 215. Cf. the same, p. 217.

50. See "Staré a nové Slovensko," Novomeský, *Publicistika*, vol. III, pp. 284–297.

51. Plevza, *KSČ*, pp. 385, 404; Clementis, *Vzduch*, vol. II, p. 248. For the later significance of the thesis "Equal with Equal," see Falt'an, *Slovenská otazka;* Jaroslav Barto, *Riešenie vzt'ahu Čechov a Slovakov*, Bratislava 1968; Plevza, *Československá štátnost'*, pp. 205–353.

52. The text appears in "Plán hospodarského, socialného a kulturného povznesenia Slovenska. Uznesenie celoslovenskéj konferencie KSČ v Bánskej Bystrici dna 17. maja 1937 po referate V. Širokého," *Na obranu*, pp. 275–297.

53. For a commentary, see Julius Šefranek, "Významná etapa narodnostnéj politiky KSČ. (K 25. vyročiu Plánu hospodarského, socialného a kulturného povznesenia Slovenska.)", *PDKČS*, II, 3 (1962), pp. 373–390.

54. *RP*, Jan. 19 and 31, 1936; Clementis, *Vzduch*, vol. II, pp. 374–376, 427–430; Novomeský, *Publicistika*, vol. II, pp. 303–313.

55. *Ibid.*, Cf. note No. 27.

56. "Pre potrebné zbliženie slovenského a českého národa na obranu republiky. Reč Viliama Širokého na zasadnutí Ústredného výboru KSČ dňa 24. oktobra 1936," *Na obranu*, pp. 199–203; *RP*, Oct. 28 and Dec. 5, 1936.

57. "Černová," *RP*, Nov. 27, 1937; Vlado Clementis, "Sidor chce totež co Hitler," *RP*, Dec. 12, 1937; Novomeský, *Publicistika*, vol. II, pp. 297–299; Viliam Široký, "Proti iredentistickemu bloku Sidor-Henlein-Eszterhazy," *Slovenské Zvesti*, March 6, 1938, in *Chteli jsme bojovat. Dokumenty o boji KSČ a lidu na obranu Československa 1938*, Prague 1963, vol. I, pp. 139–144, (hereafter, *Chteli jsme*).

58. "Do čela obrany republiky a Slovenska. Usnesení zemského vedení KSČ na Slovensku o situaci a politických úkolech strany na Slovensku, prijaté na zasedani ve dnech 30. a 31. července 1938 v Košicích," *Chteli jsme,* vol. II, p. 57.

59. Review by A. Hučková of "O vzajomných vzťahoch Čechov a Slovákov," Bratislava 1965, in *HČ,* V, 2 (1957), p. 255.

60. "Zachraňte Slovensko pred bidou a Sidorem," *RP,* June 4, 1938; "Básnik S.K. Neumann o Slovensku," *RP,* June 18, 1938; *Svoboda* (Prague), Aug. 2, 1938.

61. "L'udaci organisují protižidovské vytržnosti," *RP,* Apr. 28, 1936; "Golem a bratislavské vytržnosti," and "Delnické masy zakrikly pogromisty," *RP,* Apr. 29, 1936; Bohumír Šmeral, "Jen vláda lidové fronty bude obranou proti Hitlerovi," *RP,* May 15, 1936; Vaclav Kopecký, "Odpoved na Sidorové anti-semitické štvani," *RP,* March 13, 1937.

62. Supra, p. 31; "Leták KSČ 'Pravda o Pittsburské dohode' vydaný v predvolební kampani proti hlinkovskému prekrucovaní Pittsburské dohody," *Chteli jsme,* vol. I, pp. 329–330; "Komunistický leták ke katolikům," *Chteli jsme,* vol. I, pp. 331–333; "Slovenskú otázku treba riešit' z gruntu," *Slovenské Zvesti,* Aug. 10, 1938; "Z poslednéj cesty za Hlinkom na cestu s národom a republikou," *Slovenské Zvesti,* Aug. 21, 1938; Bohumír Šmeral, "K svědomí Slovenska," *Svoboda,* Aug. 24, 1938. *(Bohumír Šmeral, 1880–1941,* Brno 1973, p. 128.

63. Ján Křen, "Slovenská otázka v prvních letech války," *Slovenské narodné povstanie roku 1944,* Bratislava 1965, p. 109, (hereafter *SNP 1944*).

64. "Referat Klementa Gottwalda o československé otázce na zasedaní presidia exekutivy Komunistické internacionaly v Moskvě dne 26. prosince 1938, *Chteli jsme,* vol. II, p. 398, (hereafter "Referat"). Cf. Zvara, *Maďarská menšina,* p. 25.

65. Clementis, *Vzduch,* vol. II, pp. 427–430.

66. *RP,* Oct. 6 and 8, 1938; *Svoboda,* Oct. 6, 1938; "Komunisti pro jednotu Slovaků. Zemské vedení KS na Slovensku," *Svoboda,* Oct. 0, 1938. Cf. Plevza, *Československá štátnost',* pp. 152, 153; Anna Štvrtecká, *Ján Osoha,* Bratislava 1970, p. 62, (hereafter Štvrtecká, *Osoha*). For a different view, see Janáček, "O čechoslovakismu," p. IV.

67. Ferdinand Beer, et al, *Dejinná križovatka. SNP—predpoklady a výsledky,* Bratislava 1964, pp. 27, 28, (hereafter, Beer, *Dejinná*).

68. "Referát," p. 398.

## Chapter 3

1. Leaflets preserved in the *Nachlass* of Seyss-Inquart (Bundesarchiv Koblenz, File No. 43) show that during the Slovak elections-plebiscite campaign of December 18, 1938, the Communists employed the slogan of "independent Slovakia." Mrs. Anna Josko maintains that this was the CPS's slogan until January 1941, which I cannot confirm. ("The Slovak Resistance Movement," in

Victor S. Mamatey and Radomir Luža, eds., *A History of the Czechoslovak Republic, 1918-1948,* Princeton, N.J. 1973, pp. 366, 367, (hereafter Mamatey & Luža).

2. In the proclamation the Communists said: "We demand unity of the Slovak nation, from which nobody should be excluded . . . " *RP,* Oct. 9, 1938.

3. František Janáček, *Dva smery v začiatkoch národného odboja, (Oktober 1938-jun 1940),* Bratislava 1962, p. 116, (hereafter Janáček, *Dva smery*); Štvrtecká, *Osoha,* p. 62.

4. Janáček, *Dva smery,* p. 110.

5. Beer, *Dejinná,* p. 34; Ján Osoha (1901-1945), a Moravian by birth and Slovak by nationality, emigrated in 1925 to the Soviet Union. From there he returned in 1935 a trained emissary, and was active in the Communist movement until his imprisonment in 1942. Osoha perished on his way to the Mauthausen concentration camp in 1945. Neither particularly gifted nor broadly educated, yet doctrinaire and fanatic, he strongly influenced his followers.

6. See p. 35. Cf. *RP,* Oct. 9, 1938; Plevza, *Československá štátnost',* pp. 152, 153.

7. Oldřich Janeček, ed., *Z počátku odboje, 1938-1941;* Prague 1969, p. 32, (hereafter *Z počátku*); František Janáček, ed., *Národní fronta a komunisté,* Prague-Belegrad-Warszawa 1968, pp. 29, 37, (hereafter *Narodní fronta*); Cf. Kopecký, pp. 296, 297.

8. L'udovít Holotík and Miroslav Kropilák, *Slovenské Narodné Povstanie roku 1944,* Bratislava 1945, pp. 611, 617, (hereafter *SNP 1944*); *Chteli jsme,* vol. II, p. 398.

9. Štvrtecká, *Osoha,* pp. 68, 69; *Z počátku,* pp. 45, 56.

10. Jiři Doležal & Ján Křen, *Czechoslovakia's Fight,* Prague 1964, Document No. 4, pp. 21-24, (hereafter Doležal & Křen).

11. Ladislav Holdoš, "Niektoré problémy československého zahraničného odboja vo Francuzsku v rokoch 1939-1940," *HČ,* XVII, 3 (1969), pp. 396, 397, (hereafter Holdoš); Korbel, *The Communist,* p. 41.

12. T-175, R 565, 9440775.

13. Oldřich Janeček, ed., "Depeše mezi Prahou a Moskvou," *PDKSČ,* VII, 3 (1967), pp. 392, 393 (Sept. 14, 1939), and 396 (Oct. 16, 1939), (hereafter "Depeše").

14. Štvrtecká, *Osoha,* p. 86; Beer, *Dejinná,* pp. 36, 37.

15. Štvrtecká, *Osoha,* pp. 87-89.

16. Professor Korbel quotes a brochure distributed in July 1939 in the Czech lands, which included a call for the "establishment of a Czech Soviet Republic." Korbel, *The Communist,* p. 73.

17. In Fall 1939 the SS *Sicherheitdienst* seized curious leaflets celebrating the removal of the "Czech yoke" and calling for a Slovak Soviet Socialist Republic. One of the leaflets bears the signature "the Commissariat of the Slovak Red Army." Others were published in the region of Spiš, populated by the ethnic Germans, in the cities Spišské Nové Mesto and Kežmarok. T-175, R 564, 9440428, 9440572 and 9440573, R 565, 9440770, 9440771.

18. Beer, *Dejinná,* pp. 36, 37; Oldřich Janeček, ed., *Odboj a revoluce*

*1938-1945. Nástin dejín československého odboje,* Prague 1965, p. 103, (hereafter *Odboj a revoluce*).

19. See "Czechoslovak" leaflets in Anna Kociská, *Robotnická trieda v boji proti fašizmu na Slovensku, 1938-1941,* Bratislava 1964, pp. 280, 281.

20. "Depeše," p. 408.

21. "Depeše," p. 413.

22. "Depeše," pp. 411-414.

23. Štvrtecká, *Osoha,* p. 128.

24. See p. 71.

25. Krajňák, *Komunisti,* p. 172; Štvrtecká, *Osoha,* p. 111; T-175, R 564, 9440350-351.

26. "Depeše," No. B 78, Oct. 7, 1940.

27. Yeshayahu Jelinek, *The Parish Republic: Hlinka's Slovak People's Party, 1939-1945,* Boulder, Col. 1976, p. 43 (hereafter Jelinek).

28. See p. 70-75.

29. Štvrtecká, *Osoha,* p. 104; Samo Falt'an, "Niektoré otázky okolo hodnotenia SNP," *HČ,* XII, 2 (1964) p. 166, (hereafter Falt'an, "Niektoré otázky").

30. See p. 36-37.

31. Miloš Gosiorovský, "Leninizmus a riešenie slovenskéj otázky," *Nová Mysl,* XXIV, 5 (1970), p. 728; Samo Falt'an, *O Slovenskom Národnom Povstaní,* Bratislava 1964, p. 5 (hereafter Falt'an, *O SNP*).

32. The extent of the alienation of the Slovak Communists is shown in the memoirs of a volunteer to the Spanish Civil War. They regarded the Republic solely as a state practicing social oppression. Holdoš, p. 402; Cf. Beer, *Dejinná,* p. 57.

33. Falt'an, "Niektoré otázky," p. 170.

34. Gosiorovský, "K niektorým," p. 369; Samo Falt'an, "Ku Královej recenzii trocha inak," *HČ,* XIV, 4 (1966), p. 589.

35. See p. 90.

36. Štvrtecká, *Osoha,* pp. 109, 134.

37. The semi-official history of the CPS, *Prehl'ad dejín KSČ, tézy,* Bratislava 1958, pp. 246, 247, (hereafter *Prehl'ad*) claims that Bacílek's task was to oppose the slogan of Soviet Slovakia, but eventually accepted it as well. He left for the Soviet Union in March 1941, together with another functionary Karol Černocký (pp. 246, 247).

38. Jozef Jablonický, *Z ilegality do povstania,* Bratislava 1969, pp. 65, 66, (hereafter Jablonický, *Z ilegality*); Gustav Husák, *Svedectvo o Slovenskom národnom povstaní,* Bratislava 1964, p. 38, (hereafter Husák, *Svedectvo*); Martin Kvetko and Miroslav Ján Ličko, *Zborník úvah a osobných spomienok o Slovenskom národnom povstaní,* Toronto 1976, p. 114, (hereafter Kvetko & Ličko); *SNP 1944,* p. 124. Kvetko ("Na prelome dvoch ėpoch. V ilegalite a v povstaní," in Kvetko & Ličko, p. 114) gives the impression that the meeting took place in 1939, but all other sources differ.

39. *Za armádu lidu. Sborník dokumentů k bojovím tradícim našého lidu a vojenské politice KSČ,* Prague 1960, Document No. 88, pp. 180-182; Cf. the

Political Archives of the German Foreign Office, (hereafter PA), *Inland II. geheim*, vol. 83-60, Cable No. 448, Ludin to the Foreign Office, Bratislava, April 29, 1941.

40. Beer, *Dejinná*, p. 80.

41. Štvrtecká, *Osoha*, pp. 142-144.

42. Cf. Korbel, *The Communist*, p. 45.

43. *SNR 1944*, pp. 130, 131.

44. See p. 7, 8.

45. J. Křen, "Odbojové hnutí a KSS," in Janeček, *Odboj*, p. 159.

46. J. Křen, "Sovětsko-nemecká válka," in Janeček, *Odboj*, pp. 134-136.

47. Moreover, the Moscow-based radio "For Slovak Freedom" rarely mentioned a future Czech-Slovak state, and until July 1944 inclined toward nationalistic emotions. See Edo Friš, *Povstaní zdaleka a zblízka*, Prague 1965, p. 83, (hereafter Friš, *Povstaní*).

48. T-175, R 564, 9440557-558, *Hl'as L'udu*, II (Sept. 1941), pp. 3, 4.

49. British Public Records Office, F0371-29783, Dispatch, the British Embassy in Moscow to Anthony Eden, Sept. 8, 1941. Cf. T-175, R 564, 9440555-556, *Hl'as L'udu*, II (Sept. 1941), pp. 1, 2.

50. T-175, R 564, 9440649-654, *Problémy vojny a naše úkoly*.

51. Beer, *Dejinná*, p. 103; A. Benčík, O. Janeček, and J. Křen, "Pokus o sjednocení slovenského odboje," in Janeček, *Odboj*, p. 201.

52. The father of Alexander Dubček of 1968 fame.

53. Viliam Siroký, *Za st'astne Slovensko v socialistickom Československu*, Bratislava 1953, pp. 62-71. The document was tampered with, and cannot be regarded as reliable.

54. Falt'an, *O SNP*, p. 36; Štvrtecká, *Osoha*, pp. 210-211.

55. For example of descriptions of the first contacts, see Kvetko & Ličko, p. 114; Husák, *Svedectvo*, p. 39; Jablonický, *Z ilegality*, pp. 65-75; Falt'an, *O SNP*, pp. 144-147; etc.

56. Private information.

57. Sources of my evaluation are too many to be listed in detail. Since this work is designed to contribute to understanding of the national policies of Communism in Slovakia, I have not been able to analyze other topics extensively. Even in this brief summary of Communist activities, various divergencies, caused by changing times, regional varieties and socio-political differences remain undiscussed. Hence, my conclusions should be regarded as generalized.

58. On sources and the scope of my summary, see the footnote No. 57.

59. *Prehl'ad*, pp. 257-259; Beer, *Dejinná*, pp. 105-107.

60. Friš, *Povstaní*, pp. 66-69.

61. See the letter of Václav Kopecký to Ján Šverma, of Aug. 5., 1942, in Beer, *Dejinná*, pp. 120, 121.

62. Jablonický, *Z ilegality*, p. 30.

63. Kvetko & Ličko, p. 63. This writer recalls the reminiscences of his late teacher Professor Václav L. Beneš, on escape through Slovakia.

64. Cf. Friš, *Povstaní*, pp. 82, 83. London-based Communist Vlado Clemen-

tis acted very differently. In his broadcasts to the fatherland, he diligently advocated Czechoslovakia. This did not diminish his popularity in Slovakia. (*Odkazy z Londýna,* Bratislava 1947, hereafter Clementis, *Odkazy*).

65. Vladimír Huml, *Slovensko pred rozhodnutím,* Prague 1972, p. 205, (hereafter Huml, *Slovensko*).

66. Miloš Tichý, *Z bojov komunistov banskobystrickéj oblasti,* Bratislava 1966, vol. II, p. 104, (hereafter Tichý, *Z bojov*).

67. *Slovenské Národní Povstaní Dnešku,* Prague 1974, Document No. 1, pp. 15–21, (hereafter *SNP Dnešku*); Vilém Prečan, comp., *Slovenské Národné Povstanie, Dokumenty,* Bratislava 1965, No. 1, pp. 37–43, (hereafter Prečan, *Dokumenty I*).

68. Šmidke (Schmidtke), a Czech-German from Czech Silesia and a carpenter by profession, settled in Slovakia in the twenties. Prague CC CPCS sent him, with other Czechs including Gottwald and Bacílek, to propagate Communism there and to provide leadership.

69. Novomesky was Husak's senior in age and in experience. He was a noted Slovak poet.

70. The Slovak regime did not treat its adversaries with extreme severity. Until the Uprising of 1944 not a single execution took place, although beating to death of adversaries and Jews went unpunished.

71. Štvrtecká, *Osoha, pp. 266, 267.*

72. Štvrtecká, *Osoha, p. 268.*

73. Falt'an, "Niektoré otázky," p. 169.

74. Štvrtecká, *Osoha, p. 271.*

75. Prečan, *Dokumenty I,* Doc. No. 11, p. 75, No. 12, pp. 76–78; Libuše Otáhalová and Milada Červínková, comp., *Acta Occupationis Bohemiae & Moraviae. Dokumenty z historie československé politiky 1939–1943,* Prague 1966, vol. I, Doc. No. 310, p. 378, vol. II, Doc. No. 529, pp. 734, 735, (hereafter *Dokumenty z historie*); Hoover Institution, the Polish Government Collection, Box 343, Cable No. 193, Pappe to the Foreign Office, Vatican, June 8, 1943, (hereafter Polish Government).

76. US National Archives, Department of State papers, 860F.00/1009, Memorandum of Conversation, A.A. Berle Jr. with President Benes, London, May 31, 1943; *Dokumenty z historie,* vol. II, Doc. No. 507, p. 708, Doc. No. 508, p. 709.

77. Klement Gottwald, *Spisy,* Prague 1955, vol. XI, pp. 21–24, 54–57, 111–115, etc., (hereafter Gottwald, *Spisy*).

78. Polish Government, Box 675, Memo, Ministry of Information and Documentation, London, March 12, 1943; Box 343, Dispatch No. R299 Consulate General of the Polish Republic to the Foreign Office, New York, June 10, 1943.

79. *Dokumenty z historie,* vol. I, Doc. No. 13, pp. 79–81.

80. *Dokumenty z historie,* vol. II, Doc. No. 506, pp. 707–708.

81. Gottwald, *Spisy,* vol. XI, pp. 194–196.

82. Yeshayahu Jelinek, "Between Nationalism and Communism: the 'Slovak Question'," *Canadian Review of Studies in Nationalism,* II, 2 (1975), pp. 337,

338. Vasil Bilák, *Pravda zostala pravdou,* Bratislava, 1971, p. 38, (hereafter Bilák).

83. For some Communist protests against the Proclamation of June 30, 1943, see *Dokumenty z historie,* vol. I, Doc. No. 295, p. 358, Doc. No. 306, p. 374; Prečan, *Dokumenty I,* Doc. No. 24, pp. 106-110, Doc. No. 44, pp. 149-154, etc.

84. The "Flora" group sent the Memorandum of February 1943 to London. See p. 56.

85. Jablonický, *Z ilegality,* pp. 205-210, Kvetko & Ličko, pp. 32-33, 74-88. Mrs. Josko claims (Mamatey & Luža, p. 370) that it was their political standing, the support they engaged and greater experience in underground work which won the Ursíny-Lettrich group supremacy.

86. Gustav Husák, "K dokumentom z historie československéj politiky 1939-1943," *HČ,* XV, 3 (1967), pp. 422-440, 4 (1967), pp. 604-611; Cf. the L'udák Konštantín Čuleň, *Po Svätoplukovi druhá naša hlava,* Cleveland 1947, pp. 173-181, 592, 593.

87. František Janáček, "Poznámky k hodnocení čechoslovakizmu v odboji," in *Československá revoluce v letech 1944-1948,* Prague 1966, p. 79, (hereafter *Československá revoluce*); Jaroslav Opát, *O novou demokracii 1945-1948,* Prague 1966, p. 23, (hereafter Opát, *O novou*); Huml, *Slovensko,* pp. 122-125.

88. Ján Pasiak, *Riešenie slovenskéj národnostnéj otázky,* Bratislava 1962, p. 145, ft. 13, (hereafter Pasiak, *Riešenie*).

89. In the early fifties, the leaders of CPCS accused Husák, Novomeský, and others of "bourgeois nationalism." In the trials, the real views of the victims were of little importance.

90. Jozef Lettrich, *History of Modern Slovakia,* New York 1955, p. 199, (hereafter Lettrich, *History*); Jozef Lettrich, "Odboj a povstanie," in Kvetko & Ličko, pp. 75, 76.

91. Text of the agreement in Lettrich, *History,* pp. 303-305; Cf. Lettrich in Kvetko & Ličko, p. 78; Josko in Mamatey & Luža, p. 371.

92. Mamatey & Luža, pp. 371, 372.

93. *Dokumenty z historie,* vol. I, Doc. 336, p. 407; Polish Government, Box 670, Dispatch, Ministry of National Defense to the Ministry of Foreign Affairs, London, October 29, 1943; 860F.001/169, Cable No. 18, Wilson to the Secretary and Under Secretary of State, Algiers, January 3, 1944.

94. 860F.001/163, Cable No. 2264, Harriman to the President and Secretary of State, Moscow, Dec. 18, 1943; 860F.001/164, Cable No. 2284, Harriman to the President and Secretary of State, Moscow, Dec. 20, 1943. Cf. Vojtech Mastný, "The Benes-Stalin-Molotov Conversations in December 1943; New Documents," *Jahrbuecher fuer Geschichte Osteuropas,* Neue Folge, XX, 3 (Sept. 1972), pp. 367-402, (hereafter, Mastný).

95. Gosiorovský, "K niektorým," p. 377; Mastný, pp. 373, 374, 390, 395, and 401.

96. Gottwald, *Spisy,* vol. XI, pp. 259-277; Miloš Klimeš, Peter Lesjuk, Irena Malá, and Vilém Prečan, comp., *Cesta ke Květnu. Vznik lidové demokracie v*

*Československu,* Prague, Two vols., 1965, vol. I, Doc. Nos. 1, 2, pp. 35–59, (hereafter *Cesta ke Květnu*).

97. The concessions were made in London in November 1944, *Cesta ke Květnu,* vol. I, Doc. No. 92, p. 300.

98. Cf. *SNP 1944,* pp. 154–164. Although one should regard Communist sources with reservation, the argument sounds acceptable.

99. It was claimed that Beneš would prefer not to see a foreign army of liberation on the Czechoslovak territory. OSS, No. 105880, Dispatch, Hall to Langer, Nov. 27, 1944.

100. Beer, *Dejinná,* pp. 199, 200; Miroslav Ján Ličko, "K otázke spojeneckéj pomoci v Slovenskom národnom povstaní," in Kvetko & Ličko, pp. 209–233.

101. Miloš Gosiorovský, "Slovenské národné povstanie roku 1944," *ČČH,* II, 4 (1954), pp. 573–597; Bohuslav Graca, "Slovenské národné povstanie r. 1944," *HČ,* II, 1 (1954), pp. 3–38.

102. See ft. No. 52.

103. Kvetko & Ličko, p. 197.

104. Jablonický, *Z ilegality,* p. 207.

105. Rudolf Fraštacký, "Zo Slovenska cez Freya," in Kvetko & Ličko, p. 32.

106. This writer is aware that there were politicians in the Slovak State, who tried, sometimes successfully, to find channels to Western agencies. The insignificance of their personalities and the strong adverse influence of the London exiles prevented any noteworthy expansion in these attempts. There are several, very unclear, hints that ranking personalities made overtures to the West. This episode is wholly unresearched and unknown. Joseph Staško, *Slovensko po druhéj svetovéj vojne. "Aprilová dohoda r. 1946,"* S.L., 1977, pp. 12, 13, 33 (ft. 11), 34 (ft. 12) (hereafter Staško). On cooperation and preparations of the Catholic-Protestant oppositionist circles sheds an interesting light the information conveyed by Sidor to Kazemier Pappe, the Polish Ambassador by the Holy See (Polish Government, Box 343, Nr. 49/SA/86, Pappe to the Foreign Minister, June 2, 1943). Also Staško, pp. 13, 35, 36, (ft. 14–19). The author's name given to these groups is "debate groups."

107. Jozef Kirschbaum, "Osudy vyslanectiev Slovenskej Republiky," *Kalendár Jednota* 1961, pp. 109–117; the same "Diplomatic and Consular Relations of Slovakia with Neutral States," *Slovakia,* XXIII (1973), pp. 112–122; the same, "International Recognition of the Slovak Republic," *Slovakia,* I (1951), pp. 23–31.

108. Staško, pp. 12, 13; Joseph M. Kirschbaum, "My Last Diplomatic Report to the President of Slovakia," *Annual Furdek* 1972, p. 85 (hereafter Kirschbaum, "My Last"). The present writer did not find any direct proof that Tiso tried to contact the Allies. Lettrich confirmed my conclusions during a conversation in October 1965 in Washington, D.C. Yet the episode is warrant of further research.

109. T-120, R 2198, 338173, Ludin to the German Foreign Office, January 29, 1941. Cf. Staško, p. 35, ft. 13.

110. T-120, R 1318, D498510, Tiso in an interview to the pro-Nazi Dutch

priest van den Bergh—RSHA to the German Foreign Office, Dec. 10, 1940; T-175, R 524, 939465, Report SD Branch Prague to RSHA, May 21, 1943; etc.
111. Kirschbaum, "My Last," p. 85. ·
112. Cf. Kirschbaum, "My Last," pp. 82–85; See Jelinek, p. 169, ft. 7.
113. Staško p. 34, ft. 11.
114. Ferdinand Ďurčanský, "Márne sa snaží Moskva získat' Slovákov," *Literarný almanach Slováka v Amerike,* 1953, p. 43; Kirschbaum, "My Last," p. 85; Gustav Husák, *Svedectvo o Slovenskom Národnom Povstaní,* Bratislava 1964, pp. 306–308, (hereafter Husák). The story of the Communist, and possibly Russian, overtures toward the Slovak state also awaits its historian.
115. Cf. Kvetko & Ličko, pp. 65, 66.
116. Czecho-Slovakia (Č-SR) was the official name of the Second Republic. The Christmas Agreement spelled the name of the state in the same way. See P. Kollar, "Z revolučného archívu," *Pravda* (Bánska Bystrica), Sept. 12, 1944, No. 3.
117. Prečan, *Dokumenty I,* Doc. No. 112, pp. 258–261.
118. Prečan, *Dokumenty I,* Doc. No. 99, pp. 238–245.
119. Friš, *Povstaní,* pp. 76–83.
120. A.I. Nedorezov, "O nekterých otázkach narodne-osvobozeneckého boje Čechů a Slováků v druhé světové valce," in *Slovenské narodní povstaní. Sborník k 15. výročí,* Prague 1959, pp. 105–107, (hereafter *Sborník k 15. výročí*); Beer, *Dejinná,* p. 279.
121. Samo Falt'an, "Sabotáže, rozleptavanie, boj. Slovensko má partizanské tradicie, nie vojenské." *Výber z domácej a svetovéj tlače,* II (1969), pp. 24–26, (hereafter *Výber*); Jaroslav Šolc, "Cesta slovenských partizánov od celonárodného protifašistického povstania k februaru 1948," *HČ,* IX, 1 (1961), pp. 39–49.
122. *Cesta ke Květnu,* vol. I, p. 125.
123. Winston S. Churchill, *Closing the Ring,* Boston 1951, p. 452; 860F.001/164, Cable No. 2284, Harriman to the President and the Secretary of State, Moscow, Dec. 12, 1943; 860.001/169, Cable No. 18, Wilson to the Secretary and Under-Secretary of State. Algiers, January 3, 1944.
124. See p. 116, 117.
125. Cf. Husák, *Svedectvo,* pp. 522, 527.
126. T-175, R 564, 9440333, 9440606.
127. Polish Government, Box 859, Memorandum, Ministry of National Defense, Office of the Minister, Political section, Nov. 5, 1943; 860F.001/169, Cable No. 18, Wilson to Secretary and Under-Secretary of State, Algiers, Jan. 3, 1944; F0371-38941, Dispatch, the British Embassy near to the Czechoslovak Government to the Foreign Office, London, Apr. 5, 1944.
128. Mamatey & Lúža, p. 388. Taborský denied that Benes agreed to cede the territory. Eduard Taborsky, "Benes and Stalin—Moscow, 1943 and 1945," *Journal of Central European Affairs,* XIII (July 1953), p. 173, ft. 69, (hereafter Taborsky "Benes").
129. F0371-38942, Dispatch No. 1551/4, Offices of the War Cabinet to the Foreign Office, London, Sept. 5, 1944; US General Chiefs of Staff, No.

GCS 669, Memorandum by the Representatives of British Chiefs of Staff, Sept. 7, 1944; Joint Staff Planners, Memorandum No. JPS 520/1, Sept. 12, 1944.

130. OSS No. 57861, Benes' visit to Moscow, Jan. 24, 1944; 860F.001/163, Cable No. 2264, Harriman to the President and the Secretary of State, Dec. 18, 1943; 860F.001/4-2544, Memorandum of Conversation with President Benes, by Edward R. Stettinius Jr., Under Secretary of State, London, Apr. 25, 1944.

131. *SNP 1944*, p. 438; Kvetko & Ličko, pp. 186, 187; Eduard Čejka, *Intriky buržuazie and SNP*, Prague 1959, pp. 53–60, (hereafter Čejka, *Intriky*).

132. F0371-38942, Dispatch No. 151, The British Embassy near the Czechoslovak government to Eden, London, Sept. 6, 1944; Plevza, *Dokumenty I*, Doc. No. 157, pp. 331–333; Doc. No. 113, pp. 262–265; Ferdinand Ďurčanský, "Es war nur eine sowjetische Partisanenaktion," *Politische Studien*, Heft 157, p. 569, (hereafter *Ďurčanský*)," Lettrich in Kvetko & Ličko, pp. 89, 90; Taborsky, "Benes," pp. 168, 170.

133. Beer, *Dejinná*, p. 309; Edo Friš, "Moskovský pobyt K. Šmidkeho v auguste 1944," *PDKSČ*, IV, 3 (1964), pp. 439–444; Mikuláš Ferjenčík, "Moje dôjmy a skusenosti z cesty do Moskvy a zo Slovenského národného povstania," in Kvetko & Ličko, pp. 190, 191.

134. Ferjenčík in Kvetko & Ličko, pp. 190, 191.

135. Ferjenčík in Kvetko & Ličko, p. 192; Anton Rašla, "V povstaleckých štáboch," and Jan Ursíny, "Vojáci a partizáni," in *Výber*, pp. 30, 32, 33.

136. Beer, *Dejinná*, p. 299; Falt'an, *SNP*, p. 59.

137. Jablonický, *Z ilegality*, p. 61; Husák, *Svedectvo*, pp. 210–212; Prečan, *Dokumenty I*, Doc. No. 140, pp. 301–303.

138. Ján Ursíny, "Za krátky čas pôjdeme . . . ," *Matičné Čítanie*, Apr. 28, 1969; Ján Beharka, "Moje reminiscencie na SNP—Kto robil odboj a povstanie," in Kvetko & Ličko, p. 149.

139. Jablonický, *Z ilegality*, p. 62.

140. *Sborník k 15. výročí*, p. 107.

141. Čejka, *Intriky*, pp. 52, 53; Prečan, *Dokumenty I*, Doc. No. 78, pp. 210, 211; F0371-38942, Dispatch C12076/1343/112, Nichols to Eden, Sept. 12, 1944; F0371/38942, Disptach No. 52, from Bari to Resident Minister Central Mediterranean, Caserta, Sept. 9, 1944.

142. F0371-38943, Dispatch No. 169, Office of the Representative at Bari of the Minister Resident Central Mediterranean, Report Major R. Schmer, Bari, Oct. 21, 1944; Anton Rašla, *Civilista v armáde*, Bratislava 1967, pp. 153–172; Prečan, *Dokumenty I*, Doc. 409, p. 661.

143. See p. 69, 70.

144. F0371-38942, Dispatch No. 1551/4, Nichols to Roberts, London, Sept. 5, 1944; Cf. OSS No. 95382, Memorandum on conversation with Fedor Hodža and Ján Lichner, Sept. 7, 1944; Peter P. Toma, "Soviet Strategy in the Slovak Uprising of 1944," *Journal of Central European Affairs*, XIX, 2 (1959), pp. 290–298; 860F.00/3-2648, Dispatch, Yost to the Secretary of State, Vienna, March 26, 1948, Memorandum of conversation with D. Zelnich.

145. General Chiefs of Staff, No. 669, Assistance of the Slovak Army and

Partisans, Sept. 7, 1944; Combined Chiefs of Staff No. 669/1, Memorandum of the US Chiefs of Staff, Sept. 22, 1944; Joint Staff Planners, JPS 520/1, Report of JWPC, Sept. 12, 1944; F0371-38942, Memorandum, Sept. 7, 1944; F0371-38942, Note, Kerr to Vishinsky, Moscow, Sept. 9, 1944.

146. Mrs. Josko in Mamatej & Luža, p. 381.

147. Prečan, *Dokumenty I*, Doc. No. 409, pp. 659–661, and No. 433, pp. 689–691; Cf. Zdenek Fierlinger, *Ve službách ČSR*, two vols., Prague 1951, vol. II, p. 419, (hereafter Fierlinger, *Ve službách*); Paul E. Zinner, *Communist Strategy and Tactics in Czechoslovakia, 1918-1948*, New York and London 1963, p. 76, (herefter Zinner, *Communist Strategy*); Husák, *Svedectvo*, p. 393.

148. See examples Václav Král, "Západ a Slovenské Národné Povstaní," *ČČH*, XXIII, 1 (1975), pp. 51–74; Miroslav Hysko, "Zradcovská úloha buržoazie a západných imperialistov v SNP," in L'udovít Holotík, ed., *Slovenské národné povstanie, Sborník prác k 10. výročiu*, Bratislava 1954, pp. 239–261; "Ako podporovali spojenci povstanie," *Pravda* (Bratislava), Feb. 1, 1948.

149. 860F.0/11-444 Eb, William J. Donovan's Memorandum for the Secretary of State, Nov. 4, 1944; Korbel, pp. 70, 71.

150. Prečan, *Dokumenty I*, Doc. No. 212, pp. 390, 391.

151. Miloš Gosiorovský, "Úloha robotnickéj triedy a KSS v naších dejinách (s osobitným zretel'om na 30. vyročie SNP)," *HČ*, XXII, 2 (1974), p. 188.

152. *SNR 1944*, pp. 214, 215.

153. Ján Scheinost, Ant. J. Kožišek, Karel Werner, *Bánska Bystrica*, Prague 1944, p. 48; Karol Sidor, *Šest rokov pri Vatikáne*, Scranton, Pa. 1947, p. 237; Yeshayahu Jelínek, "Denník Dr. Štefana Tisu," *HČ*, XVIII, 2 (1970), p. 271; *Dokumenty, II*, Doc. No. 229, p. 465.

154. The resolution of the Congress spelled "Czecho-Slovakia" in the hyphenated form. *Pravda* (Bánska Bystrica), Sept. 17, 1944.

155. "Slovenská revolucia," *Nove Slovo*, Sept. 24, 1944.

156. Korbel, *The Communist*, p. 72; Beer, *Dejinná*, p. 402.

157. See p. 73.

158. *SNP Dnešku*, pp. 71, 72.

159. Prečan, *Dokumenty I*,Doc. No. 446, p. 708.

160. Prečan, *Dokumenty I*, Doc. No. 389, pp. 635, 636, No. 409, pp. 659–661, No. 433, p. 689, 690; *Cesta ke Květnu*, vol. I, Doc. No. 76, p. 259; Beer, *Dejinná*, p. 417.

161. Prečan, *Dokumenty I*, Doc. No. 563, p. 900; Cf. 860F.01/11-1744, Encl. No. 2 to the dispatch No. 212, Memorandum of conversation between Dr. Hubert Ripka and Mr. John H. Bruins, Nov. 15, 1944. One of my informants claimed that Dr. Husak told the audience in the city of Košice during the campaign of 1946: "We are Red Ludaks!".

162. Idea of a single state prevails in all talks of federation between Czech and Slovaks. 860F.01/11-444 BG, Dispatch, Donovan to the Secretary of State, Nov. 4, 1944; 860F.01/10-2544, Dispatch No. 201, Schoenfelt to the Secretary of State, London, Oct. 25, 1944; Polish Government, Box 352, Disptach No. 59003-8M.07/13, Tarnowski to the Foreign Minister, Oct. 23, 1944; *New York Times*, Oct. 19, 1944; etc.

163. Laco Novomeský, "Slovenská otázka," *Výber,* II (1969), p. 34; Cf. Ján Ursíny, "Vojáci a partizáni," *Výber,* II (1969), p. 33.

164. Novomeský, *Publicistika,* Vol. II, pp. 379–389. Cf. "I have never encountered a more forceful, more fiery, or more enthusiastic advocate of the Slovak cause than Laco Novomesky . . . (in) London in 1944 . . ." Edward Taborsky, *Communism in Czechoslovakia, 1948–1960,* Princeton, N.J., 1961, p. 132, (hereafter, Taborsky, *Communism*).

165. František Vnuk, *Neuveritelné sprísahanie,* Middletown, Pa., 1964, pp. 170–175; Ďurčanský; Cf. Jozef Paučo, *Tak sme sa poznali,* Middletown, Pa., 1967, p. 168; Konštantín Čuleň, *Vznik a zánik DS na Slovensku,* Middletown, Pa. 1950, p. 21.

166. Bilák, p. 66, František Vnuk, *Neuveritelné sprísahanie,* Middletown, Pa., 1964, p. 7.

167. Polish Government, Box 30, Memorandum, Ministry of National Defense, Office of the Minister, Political section, London, Nov. 14, 1944; 860F.01/11-1744, Dispatch No. 212, Schoenfeld to the Secretary of State, London, Nov. 17, 1944.

168. Prečan, *Dokumenty* I, Doc. No. 481, pp. 747–748; *Cesta ke Květnu,* Doc. No. 92, pp. 296–300, No. 93, pp. 300–302; Cf. Prečan, *Dokumenty I,* Doc. 546, pp. 837–842. Novomeský's report on his stay in England is in Husák, *Svedectvo,* pp. 430–456, Ursíny's reminiscences are in *Matičné Čítanie* (Martin), No. 12, June 1, 1969, No. 13, June 8, 1969.

169. Husák, *Svedectvo,* pp. 462, 463; Prečan, *Dokumenty I,* Docs. No. 251, pp. 797–798, No. 530, pp. 805–810.


# Chapter 4

1. Private information. See also Fierlinger, *Od Mníchova po Košice,* two vols., Prague 1946, vol. II, p. 408, (hereafter Fierlinger, *Od Mníchova*); Husák, *Svedectvo,* pp. 527, 528; Korbel, *The Communist,* pp. 99–102; Johann Wolfgang Bruegel, "Der Fall Karpatho-russland," *Europa-Archiv,* 20 (1953), pp. 6021–28.

2. Fierlinger, *Od Mníchova,* vol. II, pp. 425, 454, 474–477, 481.

3. Korbel, *The Communist,* pp. 108, 109; Zinner, *Communist Strategy,* p. 90; Jozef Jablonický, *Slovensko na prelome,* Bratislava 1965, p. 193, (hereafter Jablonický, *Slovensko*); Jozef Paučo, *Slováci a komunizmus,* Middletown, Pa. 1957, p. 178; Ferdinand Peroutka, "Jmeno, jez vyhaslo: "Šmeral," *Svědectvi,* p. 62; Jorg K. Hoensch, "Die Slowakei im Jahre 1945,"in Karl Bosl, ed., *Das Jahr 1945 in der Tschechoslowakei,* Munich-Vienna, 1971, p. 167; Polish Government, Box 365, Memorandum on Radio Kiev broadcasts, Jan. 17, 1945; etc.

4. *Čas* (Bratislava), Oct. 11, 1947; Taborsky, "Benes," p. 177.

5. 860F.01/11-1144, Dispatch, George F. Kennan to the Secretary of State, Moscow, Nov. 11, 1944. When asked, in Washington D.C., on December 17,

1975, whether he recalled the Soviet plans, Professor Kennan answered in the negative.

6. Fierlinger, *Od Mníchova,* vol. II, pp. 496, 558, 559; Cf. Radomír Lúža, "Czechoslovakia Between Democracy and Communism, 1945-1948," in Mamatey & Lúža, p. 388.

7. J. Benčík in cooperation with K. Bartošek and V. Kurala, "Utrpení a boj okupovaného Slovenska," in Janeček, *Odboj,* p. 378; Jozef Hojč, "O práci strany po zatlačení povstania do hor," PDKČS, IV, 4 (1964), pp. 582-589.

8. OSS, No. 105880, Memo of Nov. 27, 1944; *Cesty ke Květnu,* vol. I, Doc. No. 84, p. 278.

9. *Cesty ke Květnu,* vol. II, Doc. No. 171, p. 519; *SNP 1944,* p. 641.

10. Pasiak, *Riešenie,* p. 241.

11. Marta Vartiková, "Celoslovenská pracovná konferencia KSS v Košiciach ako prínos pri tvorbe vladného programu prvéj vlády Národného Frontu Cechov a Slovákov," including in two annexes Husák's speech and the resolution, *HČ,* XXIII, 2 (1975), pp. 170-200.

12. *Cesty ke Květnu,* vol. I, Doc. No. 123, pp. 336-369.

13. Cf. Bohuslav Lastovička, "Vznik a význam košického vladního programu," *ČČH,* VIII (August 1960), p. 457, ft. 23 (hereafter Lastovička). Lastovička tells how Gottwald saved Czechoslovak unity from the Slovak nationalistic-federalistic designs. On the other hand Taborsky (*Communismus,* p. 330) claims that the Communists encouraged the Slovaks to take extremist stands.

14. *Cesty ke Květnu,* vol. I, Doc. No. 130, p. 384.

15. The so-called "Leninist solution," see Husák, *Svedectvo,* p. 554.

16. Iván Škurlo, "Celoslovenská konferencia KSS v Žiline 1945, a čo jej predchádzalo," *HČ,* XIX, 2 (1971), pp. 167, 168, (Hereafter Škurlo, "Celoslovenska").

17. Korbel, *The Communist,* p. 113.

18. A pro-Soviet government established in Poland on the liberated territory. Cf. Lastovička, p. 455.

19. For the negotiations, see *Cesty ke Květnu,* vol. I, Doc. No. 132, pp. 410-418.

20. For the English text, see Lettrich, *History,* Doc. No. 41, pp. 317, 318.

21. Falt'an, "Niektoré otázky," p. 107, f. 4; Janeček, *Odboj,* pp. 385, 386; Viera Jarošová and Oldrich Jaroš, *Slovenské robotnictvo v boji o moc (1944-1948),* Bratislava 1965, p. 50, f. 34, (hereafter Jaroš & Jaroš).

22. In one of the first meetings he attended, that of the Presidium of CPS on Apr. 25, 1945, in Košice, Široký charged: "We are aggressive toward the Central government, and are compromising with home reaction." *Cesty ke Květnu,* vol. II, Doc. No. 210, p. 595, f. 13; Cf. OSS No. XL19117, Report of early August 1945.

23. OSS, No. 2651. The Position of Slovakia in the Czechoslovak State, May 25, 1945 and A56054, Report of May 13, 1945; Cf. Samo Falt'an, "Niektoré otázky revolučného vývoja na Slovensku v rokoch 1944-1948," in *Československá revoluce 1944-1948. Sborník příspěvků z konference historiků k 20.*

*Vyročí osvobození ČSSR*, Prague 1966, p. 107, (hereafter *Československá revoluce*).

24. OSS, No. A57020, Report of May 25, 1945, and No. 2651. The position of Slovakia in the Czechoslovak State, May 25, 1945.

25. Zdenek Jičinský and Jiři Grospič, *Státopravní uspořadaní vztahů českého a slovenského národa v období vypracovaní a prijetí Ústavy 9. Května*, Prague 1967, p. 137, (hereafter Jičinský & Grospič); Škurlo, "Celoslovenská," pp. 165, 166; Lúža in Mamatey & Lúža, p. 396.

26. Falťan in *Československá revoluce*, p. 202; Jablonický, *Slovensko*, p. 294.

27. Juraj Krámer, *Die Auswirkungen der slowakischen Frage auf die Partei und Innenpolitik der CSSR von 1944 bis 1968*, two vols., Cologne 1969, vol. I, pp. 24, 25, (hereafter Kramer, *Die Auswirkungen*); Jičinský & Grospič, pp. 141–144.

28. Lúža in Mamatey & Lúža, p. 396; Škurlo, "Celoslovenská," p. 165.

29. Marta Vartiková, comp., *Komunistická strana Slovenska. Dokumenty z konferencií a plén 1944–1948*, Bratislava 1971, pp. 186, 188, 189, 207, 218, 222, 229, (hereafter, *KSS*).

30. *KSS*, pp. 222–224.

31. "Komunisti v prednej linií," *Pravda* (Bratislava), Aug. 11, 1972.

32. OSS, No. XL 20996, Report of early Aug. 1945.

33. *Pravda* (Bratislava), Oct. 17, 1945; OSS, No. XL19117 and No. XL20996, reports of early Aug. 1945.

34. *KSS*, pp. 282, 283; 860F.00/11-1745, Cable No. 592, Steinhardt to the Secretary of State, Nov. 17, 1945; 860F.00/11-2445, Cable No. 624, Steinhardt to the Secretary of State, Nov. 24, 1945; 860F.00/12-2245, Dispatch No. 781, Steinhardt to the Secretary of State, Dec. 22, 1945.

35. For fear of the Russians, see 860F.00/7-3045, Dispatch No. 12 Confidential, Steinhardt to the Secretary of State, July 30, 1945; 860F.00/8-2845, Dispatch, William J. Donovan to James C. Dunn, Assistant Secretary of State, Washington, Aug. 28, 1945; 860F.00/10-145, Cable No. 404, Steinhardt to the Secretary of State, Oct. 1, 1945.

36. 860F.00/11-3045, Summary for the week Oct. 31st–Nov. 6th, 1945, No. 282, Prague, Nov. 30, 1945; 860F.00/12-645, Summary for the week Nov. 7th–Nov. 13th, 1945, No. 299, Prague, Dec. 6, 1945.

37. Gustav Husák, *Zápas o zajtrajšok*, Bratislava 1948, pp. 33–37, (hereafter Husák, *Zápas*).

38. *Pravda* (Bratislava), Nov. 16, 1945; 860F.00/12-1545, Dispatch No. 330, Steinhardt to the Secretary of State, Political situation in Slovakia, Prague, Dec. 15, 1945.

39. Pasiak, *Riešenie*, pp. 186, 187.

40. Cf. Pasiak, *Riešenie*, p. 177.

41. 760.61/6-1345, Cable No. 14, Klieforth to the Secretary of State, Prague, June 13, 1945.

42. The regular reports of Jewish institutions emphasized the anti-Semitism,

but not the dangers from the Left. Central Zionist Archive (CZA), S5/761, Moshe Baumgarten to Dr. Ben-Shalom, July 21, 1946; S6/4561, Adler-Rudl, Notes on Czechoslovakia and Austria, July 24, 1946; Maurice Pearlmann, "A Visit to Czechoslovakia," *Jewish Chronicle* (London), Nov. 22 and 29, 1946; "Jews in the New Czechoslovakia," *Jewish Chronicle* (London), Oct. 18, 1946; Cf. 860F.00/5-2746, Cable No. 893, Steinhardt to the Secretary of State, May 27, 1946.

43. Jičinský & Grospič, p. 144.

44. *Národná Obrana* (Bratislava), Apr. 12 and 13, 1946; Jaroslav Barto, *Riešenie vzťahu Čechov a Slovákov (1944-1948);* Bratislava 1968, pp. 136-154, (hereafter Barto, *Riešenie*).

45. Dr. M. Zibrín, "Kto ukrátil Slovensko o 15 mandátov," *Čas* (Bratislava), Apr. 30, 1946.

46. *Národná Obrana* (Bratislava), Apr. 5, 1946; *Čas* (Bratislava), Apr. 6, 1946.

47. Huml, *Slovensko,* pp. 35, 36; Gottwald, *Spisy,* XIII, pp. 85-89; Cf. Gustav Husák, "Dôsledne za principmi," *Nové Slovo* (Bratislava), May 31, 1946; *Pravda* (Bratislava), June 1, 1946; etc.

48. Huml, *Slovensko,* p. 28.

49. 10.3 per cent, Mamatey & Lúža, p. 154.

50. *O novou,* pp. 104, 105; Dr. Kvetko to the author in Washington, D.C., on Nov. 20, 1975.

51. Lettrich, *History,* p. 241.

52. Cf. results by regions, Huml, *Slovensko,* pp. 29, 30. Emanuel Boehm, "Východné Slovensko v boji o demokraciu," *Rozhl'ady,* I, 1 (June 1956), pp. 11-16.

53. The Communists foiled attempts to transfer branches of Czech parties into Slovakia, just as (with the support of others) they prevented establishment of the Democratic party in Bohemia-Moravia. Two new parties in Slovakia, created to compete with the established bodies, remained insignificant.

54. For April Agreement and Party of Liberty, see Staško, pp. 15-31; Iván Fiala, "Tridsiate výročie jednéj dohody," *Horizont 76* (Zurich), 3-4 (March–April 1976); Jozef Zvonar-Tieň, " 'Aprilová Dohoda' a Strana Slobody," *Slobodné Slovensko* (Cologne) 1 (January–February 1978), 2 (March–April 1978), 3-4 (May–July 1978); Karel Kaplan, "Slovenský politický katolicismus a komunisté," *Studie,* 54 (1977), pp. 454-456.

55. Gottwald, *Spisy,* vol. XIII, pp. 85-89.

56. Letter, Dr. Samuel Belluš to the author, Dec. 1, 1975. Also, letter, Dr. Martin Kvetko to the author, Nov. 20, 1975.

57. *Pravda* (Bratislava), June 23, 1946; *Čas* (Bratislava), June 26, 1946.

58. "Memorandum o Slovensku," *HC,* XVI, 2 (1968), pp. 191-193.

59. Marta Vartikova, *Od Košíc po február,* Bratislava 1968, pp. 116, 117 (hereafter Vartiková, *Od Košíc*); *KSS,* pp. 491-508.

60. *KSS,* p. 477. After the break with the Cominform, Tito and his friends regretted at least some of the excesses committed during the War and after it.

61. *KSS*, p. 497.

62. Cf. "Predseda KSS ako centralista. Na okraj štvaníc proti DS," *Čas* (Bratislava), June 15 and 16, 1946.

63. See p. 88, 89.

64. *Pravda* (Bratislava), Oct. 10, 1946; *Čas* (Bratislava), Oct. 30, 1946.

65. *Čas* (Bratislava), Sept. 9, Nov. 9 and 30, Dec. 4, 1946.

66. *Čas* (Bratislava), Nov. 29, 1946. Cf. *Pravda* (Bratislava), Nov. 19, 1946; Barto, *Riešenie*, p. 182.

67. Viliam Plevza, *Československá štátnosť a slovenská otázka v politike KSČ*, Bratislava 1971, p. 225, (hereafter Plevza, *Československá štátnosť*); Falt'an, *Slovenská otázka*, p. 229.

68. 860F.00/10-2246, Dispatch, No. 1411, Steinhardt to the Secretary of State, Oct.22, 1946; 860F.00/-346, Summary of the week Oct. 30th-Nov. 6th, 1946, No. 1150, Prague, Dec. 3, 1946; 860F.00/12-1046, Summary of the week Nov. 6th-Nov. 12th, 1946, No. 1583, Prague, Dec. 10, 1946.

69. A curious aspect of the hustle around Tiso is SNC's transfer of the amnesty decision to Prague. The institution had chosen to act that way after its repeated demands for independence from the Central authorities in Prague. 806F.00/4-1847, Cable No. 394, Steinhardt to the Secretary of State, Apr. 19, 1947; Václav Král, Comp., *Cestou k Únoru, Dokumenty*, Prague 1963, Doc. No. 45, pp. 201-203, (hereafter, Král. *Cestou)*.

70. Walter Ullmann, *The United States in Prague 1945-1948*, Boulder, CL, 1978, p. 105.

71. 860F.00/6-1147, Cables Nos. 661, 662, Steinhardt to the Secretary of State, June 11, 1947; 860F.00/6-1347, Cable No. 697, Steinhardt to the Secretary of State, June 13, 1947.

72. 860F.00/5-1647, Dispatch, Steinhard to the Secretary of State, Progress of the Non-Communist Parties, May 16, 1947.

73. Vartiková, *Od Košíc*, pp. 139, 1940.

74. 860F.00/2-1947, Dispatch No. 150, Bruins to the Secretary of State, Feb. 19, 1947; 860F.00/2-2147, Dispatch No. 1890, Bruins to the Secretary of State, New developments in Czech-Slovak Relations, Prague, Feb. 21, 1947.

75. 860F.00/3-447, Dispatch No. 1912, Bruins to the Secretary of State, March 4, 1947; 860F.00/3-1047, Cable A-135, Bruins to Secretary of State, March 10, 1947.

76. 860F.00/2-1947, Dispatch No. 150, Bruins to the Secretary of State, Feb. 19, 1947; 860F.00/2-2147, Dispatch No. 1890, Bruins to the Secretary of State, New developments in Czech-Slovak Relations, Prague, Feb. 21, 1947; *Foreign Relations of the United States 1947*, vol. IV, Washington D.C. 1972, p. 197; 860F.00/3-447, Dispatch No. 1972, Bruins to the Secretary of State, March 4, 1947.

77. *Pravda* (Bratislava), Feb. 4, 1947.

78. 860F.00/5-947, Cable A-314, Steinhardt to the Secretary of State, May 16, 1947; 860F.00/5-2947, Dispatch No. 2477, Steinhardt to the Secretary of State, Prague, May 25, 1947.

79. *Čas* (Bratislava), Aug. 5, 1947.

80. *Pravda* (Bratislava), Feb. 4, and June 6, 1947; Cf. Gottwald, *Spisy*, vol. XIV, pp. 43–47.

81. "Rok skúšky," *Nové Slovo*, Jan. 4, 1947.

82. Král, *Cestou*, Doc. No. 45, pp. 201–203.

83. See examples Král, *Cestou*, Doc. No. 49, pp. 208, 209; *Národná Obroda* (Bratislava), Dec. 11, 1947.

84. 860F.00/7-1547, Dispatch No. 904, Steinhardt to the Secretary of State, July 15, 1947; *Pravda* (Bratislava), Oct. 9, 1947; *Čas* (Bratislava), Oct. 14, 1947; Jaroš & Jaroš, p. 232.

85. *Foreign Relations*, vol. IV, p. 227.

86. Vartiková, *Od Košíc*, p. 140.

87. 860F.00/10-3147, Cable No. 1444 and Airgram No. A-858, Steinhardt to the Secretary of State, Oct. 31, 1947; 860F.00/11-347, Cable No. 1451, Oct. 3, 1947; 860F.00/11-1247, Cable No. 1504, Steinhard to the Secretary of State, Nov. 12, 1947; 860F.00/11-1947, Airgram No. A-905, Steinhardt to the Secretary of State, Nov. 19, 1947; 860F.00/11-2447, Airgram No. A-927, Steinhardt to the Secretary of State.

88. Jaroš & Jaroš, p. 233; Cf. Král, *Cestou*, Doc. No. 74, Nov. 8, 1947; 860F.00/11-1247, Cable No. 1513, Steinhardt to the Secretary of State, Nov. 12, 1947.

89. Vartiková, *Od Košíc*, pp. 171, 172.

90. *Foreign Relations*, vol. IV, p. 339. Although it is easy to agree with Steinhadt, the reader of the American diplomatic correspondence is often surprised by the unrealistic, nay doctrinaire, reporting. Typical were the dispatches of Charles W. Yost, who in letters to the superiors appeared to be fighting the Cold War. See for example 860F.00/9-347, Dispatch No. 3032, Charles W. Yost to the Secretary of State, Sept. 3, 1947.

91. 860F.00/1-1448, Airgram No. A-42, Bruins to the Secretary of State, Jan. 14, 1948; 860F.00/1-2948, Airgram No. A-91, Bruins to the Secretary of State, Jan. 29, 1948; 860F.00/1-2948, Cable No. 85, Bruins to the Secretary of State, Jan. 29, 1948; 860F.00/2-448, Airgram No. A-112, Bruins to the Secretary of State, Feb. 4, 1948. Karel Kaplán, "Narodní fronta 1945–1948," *Studie*, 56 (1978), p. 108; the same, "Slovenský katolicizmus a komunisté," *Studie*, 54 (1977), p. 465; Lastovička, p. 461.

92. *Nové Slovo* (Bratislava), Feb. 21, 1948.

93. *Národná Obrana* (Bratislava), Apr. 9 1946.

94. Král, *Cestou*, Doc. No. 117, pp. 349–350.

95. Král, *Cestou*, pp. 177–181.

96. *Národná Obrana* (Bratislava), May 8, 1948.

97. *Pravda* (Bratislava), March 11, 12, 14, etc., 1948.

98. *Pravda* (Bratislava), April 17 and 23, 1948.

99. Eduard Kučera, *K některým otázkam autonomie a postavení Slovenska v rámci Československé republiky*, Prague 1954, pp. 37, 38, (hereafter Kučera, *K některým*).

100. Kučera, *K některým*, pp. 17–34.

101. *KSS*, pp. 699–728; Cf. Král, *Cestou*, pp. 215–229.

102. In a letter to the Central Committee of CPCS in 1963, Husák recounted his story. Parts of the present work, based on Husák's letter, go without reference—according to the stipulations of the holders. A copy of this document was deposited in the mean-time at the Herder Institute, Marburg, West Germany.

## Chapter 5

1. Livia Rothkirchen, "The Czechoslovak Government in Exile: Jewish and Palestinian Aspects in the Light of Documents," *Yad Vashem Studies*, IX, 1973, pp. 157-200.

2. "Neoslavizmus komunistov," *Národná Obrana* (Bratislava), Apr. 2, 1946.

3. Zvara, *Mad'arská*, p. 50.

4. L'ubomír Lipták, ed., "Z kroniky predmnichovských dni (z denniku A. Markuša)," *HČ*, XVIII, 5 (1970), pp. 379-405; Ladislav Lipscher, "Účast'židov na hnutí odporu na Slovensku," in Kvetko & Ličko, p. 307, f. 1, and letter Dr. Ladislav Lipscher to the author, Nov. 23, 1976.

5. i.e. "Aryanization," sequestration of property of the Jews. T-175, R 564, 9440595,9440253.

6. T-175, R 564, 9440627. In Czechoslovakia, industrialists in several branches were nicknamed "barons." Hence *uhlobaróni*, "coal-barons," i.e. the owners of coal mines, and *cukrobaróni*, "sugar-barons," i.e. owners of sugar mills. Cf. T-175, R 564, 9440300, July 1941, "In the Soviet Union no Jews have millions, factories, and estates; in Germany and Slovakia they do!".

7. Yaakov Ronen (Rosenberg), Kibbutz Ha-Ogen, Israel, Interview of July 21, 1961, in Institute on Contemporary Jewry, *Oral History Division Catalogue* No. 2, Interview No. 80.

8. Krajňák, *Komunisti*, p. 136; T-175, R 564, 9440219-221.

9. Tichý, *Z bojov*, vol. I, p. 113. The author has discussed the topic with some of the surviving Jewish Communists from Slovakia living in Israel. Mr. Šimon Čermák (Porges) told him the story of a young Communist from Prievidza, Cathrine Rosenthal, who was adviced by the local secretary of the party Ján Svítok" to go with the masses. Katka died in Auschwitz. See Yeshayahu Jelinek, "The Communist Party of Slovakia and the Jews: Ten Years (1938-1948)," *East Central Europe*, V, 2 (1978), p. 192.

10. *Odboj a revolucé 1938-1945*, Prague 1965, pp. 203, 207. The commander of the first CPS guerilla group "Janko Král,"was Alexander Markuš (Markus). There were Jewish members in the "Vihorlat" and "Sitno" groups. All three groups existed in 1942.

11. On Jews in Slovak resistance, see Yeshayahu Jelinek, "The Role of the Jews in Slovakian Resistance," *Jahrbuecher fuer Geschichte Osteuropas*, Neue Folge, XV, 3 (Sept. 1967), pp. 415-422; Emil F. Knieža, "The Resistance of Slovak Jews," in Juri Suhl, ed., *They Fought Back*, New York 1967, pp. 191-196; Lipscher in Kvetko & Ličko.

12. "Neznámi dokument z Povstania," *Nové Slovo* (Bratislava), Aug. 14, 1969.

13. Gottwald, *Spisy*, vol. XI, pp. 178, 179.

14. Clementis, *Odkazy*, pp. 129, 130, 407–411.

15. *KSS*, pp. 17–19.

16. "Vrátit' l'udu," *Pravda* (Bratislava), Sept. 24, 1944.

17. CZA, S26/1081, Leo Hermann to the Jewish Agency in Jerusalem, Nov. 19, 1944.

18. Gottwald, *Spisy*, vol. XI, p. 270.

19. *Pravda* (Košice), Feb. 13, 1945.

20. *HČ*, XIII, 2 (1975), p. 194.

21. One of them, Oto Krajňák (Klein), was a member of the Second CC CPS.

22. Husák, *Svedectvo*, p. 559.

23. Široký's brother-in-law Julius Bránik (Maibaum) held some of the leading functions in CPS.

24. *Čas* (Bratislava), the organ of DP, did not miss a week without a veiled or open attack on the Jews—particularly in the column "Do živého" (Into the Living Flesh). The Democratic Commissioner Kornel Filo and other officials frequently undermined Jewish interest. Archive Winterstein (AW, File II/7, SRP and USŽNO: A Proposal for Fast and Easy Implementation of the Law of Restitution No. 128/1946 in Slovakia, July 19, 1946). Cf. also OSS, No. XL20996, early Aug. 1945; OSS, No. 3380, Status and Prospects of Slovak Reconstruction, Sept. 20, 1945.

25. AW, Session of the Executive Board of Association of Racially Persecuted, Aug. 10 and Sept. 14, 1945.

26. Yeshayahu Jelinek, "Between Assimilation and Emigration: the Authorities, the Population, and the Remnant of the Jews in Slovakia, 1945–1949," *Proceedings of the Sixth World Congress of Jewish Studies,* Jerusalem 1976, vol. II, pp. 249–256.

27. CZA, S5/725, Raffi Friedl to the Executive of Jewish Agency, Prague, July 15, 1947, and the same S5/752, of Oct. 12, 1947.

28. T-175, R 564, 9440565, 9440627.

29. Juraj Zvara, "K problematike postavenia mad'arskéj narodnostnéj skupiny v ČSR v období boja za upevnenie l'udovéj demokracie a rozširenia moci robotnickéj triedy (1945–1948)," *HČ*, XXII, 1 (1964), pp. 28–49, (hereafter Zvara, "K problematike").

30. See "Ide o Mad'arsko," *Pravda* (Bánska Bystrica), Sept. 24, 1944.

31. Purgát, *Od Trianonu*, p. 223.

32. Cf. *KSS*, p. 89.

33. Zvara, *Mad'arská*, p. 57; Purgát, *Od Trianonu*, p. 255; Marta Vartiková, *Od Košíc po februar*, Bratislava 1968, p. 66, (hereafter Vartiková, *Od Košíc*); Jablonický, *Slovensko*, p. 407; OSS, No. XL19117, early Aug. 1945.

34. *RP*, Dec. 12, 1937, *Pravda* (Bratislava), July 10, 1945; *KSS*, p. 215; Cf. 860F.00/10-847, Oct. 21, 1947.

35. Purgát, *Od Trianonu*, pp. 263, 264; *SNP 1944*, p. 531; Jablonický, *Slovensko*, pp. 404, 405.

36. *KSS*, p. 669; Zvara, "K problematike," p. 33, and *Mad'arská*, p. 63.

37. Zvara, "K problematike," pp. 29, 30; Jablonický, *Slovensko*, p. 373.

38. Purgát, *Od Trianonu*, pp. 250, 251; Jablonický, *Slovensko*, p. 370.

39. See p. 4.

40. 860F.001/170, Cable No. 32, Wilson to the Secretary and Under Secretary of State, strictly confidential, Algiers, Jan. 4, 1944; cf. Lastovička, p. 451. In 1945, the Prague-based *Svobodné Noviny* demanded in an Editorial territorial adjustments on the Hungarian border in favour of Slovakia and Moravia. (860F.00/8-1445, Summary No. 35, July 18-24, 1945).

41. 860F.00/1-746, Summary No. 377, Dec. 19-25, 1946; 860F.00/9-546, Airgram No. A-1254, Jefferson Caffery to the Secretary of State, Paris, Sept. 9, 1946.

42. *KSS*, p. 91.

43. *Pravda* (Bratislava), July 25, Sept. 16, 1945, Apr. 13, 1947, etc.

44. *Pravda* (Bratislava), July 25, 1945, called on the "steeled sons of the Slovak mountains" to stand guard on the Danube. One is reminded of the *Wacht am Rein . . .*

45. Husák, *Svedectvo*, p. 548.

46. *Pravda* (Bratislava), Nov. 29, 1945, Christmas 1945, Sept. 13, 1946; Zvara *Mad'arská*, p. 57.

47. OSS, No. 3380, Report of Sept. 20, 1945.

48. Cf. Martin Vietor, "K problematike mad'arskéj menšiny v rokoch okupacie a po oslobodení ČSR," *Československá revoluce*, pp. 153-157. Cf. Zvara, *Mad'arská*, pp. 68-81, 410, 411, and "K problematike," pp. 33-46.

49. Mastný, p. 402.

50. *Pravda* (Bratislava), Sept. 5, 1945, and June 4, 1946; 860F.00/6-446, Cable No. 959, Bruins to the Secretary of State, June 4, 1946; 860F.00/8-3046, Cable No. 1599, Steinhardt to the Secretary of State, Aug. 30, 1946.

51. Kopecký, *ČSR*, pp. 400, 401; Zvara, *Mad'arská*, p. 80.

52. *Pravda* (Bratislava), Feb. 9, 1946, Oct. 2, 1947; Kopecký, *ČSR*, pp. 400, 410; 860F.00/10-247, Cable No. 777, Steinhardt to the Secretary of State, Oct. 3, 1947.

53. OSS, No. XL40409, Feb. 12, 1946; Zvara, *Mad'arská*, p. 76.

54. Huml, *Slovensko*, pp. 99, 220, f. 24.

55. Opat, *O novou*, p. 86; C. 840.4016/9-1545, Dispatch No. 297, Schoenfeld to the Secretary of State, Budapest, Sept. 15, 1945.

56. 860F.00/7-245, Dispatch No. 35, Klieforth to the Secretary of State, Prague, July 2, 1945.

57. Huml, *Slovensko*, p. 99.

58. *Pravda* (Bratislava), May 17, and Sept. 15, 1946.

59. Zvara, *Mad'arská*, p. 56; OSS, No. XL19112, early Aug. 1945.

60. *Pravda* (Bratislava), Feb. 14, 1946, July 9, and 24, July, 1947; *Čas* (Bratislava), June 27 an 28, 1946; Huml, *Slovensko*, p. 100.

61. *Pravda* (Bratislava), June 25, and Sept. 23, 1947; *Národná Obrana* (Bratislava), Oct. 7, 1947, and Jan. 14, 1948.

62. Decree of the President of the Republic No. 5, May 19, 1945, and No. 8, Aug. 2, 1945; *Pravda* (Bratislava), Aug. 7, 1945.

63. Zvara, "K problematike," p. 38; Huml, *Slovensko,* p. 100, gives the number 410,000.

64. 860F.00/8-547, Airgram No. A-601, Yost to the Secretary of State, Aug. 14, 1947; OSS, No. XL40409, Feb. 12, 1946. Joining the CPS was a guarantee that "re-Slovakization" would be accepted, and one will be left at home undisturbed.

65. *RP,* Oct. 25, 1925.

66. *KSS,* p. 78.

67. Slovak historiography occasionally returns to the problems of the Magyar minority. The writers repeatedly display both nationalistic bias and sophistry. For a study critical on Czechoslovakia and its Communists, see Sándor Bazogh, "Az 1946, február 27-i magyar-csehszlovák lakossagcsere egyezmeny," Tortenelmi Szemie, 22 (1979) pp. 59-87.

68. Gejza Lacko, "Komunisté kremnického okresu v boji proti fašizmu," in *Sborník k 15. výročí,* pp. 175-179; Krajňák, *Komunisti,* pp. 78-81; Filip Holka, *Narodnooslobodzovací boj na Ponitrí,* Bratislava 1967, pp. 70, 89.

69. See microfilms T-175, Rolls 564 and 565.

70. T-175, R 564, 9440410-414, 9440588-589, 9440514-533, etc.

71. Kvetko & Ličko, pp. 333, 334.

72. Wolfgang Venohr, *Aufstand fuer die Tschechoslowakei. Der slowakische Freiheitskampf von 1944,* Hamburg 1969, p. 216. Cf. Ursíny, *Matičné Čítanie,* Apr. 28, 1964. Atrocities committed against the civilian German population find only sporadic mention in contemporary scholarship.

73. See p. 114.

74. *Pravda* (Bratislava), Feb. 12, 1947.

75. *Pravda* (Bratislava), Feb. 14, 1946.

76. *Pravda* (Bratislava), May 27, 1945. Hungarian monarchs invited Germans to Slovakia to develop local mining and industry in the late Middle Ages.

77. Huml, *Slovensko,* p. 173; 860F.00/9-2145, Dispatch No. 111, Steinhardt to the Secretary of State, Sept. 21, 1945; OSS No. L57726, July 7, 1945; *Pravda* (Bratislava), March 9, 1947; Gottwald, *Spisy,* vol. XII, pp. 365, 392.

78. T-175, R 564, 9440333, 9440606.

79. Beer, *Dejinná,* p. 77; T-175, R 522, 9391612.

80. Iván Bajcura, *Ukrajinská otázka v ČSSR,* Košice 1967, p. 73, (hereafter Bajcura, *Ukrajinská*).

81. Janeček, *Odboj,* pp. 361, 362; Bajcura, *Ukrajinská,* p. 74; Karel Bartošek, "Československá spoločnosť a revoluce," in *Československá revoluce,* p. 31; The Soviet officers were later described as working for Lavrentij Berja.

82. Beer, *Dejinná, p. 485; Bajcura, Ukrajinská,* p. 75; *KSS,* pp. 130-138; Kvetko & Ličko, p. 182; Fierlinger, *Ve službách,* vol. II, 495.

83. Prjaševščina, or the Prešov region, a controversial title, denotes the area in Slovakia populated by the alleged Ukrainians. Cf. Paul R. Magocsi, *An Historiographical Guide to Subcarpathian Rus',* Cambridge, Mass. 1976, p. 202; Bajcura, *Ukrajinská,* p. 72.

84. Bajcura, *Ukrajinská,* pp. 73-75; Jablonický, *Slovenská,* pp. 286-288; Beer, *Dejinná,* pp. 474, 484, 485; *Cesty ke Květnu,* vol. II, pp. 678-681.

85. Bajcura, *Ukrajinská,* p. 75; Beer, *Dejinná,* p. 485.

86. Cf. Janeček, *Odboj*, p. 363.

87. *KSS*, pp. 90, 112.

88. Cf. *Pravda* (Bratislava), March 1, 1945. Later Kopecký charged Husák and his friends with persecution of the Ukrainians. (Kopecký, *CSR*, p. 401.).

89. Bajcura, *Ukrajinská*, pp. 98, 99; Jablonický, *Slovenská*, pp. 286-288; Beer, *Dejinná*, pp. 484, 485.

90. Jablonický, *Slovenska*, p. 259.

91. *Pravda* (Bratislava), Oct. 13, and Nov. 16, 1945; 860F.9111/11-1345, Dispatch No. 226, Steinhardt to the Secretary of State, Nov. 1945; Bajcura, *Ukrajinská*, pp. 77, 78, 84.

92. Bajcura, *Ukrajinská*, p. 80.

93. Vartiková, *Od Košíc*, p. 13, Bajcura, *Ukrajinská*, pp. 72, 76.

94. Joblonický, *Slovenská*, pp. 259, 260; Bajcura, *Ukrajinská*, pp. 76-79, 91-93; Cf. Yeshayahu Jelinek, "Slovakia and its Minorities 1939-1945: People With and Without National Protection," *Nationality Papers*, IV, 1 (1976), pp. 3-6.

95. Bajcura, *Ukrajinská*, p. 77. Many of the emigrants gladly returned to Slovakia in 1960 and after. (Zdenka Štastná, "Na vychodní vyspě," *Reporter* (Brno), IV, 10 (March 3, 1969).

96. Bajcura, *Ukrajinská*, p. 77; *Pravda* (Bratislava), Aug. 6, Oct. 17 and 18, 1946, Apr. 13, 1947.

97. 860F.00/12-947, Airgram No. A-983, Bruins to the Secretary of State, Dec. 9, 1947; Bajcura, *Ukrajinská*, pp. 89-91.

98. *Pravda* (Bratislava), Apr. 20, 1948; Bajcura, *Ukrajinská*, p. 98.

## Chapter 6

1. *50. výročí Československé Republiky. Materialy z vedecké konference*, Prague 1968, vol. II, p. 213.

# BIBLIOGRAPHY

## Documents, Unpublished and Published

The Hebrew University of Jerusalem, The Institute on Contemporary Jewry. Oral History Division Catalogue No. 2 (English), Jerusalem 1965, No. 1 (Hebrew), Jerusalem 1965. *Jewish Resistance Activity in Slovakia during World War II.* The Interviewer: Yeshayahu Jelinek. Copies of 44 testimonies, and transcripts of two symposia listed in the catalogue No. 2 are in the possession of the writer.

The Hoover Institution on War, Revolution and Peace, Stanford, California, USA. The Polish Government Collection, Boxes Nos. 35, 227, 343 and 352.

*Nachlass* Dr. Vojtech Winterstein, the late President of the (Slovak) Association of Racially Persecuted by the Fascist Regime, Bratislava, Czechoslovakia. Held privately.

Political Archives of the Foreign Office, Bonn, FGR. Section *Inland II, geheim—Kommunismus, Slowakei.*

Central Zionist Archives, Jerusalem, Israel. Sections S5 and S26.

Mr. Emanuel Frieder, formerly President of the (Slovak) Union of Jewish Religious Congregations, Natania, Israel. Collection of documents of Jewish organizations and public life in Slovakia, 1940-1949. In possession of the owner.

Federal Archives of FGR, Koblenz, FGR. *Nachlass* Arthur Seyss-Inquart.

The Public Record Office, London, England. The British Foreign Office documents, Section F0371-38941, 38942 and 38943.

U.S. National Archives and Record Service, Washington, D.C., USA. World War II Records Division, German Records Microfilmed at Alexandria, Va. Microcopy T-175, Reichsfuehrer SS and Chief of the German Police, Heinrich Himmler, Rolls Nos. 564 and 565. Modern Military Records Division Nos. CCS 669; JCS 1056; JPS 520 and 545; OPD 165.

Modern Military Records Division. Office of Strategic Services (OSS) Collection.

Department of State Papers, Section 860F.

Yad Vashem, Martyrs and Heroes Memorial Authority Archives, Jerusalem, Israel. Microfilm No. JM 2211.

Amort, Čestimír, comp., *Dokumenty o vztazích československého lidu k narodum SSSR v letech 1917-1945. Velká víra a nádeje.* Prague 1968.

*Chteli jsme bojovat. Dokumenty o boji KSČ a lidu na obranu Československa 1938.* Two volumes. Prague 1963.

*Thesen und Resolutionen des III. Weltkongresses der kommunistische Internationale (Moskau, 22. Juni bis 12. Juli 1921).* Hamburg 1921.

*Die Taetigkeit der Exekutive des Praesidiums des EK der kommunistische Internationale vom 13. Juli bis 7. Februar 1922.* Petrograd 1922.

*Thesen und Resolutionen des IV. Weltkongreses der kommunistische Internationale, Moskau, vom 5. November bis 5. Dezember 1922.* Hamburg 1923.

*Bericht ueber den IV. Kongress der kommunistische Internationale, Petrograd-Moskau vom 5. November bis 5. December 1922.* Hamburg 1923.

*Protokoll der Konferenz der Erweiterten Exekutive der Kommunistischen Internationale, Moskau 12-23. Juni 1923,* Hamburg 1923.

*Protokoll, Fuenfter Kongress der kommunistischen Internationale (8. Juli-17. Juli 1924),* Two volumes. Hamburg (?) 1924 (?).

*Protokoll erweiterte Exekutive der kommunistische Internationale, Moskau, 21 Maerz-6 April 1925,* Hamburg 1925.

*Sechster Weltkongress der Kommunistischen Internationale, Moskau, 17. Juli-1. September 1928,* Three volumes. Hamburg-Berlin 1928.

*Foreign Relations of the United States 1947,* Vol. IV, Washington, D.C. 1972.

Husár, Jozef, *Zjazd v L'ubochni 1921, Dokumenty,* Bratislava 1969.

Janáček, Oldrich, ed., "Depeše mezi Prahou a Moskvou," *Příspěvky k dejinám KSČ,* 3, VII, 1967, pp. 375-433.

*Klement Gottwald ve vzpomínkach a dokumentech,* Brno 1972.

Klimeš, Miloš, Petr Lesjuk,Irena Malá and Vilém Prečan, Comp., *Cesta ke Květnu. Vznik lidové demokracie v Československu,* Two volumes, Prague 1965.

Klimeš, Miloš, and Vilém Prečan, "Z nových dokumentů k Slovenskému Narodnému Povstaní," *Příspěvky k dejinám KSČ,* 1, IV (1964), pp. 72-85.

Král, Václav, *Cestou k Únoru, Dokumenty.* Prague 1963.

———, *Cesta k Leninismu, prameny k dejinám KSČ v letech 1921-1929,* Prague 1971.

Mastný, Vojtech, "The Benes-Stalin-Molotov Conversations in December 1943: New Documents," *Jahrbuecher fuer Geschichte Osteuropas,* Neue Folge, XX, 3 (Sept. 1972), pp. 367-402.

"Neznámi dokument z Povstania," *Nové Slovo,* August 14, 1969, No. 33.

Novák, Oldřich, Oldřich Sládek and Jaroslav Žižka, *KSČ proti nazismu. KSČ v dokumentech nacistických bezpečtnostných a zpravodajských organu,* Prague 1971.

Otahlová, Libuše, and Milada Červinková, comp., *Acta Occupationis Bohemiae & Moraviae. Dokumenty z historie československé politiky 1939-1943,* Two volumes, Prague 1966.

*Stenographische Protokolles des Abgeordnetenhaus,* Prague.

Prečan, Vilém, comp., *Slovenské Narodné Povstanie, Dokumenty.* Bratislava 1965.

———, *Slovenské Narodné Povstanie, Dokumenty. Nemci a Slovensko 1944.* Bratislava 1971.

*Protokol III. řádného sjezdu Komunistické strany Československa. (Prameny k dejinám KSČ). 26.-28. zaři 1925.* Prague 1967.

*Protokol V. řádného sjezdu Komunistické strany Československa. (Prameny k dejinám KSČ). 18.-23. února 1929.* Prague 1971.

*Protokol VI. řádného sjezdu KSC konaního v Praze ve dnech 7. az 11. března 1931,* Prague 1931 (?).

*Protokol VII. řádného sjezdu Komunistické strany Československa. (Prameny k dejinám KSČ). 11.-14. dubna 1936.* Prague 1967.

Ratkoš, Peter, Jozef Butvín, and Miroslav Kropilák, *Naše dejiny v prameňoch.* Bratislava 1971.

*Slovenské Národné Povstanie Dnešku.* Prague 1974.

*Sborník dokumentů k I. svazku Spisů Klementa Gottwalda. Za bolševickou orientaci KSČ.* Prague 1953.

*Sborník dokumentů k II., III., IV., a V. sväzků Spisů Klementa Gottwalda. Za chléb, práci, pudu a svobodu.* Prague 1954.

*Sborník dokumentů k dejinám KSČ v letech 1934-1938 a k VI., VII., a VIII. svazku Spisů Klementa Gottwald. Na obranu republiky proti fašizmu a valce.* Prague 1955.

*Učebné texty pre študium dejín KSČ.* Bratislava 1959 (?).

*Únor 1948. Sbornik dokumentů.* Prague 1958.

Vartiková, Marta, comp., *Komunistická strana Slovenska. Dokumenty z konferencií a plén 1944-1948.* Bratislava 1971.

*Za armádu lidu Sborník dokumentů k bojovím tradicím našého lidu a vojenské politice KSČ.* Prague 1960.

*Založení KSČ: sborník dokumentů ke vzniku a založení KSČ, 1917-1924.* Prague 1954.

## Newspapers and Periodicals

*Čas* (Bratislava), Organ of the Slovak Democratic Party, 1944-1948.

*Delnická Osvěta* (Prague), Monthly of the Social Democratic Party in Czechoslovakia, 1925, 1926, 1927.

*Horizont* (Zurich), Slovak emigrant journal, 1976, 1977, 1978.

*Jewish Chronicle* (London), 1945-1949.

*Literarní Listy, LL, L* (Prague), Organ of the Association of Czech Writers, 1968, 1969.

*Moderní Stát* (Prague), Weekly, 1929-1937.

*Národná Obrana* (Bratislava), Organ of the Slovak National Council, 1945-1948.

*Prager Rundschau* (Prague), Weekly, 1931-1938.

*Pravda* (Bratislava), Organ of the Communist Party of Slovakia, 1944-1948.

*Pravda Chudoby* (Žilina), Journal of the Communist Party in Slovakia, 1923.

*Reporter* (Brno), Weekly, 1968, 1969.

*Rozhl'ady* (New York), Semi-Annual, 1956-1958.

*Rudé Právo* (including *Rudé Právo Večerník, Rudý Večerník* and *Pražský Pondelník*) (Prague), Organ of the Communist Party of Czechoslovakia, 1920–1938.
*Slobodné Slovensko* (Cologne), Slovak emigrant journal, 1978, 1979, 1980.
*Slovák* (Bratislava), Organ of Hlinka's Slovak People's Party, 1938–1945.
*Slovenské Pohl'ady* (Bratislava), Monthly, 1919–1938.
*Svoboda* (Prague), A Communist daily,1938
*Szakszervezeti Munkas* (Prague), Communist Trade Unions journal, 1925.
*Tribúna* (Bratislava), Weekly, 1947–1949.
*Véstník SŽNO* (Prague), Monthly, 1945–1949.


## Memoires, Autobiographies, Publications and Speeches

Beneš, Eduard, *From Munich to New War and New Victory*, London 1954.
Bilák, Vasil, *Pravda zostala pravdou. Prejavy a články, okober 1967-december 1970*, Bratislava 1971.
Churchil, Winston S., *Closing the Ring*, Boston 1951.
Clementis, Vladimir, *Vzduch naších čias*, Two Volumes, Bratislava, 1967.
———, *Odkazy z Londýna*, Bratislava 1947.
Fierlinger, Zdenek, *Ve službách ČSR. Paměti s druhého zahraničního odboje*, Prague 1951.
———, *Od Mníchova po Košice*, Prague 1946.
Gottwald, Klement, *Spisy*, Eight Volumes, Prague 1955.
———, *Výbor z díla*, Prague 1971.
——— *Vojenská politika KSČ*, Prague 1972.
Husák, Gustav, *Zápas o zajtrajšok*, Bratislava 1948
———, *Svedecto o Slovenskom Národnom Povstaní*, Bratislava 1964.
Juriga, Ferdiš, *Blahozvest' kriesenia slovenského národa a slovenskéj krajiny*, Trnava 1937.
Kopecký, Václav, *ČSR a KSČ*, Prague 1960.
Novomeský, Ladislav, *Publicistika*, Four Volumes, Bratislava 1967–1972.
Široký, Viliam, *Za šťastné Slovensko v socialistickom Československu*, Bratislava 1953.
Ursíny, Ján, "Spomienky," *Matičné Čítanie* (Martin), No. 9, April 28, 1969; No. 10, May 12, 1969; No. 11, May 25, 1969; No. 12, June 10, 1969.


## Monographs and Symposia

Amort, Čestimír, *SSSR a osvobození Československa*, Prague 1970.
Bajcura, Ivan, *Ukrajinská otázka v ČSSR*, Košice 1967.
Barto, Jaroslav, *Riešenie vzt'ahu Čechov a Slovákov (1944–1948)*, Bratislava 1968.
Beer, Ferdinand, *et al., Dejinná križovatka. SNP—predpoklady a výsledky*, Bratislava 1964.

Borkenau, Franz, *Der europaeische Kommunismus,* Munich 1952.

Cambel, Samuel, *Revolučný rok 1945,* Bánska Bystrica 1965.

———, Agrárna otázka na Slovensku a naša revolucia 1945-48, Bratislava 1960.

Čejka, Eduard, *Intriky buržoazie a SNP,* Prague 1959.

*Československá revoluce v letech 1944-1948,* Prague 1966.

Čuleň, Konštantín, *Boj Slovákov o slobodu,* Bratislava 1944.

———, *Po Svätoplukovi druhá naša hlava,* Middletown, Pa. 1947.

———, *Vznik a zánik Demokratickéj strany na Slovensku,* Middletown, Pa. 1950.

*Dejiny Komunistickéj strany Československa,* Prague 1961.

*Dejiny KSČ. Študijná príručka,* Prague 1967.

Dérer, Ivan, *Slovenský vývoj a ľudacká zrada,* Prague 1946.

Doležal, Jiři, ed., *Z bojů za svobodu,* Prague 1963.

Doležal, Jiři, and Ján Křen, *Czechoslovakia's Fight,* Prague 1964.

Dudaš, Andrej, *Rusinská otázka a jej pozadie,* Buenos Aires S.A.

Falťan, Samo, *O Slovenskom Národnom Povstaní,* Bratislava 1964

Filo, Milan, *Boj KSČ na Slovensku za obranu republiky v rokoch 1937-1938,* Bratislava 1960.

Franek, Otakar, and Antonin Verlík, eds., *Bohumír Šmeral,* Brno S.A.

Friš, Edo, *Povstanie z daleka a z blizka,* Prague 1965.

Gosiorovský, Miloš, *Dejiny slovenského robotnického hnutia (1948-1918),* Bratislava 1956.

Grna, Jozef, *Sedm roků na domáci fronte,* Brno 1968.

Hoensch, Jörg, K., *Die Slowakei und Hitlers Ostpolitik,* Cologne-Graz 1965.

Hajek, Miloš, *Jednotná fronta. K politické orientaci Komunistické internacionaly v letech 1921-1935,* Prague 1969.

Holka, Filip, *Narodnooslobodzovací boj na Ponitrí,* Bratislava 1967.

Holotík, L'udovit, ed., *Slovenské národne povstanie. Sborník prác k 10. výročiu,* Bratislava 1954.

Holotík, L'udovit, and Miroslav Kropilák, eds., *Slovenské narodné povstanie roku 1944,* Bratislava 1965.

Holotíková, Zdenka, *Klement Gottwald na Slovensku v rokoch 1921-1924,* Bratislava 1953.

Horka, František, ed., *Ze čtyreceti let zápasu KSČ; historické studie,* Prague 1961.

Huml, Vladimír, *Slovensko před rozhodnutím,* Prague 1972.

Ilok, Štefan, with Lester Tanzer, *Brotherhood of Silence. The Story of an Anti-Communist Underground,* Washington, D.C. 1963.

*Istoria vengerskovo revoliucionovo rabochevo dvizhenia,* Moscow 1970.

Jablonický, Jozef, *Slovensko na prelome. Zápas a víťazstvo narodnéj a demokratickéj revolucie na Slovensku,* Bratislava 1965.

———, *Z ilegality do povstania,* Bratislava 1969.

———, *Študie (Zborník o Slovenskom národnom povstaní, Zvazok II),* Toronto, 1980.

Jablonický, Jozef, a Miroslav Kropilák, *Slovník Slovenského Národného Povstania,* Bratislava 1970.

Janaček, František, *Dve smery v začiatkoch národného odboja (Oktober 1938–jun 1940)*, Bratislava 1962.

Janáček, František, ed., *Narodní fronta a komunisté*. Prague-Belgrade-Warszaw 1968

Janeček, Oldřich, ed., *Odboj a revoluce 1938–1945. Nástin dejín československého odboje*, Prague 1965.

————, ed., *Z počatků odboje 1938–1941*, Prague 1969.

Jarošová, Viera, and Oldřich Jaroš, *Slovenské robotnictvo v boji o moc (1944–1948)*, Bratislava 1965.

Jelinek, Yeshayahu, *The Parish Republic: Hlinka's Slovak People's Party, 1939–1945*, Denver, Ccl. 1976.

Jičinský, Zdenek, and Jiři Grospič, *Statopravní usporadaní vztahů českého a slovenského národa v obdobi vypracovaní a prijetí Ústavy 9. května*, Prague 1967.

Kabelík, Ján, ed., *Slovenská čítanka*, Prague 1925.

Kalvoda, Josef, *Czechoslovakia's Role in Soviet Strategy*, Washington, D.C. 1978.

Kaplan, Karel, *Der tschoslowakische Weg zum kommunistischen Machtpolitik 1945–1948*, Munich 1979.

Kirschbaum, Joseph M., ed., *Slovakia in the 19th and 20th Centuries*, Toronto 1973.

Kladiva, Jaroslav, ed., *Československá revoluce v letech 1944–1948*, Prague 1966.

Klimeš, Miloš, Václav Král and Marcel Zachoval, *Otázky narodní a demokratické revoluce v ČSR*, Prague 1955.

Kociská, Anna, *Robotnická trieda v boji proti fašizmu na Slovensku, 1938–1941*, Bratislava 1964.

Korbel, Josef, *The Communist Subversion of Czechoslovakia. The Failure of Coexistence*, Princeton, N.J. 1959.

Krajňák, Oto, *Komunisti bratislavskéj oblasti v boji proti fašizmu v rokoch 1938–1942*, Bratislava 1959.

Krámer, Juraj, *Die Auswirkung der slowakischen Frage auf die Partei und Innenpolitik der CSSR von 1944 bis 1968*, Two volumes, Cologne 1969.

Krechler, Vladimir, *Priručný slovník k dejinám KSČ*, Prague 1964.

Kučera, Eduard, *K niektorým otázkam autonomie a postavení Slovenska v rámci Československé republiky*, Prague 1954.

Kuhn, Heinrich, *Der Kommunismus in der Tschechoslowakei*, Cologne 1965.

Kvetko, Martin, *Dohody o štátopravnom usporiadaní pomeru Čechov a Slovákov v oslobodenéj vlasti*, Bratislava 1947.

————, *K základom ustavného pomeru česko-slovenského*, Bratislava 1947.

Kvetko, Martin, and Miroslav Ján Ličko, eds., *Zborník úvah a osobných spomienok o Slovenskom Národnom Povstaní*, Toronto 1976.

Lettrich, Jozef, *History of Modern Slovakia*, New York 1955.

Lipscher, Ladislav, *K vývinu politickéj správy na Slovensku v rokoch 1918–1938*, Bratislava 1966.

Liptak, L'ubomir, *Slovensko v 20. storočí*, Bratislava 1968.

―――, *Czechs and Slovaks―Two Nations in One State*, Bratislava 1970.

McKenzie, Kermit E., *Comintern and World Revolution, 1928-1934*, London-New York 1964.

Mamatey, Victor S., and Radomír Lúža, eds., *A History of the Czechoslovak Republic*, Princeton, N.J. 1973.

Mencl, Vojtech, and Oldřich Sládek, *Dny odvahy, Z historie Revolučný skupiny Předvoj*, Prague 1966.

Mésaroš, Julius, ed., *Slováci a ich národný vývoj*, Bratislava 1966.

Mikus, Joseph A., *Slovakia, A Political History 1918-1950*, Milwaukee, Wisc. 1963.

Millar, Peter, *Prager Winter*, Vienna 1977.

Motoška, Vladimír, *SNP a uvedomovací proces v národe*, Bánska Bystrica 1967.

Myant, M.R., *Socialism and Democracy in Czechoslovakia 1945-1948*, Cambridge 1981.

Netík, Jaroslav, and J. Franko, *Communism and Slovakia*, Munich 1960.

Novák, L'udovit, *Jazykovedné glosy k československéj otázke*, Turčiansky Sv. Martin 1935.

*O vzajomnych vzťahoch Čechov a Slovákov. Sborník z konferencie HU SAV*, Bratislava 1956.

Olivová, Vera, *The Doomed Democracy. Czechoslovakia in a Disrupted Europe 1914-1938*, London 1972.

Opat, Jaroslav, *O novou demokracii, 1945-1948*, Prague 1966.

*50 let KSČ. Materialy z ideologické konferencie k 50. vyročí slučovacího sjezdu KSČ a k 75. vyročí narození Klementa Gottwalda konané 19.-21. řijna 1971 v Praze*, Prague 1972.

*50. vyročí Československé Republiky. Materialy z vedecké konference*. Two volumes, Prague 1968.

Pašiak, Ján, *Riešenie slovenskéj národnostnéj otázky*, Bratislava 1962.

Paučo, Jozef, *Slováci a komunizmus*, Middletown, Pa. 1957.

Peroutka, Ferdinand, *Budovaní státu*, Four volumes, Prague 1933-1936.

Plevza, Viliam, *KSČ a revolučné hnutie na Slovensku, 1929-1938*, Bratislava 1965.

―――, *Československá štátnosť a slovenská otázka v politike KSČ*, Bratislava 1971.

―――, ed., *Prehl'ad dejin KSČ na Slovensku*, Bratislava 1971.

Prečan, Vilém, *Slovenský, katolicizmus pred februarom 1948*, Bratislava 1961.

*Prehl'ad dejin KSČ; tezy*, Bratislava 1958.

*Príspevky k dejinám východného Slovenska. Materialy zo IV. sjazdu slovenských historikov v Košiciach dna 28.-30. VI. 1962*, Bratislava 1964.

Purgat, Juraj, *Od Trianonu po Košice. (K mad'arskej otazke v Československu.)* Bratislava 1970.

Rašla, Anton, *Civilista v armáde*, Bratislava 1967.

Reimann, Paul, *Geschichte der Komunistische Partei der Tschechoslowakei*, Hamburg 1931.

―――, *Dejiny komunistické strany Československa*, Prague 1931.

————, *et al., Dejiny Komunistické strany Československa,* Prague 1961.

Scheinost, Jan, Antonin J. Kozisek, and Karel Werner, *Bánska Bystrica,* Prague 1944.

Seton-Watson, Richard William, *Slovakia Then and Now,* London 1931.

*Slovenská Národná Rada 1943-1949,* Bratislava 1949.

*Slovenské narodní povstaní. Sbornik k 15. výročí.* Prague 1959.

Staško, Joseph, Slovenko po druhéj svetovéj vojne. "Aprilová dohoda" r. 1946, New York, 1977.

Steiner, Eugen, *The Slovak Dilemma,* Cambridge 1973.

Štvrtecká, Anna, *Ján Osoha,* Bratislava 1970.

Süle, Tibor, *Sozialdemokratie in Ungarn. Zur Rolle der Intelligenz in der Arbeiterbewegung 1899-1910,* Cologne-Graz 1967.

Táborský, Edward, *Communism in Czechoslovakia 1948-1960,* Princeton, N.J. 1961.

Tichý, Miloš, *Z bojov komunistov bánskobystrickéj oblasti,* Bratislava, Volume one: 1962, volume two: 1966.

Tokes, Rudolf, *Bela Kun and the Hungarian Soviet Republic,* New York 1967.

Ullman, Walter, *The United States in Prague 1945-1948,* Boulder, Colo., 1978.

*V bojich se zocelila KSČ,* Prague 1956.

Vartiková, Marta, *Roky rozhodnutia. K dejinám politického boja pred februarom 1948,* Bratislava 1962.

————, *Od Košíc po februar,* Bratislava 1968.

Venohr, Wolfgang, *Aufstand fuer die Tschechoslowakei. Der slowakische Freihetskampf von 1944,* Hamburg 1969.

Vietor, Martin, *Slovenská sovietská republika v 1919; príčiny jej vzniku a jej vplyv na d'alší vývoj robotnického hnutia v ČSR,* Bratislava 1955.

Volgyes, Ivan, ed., *Hungary in Revolution, 1918-1919,* Lincoln, Nebraska 1971.

Vnuk, František, *Neuveritelné sprísahanie,* Middletown, Pa. 1964.

————, *Kapitoly z dejín domunistickéj strany Slovenska,* Middletown, Pa. 1968.

*Z dejín obdorového hnutia na Slovensku (1944-1946),* Bratislava 1970.

*Za svobodu do nové Československé republiky,* Prague 1945 (?).

Zinner, Paul, E., *Communist Strategy and Tactics in Czechoslovakia, 1918-1948,* New York-London 1963.

*Živé tradicie. Kapitoly z narodne-osvobozeneckého a protifašistického boje našého lidu.* Prague 1964.

Zvara, Juraj, *Maďarská mensina na Slovensku po roku 1945,* Bratislava 1969.


## Essays in Periodical Literature

Balogh, Sandor, "Az 1946. február 27-i magyar-czehszlovák lakosságcsere egyzmeny," *Történelmi Szemle,* XXII (1979), pp. 59-87.

Barnovský, Michal, "Problematika industrializacie Slovenska v rokoch 1945-1950," *Historický Časopis,* XVI, 2 (1968), pp. 169-195.

————, "K otázke rozvoja kovorobného a strojárenského priemyslu na Slovensku v rokoch 1945-1948," *Historický Časopis,* XIV, 4 (1966), pp. 517-551.

Beer, František, "Karol Šmidke," *Příspěvky k Dejinám KSČ,* VII, 3 (1967), pp. 445-448.

Benes, Vaclav, "Pan-Slavism and Czechoslovak Policy During World War II," *Indiana Slavic Studies,* I (1956), pp. 137-164.

Bistrický, Josef, "The Slovaks and Dr. Joseph Lettrich," *Slovakia,* I, 2 (1951), pp. 48-52.

Bohm, Emanuel, "Vychodné Slovensko v boji o demokraciu," *Rozhl'ady,* I, 1 (June 1956), pp. 11-16.

Bouček, M., and Miloš Klimeš, "Narodní fronta Čechů a Slováků a slovenská otázka pred Únorem 1948," *Historický Časopis,* XXI, 1 (1973), pp. 1-20.

Bruegel, Johann Wolfgang, "Der Fall Karpathorussland," *Europa-Archiv,* XX (1953), pp. 6021-6028.

———, "Vor zehn Jahren in der Slowakei. Ein unbekantes Kapitel kommunist Verrats," *Die Zukunft,* 1954, pp. 253-259.

Celko, Jaroslav, "Politické machinácie katolického kléru na Slovensku v rokoch 1945-1948 (Pokus o vytvorenie katolickej politickéj strany)." *Historický Časopis,* VIII, 1 (1960), pp. 88-109.

"Česká otázka ve 20. století. Diskuse 17. unora 1967," *Príspévky k Dejinám KSČ,* VII, 3 (1967), pp. 463-477.

Czizmadia, Dezider, "K problému vzt'ahov československých a madarských pokrokových síl medzi dvoma svetovými vojnami (1918-1938)," *Historický Časopis,* XVIII, 1 (1970), pp. 406-426.

Dubský, Vladimír, "Utvarení politické linie KSČ v období Šmeralová vedení," *Príspévky k Dejinám KSČ,* VII, 5 (1967), pp. 645-668; VII, 6 (1967), pp. 803-838.

———, "Historický význam V. sjezdu KSČ," *Československý Časopis Historický,* VII, 1 (1958), pp. 1-24.

Dubský, Vladimír, and Ladislav Niklíček, "Poznámky k článku J. Mlynárika," *Československý Časopis Historický,* XII, 5 (1964), pp. 687-699.

Ďurčanský, Ferdinand, "Es war nur eine sowjetische Partisanenaktion," *Politischen Studien,* 157, pp. 567-575.

———, "Márne sa snaží Moskva získat Slovákov," *Literarný Almanach Slováka v Amerike,* 1953.

Faltán, Samo, "Ku královej recenzií trocha inak," *Historický Časopis,* XIV, 4 (1966), pp. 585-595.

———, "Niektoré otázky okolo hodnotenia SNP," *Historický Časopis,* XII, 2 (1964), pp. 161-185.

Fiala, Jan, "Banderovci a politická kríze v Československu v roce 1947," *Revue Dejin Socialismu,* IX, 5 (1969), pp. 707-720.

Filo, Milan, "Údalosti v Rumanovéj r. 1920," *Historický Časopis,* I, 1 (1953), pp. 106-116.

"Fraternite. Rozhovor s Jánem Mlynárikem," *L,* II, 15, 17 April 1969.

Friš, Edo, "Moskovský pobyt K. Šmidkeho v auguste 1944," *Príspévky k Dejinám KSČ,* IV, 3 (1964), pp. 439-444.

Gašpar, Tido J., "Triedenie duchov," *Slovenské Pohl'ady,* XLVIII, 7-8 (July-August 1932), pp. 496-502.

Gosiorovský, Miloš, "K niektorým otázkam vzťahu Čechov a Slovákov v politike Kumunistickéj strany Československa," *Historický Časopis*, XVI, 3 (1968), pp. 354–406.

——, "Slovensko a V. sjazd KSČ," *Československý Časopis Historický*, I, 1 (1953), pp. 4–15.

——, "Úloha robotníckéj triedy a KSČ v našich dejinách (s osobným zreteľom na 30. výročie SNP)," *Historický Časopis*, XXII, 2 (1974), pp. 179–194.

——, "Leninizmus a riešenie slovenskéj otázky," *Nová Mysl*, XXIV, 5 (1970), pp. 721–731.

——, "Slovenské národné povstanie roku 1944," *Československý Časopis Historický*, II, 4 (1954), pp. 573–597.

Gráca, Bohuslav, "Slovenské narodné povstanie r. 1944," *Historický Časopis*, II, 1 (1954), pp. 3–38.

——, "O vzniku a boji KSČ za predmnichovskéj ČSR," *Historický Časopis*, IX, 2 (1961), pp. 181–200.

Hoensch, Jörg K., "Die Slowakei im Jahre 1945," in Karl Bosl, ed., *Das Jahr 1945 in der Tschechoslowakei*, Munich-Vienna 1971, pp. 159–199.

Hofmann, Pavel (Záviš Kalandra), "Na trech urovních," *Reporter* (Brno), IV, 12, March 3, 1969.

Hojč, Jozef, "O práci strany po zatlačení povstania do hôr," *Príspevky k Dejinám KSČ*, IV, 4 (1964), pp. 582–589.

Holdoš, Ladislav, "Niektoré problémy československého zahraničného odboja vo Francuzsku v rokoch 1939–1940," *Historický Časopis*, XVII, 3 (1969), pp. 399–419.

Holotík, Ľudovít, "Ohlas velkéj oktobrovéj socialistickéj revolucie na Slovensku od konca roku 1917 do vzniku ČSR," *Historický Časopis*, V, 4 (1957), pp. 425–450.

——, "Oktobrová revolucia a revolučné hnutie na Slovensku koncom roku 1918," *Historický Časopis*, XV, 4 (1967), pp. 489–511.

——, "Sjazd socialnodemokratickéj strany (ľavice) na Slovensku v januari 1921," *Historický Časopis*, XI, 3 (1963), pp. 337–365.

——, "Slovenská otázka v dejinách KSČ," *Historický Časopis*, XIX, 4 (1971), pp. 481–494.

——, "Súčasný stav a problémy slovenskéj historiografie," *Historický Časopis*, XIV, 1 (1966), pp. 1–9.

——, "Zápas o charakter republiky—revolučný Hlohovec roku 1920," *Historický Časopis*, XIV, 2 (1966), pp. 219–250.

Holotíková, Zdenka, "Bolševizačný proces KSČ v rokoch 1924–1929," *Historický Časopis*, V, 2 (1957), pp. 204–219.

——, "Niektoré problémy slovenskéj politiky v rokoch 1921–1925," *Historický Časopis*, XIV, 3 (1966), pp. 412–463.

——, "The Slovak Question and Czechoslovak Communist Party in pre-Munich Czechoslovakia," *Studia Historica Slovaca*, IV (1966), pp. 139–158.

——, "K činnosti a ideologii ľudackých odborov na Slovensku v radcch robotníckéj triedy (1921–1945)," *Historický Časopis*, IX, 2 (1961), pp. 50–67.

Hradilák, Zdenek, "Místo v dejinách: Čtyricet let od V. sjezdu KSČ," *Reporter* (Brno), IV, 7 (February 20, 1969), pp. 14–16.

Hrbata, František, and Ladislav Niklíček, "Na ceste k VII. kongresu Kominterny," *Československý Časopis Historický*, XIII, 4 (1965), pp. 655–682.

――――, "Nádeje a skutečnost. Bezprostrední vliv VII. kongresu Kominterny v mezinarodním delnickém hnutí," *Československý Časopis Historický*, XV, 5 (1967), pp. 667–690.

Huebl, Milan, "Konflikt nebo jednota," *LL*, I, 3 (March 14, 1968).

――――, "Slovenské narodní povstaní—začátek narodní a demokratické revoluce v Československu," *Historický Časopis*, XII, 4 (1964), pp. 519–534.

Husák, Gustav, "K dokumentom z historie československéj politiky 1939–1943," *Historický Časopis*, XV, 3 (1967), pp. 422–440.

Jablonický, Jozef, "Slovenské národné povstanie—nová fáza v riešení vzajomných vzťahov medzi Čechmi a Slovákmi," *Historický Časopis*, XII, 3 (1964), pp. 313–328.

――――, "Politická situacia na východnom Slovensku od oslobodenia do vyhlásenia Košického vládneho programu," *Historický Časopis*, XI, 4 (1963), pp. 529–551.

Janáček, František, "Poselství Vladimíra Clementisa," *Reporter* (Brno), IV, 11 (March 20, 1969).

――――, "O čechoslovakismu a čechoslovenství (1918–1938–1968)," *Reporter* (Brno), IV, 7 (February 20, 1969).

Jankovec, Volfgang, "Nové Slovensko," *Delnická Osvěta*, XXIV, 9–10 (1938), pp. 322–327.

Jelinek, Yeshayahu, "The Role of the Jews in Slovakian Resistance," *Jahrbuecher fuer Geschichte Osteuropas*, Neue Folge, XV, 3 (1967), pp. 415–422.

――――, "Between Nationalism and Communism: the 'Slovak Question'," *Canadian Review of Studies in Nationalism*, II, 2 (1975), pp. 334–341.

――――, "Between Assimilation and Emigration: the Population, the Authorities, and the Holocaust Survivors in Slovakia, 1945–1948," *Proceedings of the Sixth World Congress of Jewish Studies*, Jerusalem 1976, Vol. two, pp. 249–256.

――――, "The Communist Party of Slovakia and the Jews: Ten Years (1938–1948)," *East Central Europe*, V, 2 (1978), pp. 186–202.

Jirásek, Josef, "Československá otázka na Slovensku," *Delnická Osvěta*, XII, 1 (Jan. 1926), pp. 31–34, and 2 (Feb. 1926), pp. 264–266.

Kalina, Robert, "Slovenské národné povstanie—proti komu a začo?" *Svědectví*, XII, 48 (1974), pp. 669–694.

Kaplan, Karel, "Narodní fronta 1945–1948," *Studie*, 56 (1978), pp. 81–114.

――――, "Úvahy o nevyhnutelnosti unora," *Svědectvi*, 55 (1978), pp. 343–364.

――――, "Slovenský politický katolicismus a komunisté," *Studie*, 54 (1977), pp. 452–469.

Kirschbaum, Joseph M., "International Recognition of the Slovak Republic," *Slovakia*, I (1951), pp. 23–31.

――――, "Osudy vyslanectiev Slovenskéj Republiky," *Kalendár Jednota*, 1961, pp. 109–117.

――――, "My Last Diplomatic Report to the President of Slovakia, *Annual Furdek*, 1972, pp. 81–87.

――――, "Diplomatic and Consular Relations of Slovakia with Neutral States,"

*Slovakia,* XXIII (1973), pp. 111-122.

Kirschbaum, Stanislav J., "The Slovak Republic and the Slovaks," *Slovakia,* XXIX (1980-1981), pp. 11-38.

Kašpar, Ján, "Členská základna Komunistické strany Československa v letech 1945-1949," *Československý Časopis Historický,* XIX, 1 (1971), pp. 1-25.

Klír, Miroslav, "Dr. Bohumír Šmeral," *Přispěvky k Dejinám KSČ,* V, 6 (1965), pp. 930-939.

———, "Úloha Bohumíra Šmerala pri vypracovaní strategickotaktické orientace KSČ," *Přispěvky k Dejinám KSČ,* V, 1 (1965), pp. 28-33.

Knieža, Emil F., "The Resistance of Slovak Jews," in Juri Suhl, ed., *They Fought Back,* New York 1967, pp. 191-196.

Kociská, Anna, "Robotníci bratislavských závodov v boji proti fašizmu v rokoch 1939-1940," *Historický Časopis,* IV, 1 (1956), pp. 24-49.

Král, Václav, "Západ a Slovenské Národné Povstaní," *Československý Časopis Historický,* XXIII, 1 (1975), pp. 51-74.

———, "Prínce Slovenského národního povstaní ke vztahům československo-sovětským," *Slovanský Přehled,* LXI, 1 (1975), pp. 1-29.

———, "Československo-sovětske vztahy v obdobi príprav Slovenskóho narodního povstaní," *Slovanský Přehled,* LX, 8 (1978), pp. 273-296.

Krámer, Juraj, and Ján Mlynárik, "Revolučné hnutie a národnostná otázka na Slovensku v dvadsiatých rokoch," *Historický Časopis,* XIII, 3 (1965), pp. 423-443.

Kropilák, Miroslav, "Vedecká konferencia o Slovenskom Národnom Povstaní," *Historický Časopis,* II, 1 (1954), pp. 105-138.

Kulíšek, Vladimír, "Úloha čechoslovakizmu ve vztazích Čechů a Slovaků (1918-1938)," *Historický Časopis,* XII, 1 (1964), pp. 50-74.

Lamberg, Robert F., "Slovenský stat a extremisti," *Svědectví,* VI, 24 (1964), pp. 357-370.

Lastovička, Bohuslav, "Vznik a význam Košického vládního programu, *Československý Časopis Historický,"* VIII, 2 (August 1960), pp. 449-471.

Ličko, Miroslav, "Nove publikacie: Slovenské národné povstanie—proti komu a začo?" *Naše Snahy,* XI (May-June 1975), pp. 12-14.

Lipták, Ľubomír, "Z kroniky predmnichovských dní (z denníka A. Markuše)," *Historický Časopis,* XVIII, 5 (1970), pp. 379-405.

———, "Slovenský štát a protifašistické hnutie v rokoch 1939-1943," *Historický Časopis,* XIV, 2 (1966), pp. 161-218.

Lúža, Radomír, "The Communist Party of Czechoslovakia and the Czech Resistance 1939-1945," *Slavic Review,* XXVIII, 4 (1961), pp. 561-576.

———, "February 1948 and the Czechoslovak Road to Socialism," *East Central Europe,* IV, 1 (1977), pp. 44-55.

Magosci, Paul R., "Rusyns and the Slovak State," *Slovakia,* XXIX (1980-1981), pp. 39-44.

Mencl, Vojtech, "K historií II. sjezdu KSC," *Československý Časopis Historický,* III, 4 (1955), pp. 557-593.

Mlynárik, Jan, "O Slovácich v první republice," *Reporter* (Brno), IV, 19 (May 15, 1969).

———, "O hlavnom nebezpečí," *Reporter* (Brno), IV, 8 (February 27, 1969).

———, "Dr. Bohumír Šmeral a slovenská národná otázka v počiatkoch komunistického hnutia," *Československý Časopis Historický*, XV, 4 (1967), pp. 653–666.

———, "Hnutie nezamestaných na Slovensku v rokoch 1919–1929," *Historický Časopis*, XI, 2 (1963), pp. 195–235.

———, "K niektorým otázkam revolučného hnutia v Československu v rokoch 1918-1938," *Československý Časopis Historický*, XII, 2 (1964), pp. 206-216.

———, "K otázkam všeľudového protikapitalistick ého hnutia na Slovensku v rokoch 1931-1933. (Historia Sjazdu pracujuceho ľudu Slovenska.)" *Československý Časopis Historický*, X, 3 (1962), pp. 339-366.

———, "Robotnické hnutie na Slovensku roku 1920. (Od parlamentných volieb do decembrového generalného štrajku)," *Historický Časopis*, VIII, 1 (1960), pp. 26-87.

———, "Vývoj robotnického hnutia na strednom Slovensku v rokoch 1918-1920," *Historický Časopis*, IV, 3 (1956), pp. 296-330.

———, "Vyvrcholenie hnutia nezamestaných na Slovensku v rokoch 1929-1933," *Historický Časopis*, XIV, 1 (1966), pp. 37-74.

Peroutka, Ferdinand, "Jmeno, jež vyhaslo: Šmeral," *Svědectví*, XI, 41 (1971), pp. 59-67.

Plevza, Viliam, "K niektorým otázkam vývinu komunistického hnutia za predmníchovskéj ČSR," *Historický Časopis*, XIII, 4 (1965), pp. 489–516.

———, "Príspevok o činnosti davistov v revolučnom hnutí za predmníchovskéj ČSR," *Historický Časopis*, XII, 1 (1964), pp. 1-27.

———, "Vytvorenie celoslovenského kraja KSČ a revolučného hnutia na Slovensku na začiatkoch tridsiatých rokov," *Historický Časopis*, X, 2 (1962), pp. 165-197.

Pokorný, Ctibor, "Der Kommunismus und die Slowaken," in *Die Slowakei als mitteleuropaische Problem in Geschichte und Gegenwart*, Munich, 1965, pp. 189-198.

Prečan, Vilém, "Nacistická politika a Tisuv režim v predvěčer Povstani" *Historie Vojenství*, VI (1969), pp. 1028-1146.

Samák, Ján, "O česko-slovenskéj otázke trochu inač," *Svědectví*, IX (1969), pp. 275-291.

Šefránek, Julius, "Významná etapa národnostnéj politiky KSČ. (K 25. výročiu Plánu hospodarského, socialného a kulturného povznesenia Slovenska.)," *Přispěvky k Dejinám KSČ*, II, 3 (1962), pp. 373-390.

Skilling, H. Gordon, "The Formation of a Communist Party in Czechoslovakia," *The American Slavic and East European Review*, XIV, 3 (1955), pp. 346-358.

———, "The Comintern and Czechoslovak Communism: 1921-1929," *The American Slavic and East European Review*, XIX, 3 (1960), pp. 234-247.

———, "Gottwald and the Bolshevization of the Communist Party of Czechoslovakia 1929-1939," *Slavic Review*, XX, 4 (1961), pp. 641-655.

———, "Communism and Czechoslovak Tradition," *Journal of International Affairs*, XX, 1 (1966), pp. 118-136.

Škurlo, Ján, "Celoslovenská konferencia KSS v Žiline 1945 a čo jej predchádzalo," *Historický Časopis*, XIX, 2 (1971), pp. 145–176.

Šolc, Jaroslav, "Cesta slovenských partizánov od celonarodného protifašistického povstania k februaru 1948," *Historický Časopis*, IX, 1 (1961), pp. 29–49.

Šťastná, Zdenka, "Na východné vyspě," *Reporter* (Brno), IV, 10 (March 13, 1969).

Štvrtecká, Anna, "V. sjazd slovenských historikov a jeho podnety," *Přispěvky k Dejinám KSČ*, V, 5 (1965), pp. 832–834.

Taylor, A.J.P., "Czechoslovakia Today. The Position of the Slovaks," *Manchester Guardian*, Aug. 9, 1946.

Toma, Peter A., "The Slovak Soviet Republic of 1919," *American Slavic and East European Review*, XVII, 2 (April 1958), pp. 203–215.

———, "Soviet Strategy in the Slovak Uprising," *Journal of Central European Affairs*, XIX (1959–1960), pp. 290–298.

Tomčik, Miloš, "Vzájemnost neni mrtva," *L*, 8, February 27, 1969.

Ušiak, Ján, "Boj KSČ s Hlinkovou Slovenskou L'udovou Stranou o vplyv na masy v období nástupu fašizmu," *Přispěvky k Dejinám KSČ*, 1963, III, 5 (1963), pp. 710–729.

Vaculík, L'udovik, "Ponekud neklidne," *L*, 18, May 7, 1969.

Vartiková, Marta, "Boj Komunistickéj strany Československa za uskutočňovanie zásad Magny Charty slovenského národa," in *Prispevky k dejinám l'udovéj demokracie v ČSR*, Bratislava 1955, pp. 185–235.

———, "Čekoslovenská pracovná konferencia KSS v Košiciach ako prínos pri tvorbe vládneho programu prvéj vlády Národného Frontu Čechov a Slovákov," *Historický Časopis*, XXIII, 2 (1975), pp. 170–200.

———, "Kulturná politika slovenských komunistov v prvom roku oslobodenia," *Přispěvky k Dejinám KSČ*, VI, 4 (1966), pp. 514–532.

———, "K otázke vzťahu Čechov a Slovákov na jar 1945," *Revue Dejin Sozializmu*, IX, 1 (1969), pp. 63–79.

———, "Príspevok k odhaleniu protil'udovéj politiky demokratickéj strany," *Historický Časopis*, I, 2 (1953), pp. 289–306.

———, "O vývoji robotnickéj triedy na Slovensku v l'udovodemokratickom období (1945–1960)," *Historický Časopis*, VII, 3 (1960), pp. 469–482.

Vietor, Martin, "K tridsiatemu piatemu výročiu Slovenskéj republiky rád," *Historický Časopis*, II, 2 (1954), pp. 161–190.

Vnuk, František, "Fifty years of Communist Party of Slovakia (1918–1968)," *Slovakia*, 1969, pp. 125–178.

———, "K činnosti komunistov na Slovensku v rokoch 1939-1944," *Kalendár Jednota*, 1963, pp. 83-93.

Vrabic, Emil, "Obnova priemyselnéj výroby na Slovensku roku 1945," *Historický Časopis*, XVII, 2 (1969), pp. 233–269.

Zvara, Juraj, "K problematike postavenia maď'arskej národnostnéj skupiny v ČSR v období boja za upevnenie l'udovéj demokracie a rozširenia moci robotnickéj triedy (1945–1948)," *Historický Časopis*, XXII, 1 (1964), pp. 28–49.

# INDEX